THE GREATEST OF EVILS

SOCIAL INSTITUTIONS AND SOCIAL CHANGE
An Aldine de Gruyter Series of Texts and Monographs
EDITED BY
Michael Useem • James D. Wright

THE GREATEST OF EVILS

Urban Poverty and the American Underclass

Joel A. Devine and James D. Wright

ALDINE DE GRUYTER

New York

About the Authors

Joel A. Devine is Associate Professor of Sociology, Tulane University. The author of numerous journal articles, he is presently studying the increasing chronicity of poverty, alcohol, and drug abuse among the homeless and the urban underclass.

James D. Wright is Charles and Leo Favrot Professor of Human Relations, Department of Sociology, Tulane University. He is the author of numerous journal articles and author (or coauthor) of over twelve books including: *Address Unknown: The Homeless in America; Under the Gun; Weapons, Crime, and Violence in America; Armed and Considered Dangerous: A Survey of Felons and Their Firearms;* and *The State of the Masses* (all: Aldine de Gruyter).

ALDINE DE GRUYTER
A division of Walter de Gruyter, Inc.
200 Saw Mill River Road
Hawthorne, New York 10532

This publication is printed on acid-free paper ♾

Library of Congress Cataloging-in-Publication Data
Devine, Joel A., 1953–
    The greatest of evils : urban poverty and the American underclass
/ Joel A. Devine and James D. Wright.
        p.   cm. — (Social institutions & social change)
    Includes bibliographical references and index.
    ISBN 0-202-30473-6. — ISBN 0-202-30474-4 (pbk.)
    1. Urban poor—United States.   2. Poverty—United States.
3. United States—Social policy—1980–   I. Wright, James D.
II. Title.   III. Series: Social institutions and social change.
HV4045.D48   1993
362.5′0973—dc20   93-6873
                                                                          CIP

Manufactured in the United States of America

10 9 8 7 6 5 4 3 2 1

To Lise, Jake, Ethan, Chris, Matt, and Derek

"The greatest of evils and the worst of crimes is poverty."
George Bernard Shaw, *Major Barbara*

Contents

   POVERTY   49

      The Working Poor   49
      The Rural Poor   62
      The Elderly Poor   65
      Poverty among Children   68
      Summary   71

4 WHO AND WHAT IS THE URBAN
   UNDERCLASS?   77

      Underclass and the Lumpen-Proletariat   79
      The Underclass and the New Urban Reality   81
      Defining the Underclass   82
      How Big Is the Underclass?   91
      A Caveat on Geography, Region, and City
         Size   92
      Conclusions   93

5 THE PERSISTENCE OF POVERTY   95

      The Panel Study of Income Dynamics (PSID)   97
      Operationalizing Chronicity   97
      Analyzing Persistent Poverty   102
      Summary   115
      A Footnote on Homelessness   118

6 THE INNER LOGIC OF THE UNDERCLASS   123

      Out-of-Wedlock Births   132
      Welfare   142
      Unemployment, Subemployment, and
         Labor Force Participation   148
      Educational Attainment   158
      Drug Abuse and the Drug/Crime
         Connection   163
      Crime and Victimization   173
      Summary   185

Preface

We began this book almost three years ago. Today the analysis and message are even more timely than when we began, for the most recent picture is even more grim. A recession and the technical nonrecession that has followed have only exacerbated already disturbing trends in poverty. In 1991, 35.7 million Americans were impoverished, 2 million more people than in 1990. This translates into 14.2% of the population. Data for 1992 will not be available for some time, but the continued stagnation of the economy virtually ensures an even higher figure. Equally disturbing, the rate of poverty among children has worsened and the physical and social deterioration of our central cities continues unabated. Though speculative, the eventual release of tract and block-level data from the 1990 decennial census will presumably show further and deeper concentrations of poverty within minority communities.

That some recent economic indicators have shown signs of growth—however minimal—is, of course, encouraging. Even a modest economic turnaround will reduce the temporary, cyclical component of our poverty problem. Economic growth has long been recognized as the best antidote to unemployment and poverty.

At the same time, as this book documents, most of our poverty owes to more than the latest recession. As such, its alleviation requires more active and targeted interventions that pursue the longer-term solutions necessitated by more deeply rooted and entrenched problems in the structure and organization of our political economy.

This preface is being written two days after the American electorate rejected the complacency of the Bush administration and seemingly endorsed a more active response to the nation's economic woes. While Bill Clinton's victory in the electoral college is impressive, his popular vote falls well short of a mandate—despite his apparent appeal among widely diverse segments of the electorate. More to the point, neither Clinton's platform nor his election can be construed to constitute support for aggressive social activism.

Had George Bush been reelected, we could safely (though somewhat sadly) assume that our policy recommendations would be entirely ignored and that the ideas we offer for consideration would be just as timely and necessary in the six to twelve months that will elapse between this writing and the book's publication. With a Clinton administration we are somewhat more optimistic about the fate of a number of the proposals we advance, or at least something that resembles them.

Though President Clinton's agenda is different in numerous respects from our own, it is clear that he recognizes the need to move ahead on a jobs and infrastructure program. Within the first hundred days of his administration we can expect legislation that simultaneously seeks to attack unemployment and arrest the further deterioration of our physical infrastructure. Similarly, a Clinton administration can be expected to expand Head Start and other educational programs and opportunities from preschool through university level. Job training and retraining programs will also square well with the new administration, and welfare reform is high on the president-elect's wish list. In addition, we can safely expect a concerted effort to achieve some modicum of health care reform. Extension of at least minimal coverage to all Americans and cost-containment provisions are probable. Moreover, we fully expect the new administration to be truly kinder and gentler than the last, to attempt to promote a sense of inclusion rather than exclusion, to attempt to invigorate a politics of all of us rather than the divisive mentality that celebrates the "us" and denigrates the "them."

As such, we are cautiously optimistic about the directions and policies a Clinton administration is likely to pursue. However, we are not so optimistic as to think that events will overtake the relevance of this book, our diagnoses, and our prescriptions. The new administration will undoubtedly approach the poverty problem with some timidity. Deficits, the needs of the middle class, and a lack of necessary political capital will ensure that. Later, if economic stabilization has been achieved, the necessary economic and political capital will have been secured. At minimum, however, the new administration starts from the premise that our national fate and well-being cannot be achieved by insulating ourselves from the poverty in our midst, squandering our critical human resources, and failing to educate our populace. That in itself represents a promising new beginning.

Joel A. Devine
James D. Wright

Acknowledgments

Our individual interests in poverty are longstanding, but our separate thoughts about it owe much to the vital work done at the Institute for Research on Poverty at the University of Wisconsin, a part of our common but separate maturation as researchers. We acknowledge this common intellectual debt and the important work done under the auspices of IRP over many years. It was not until 1988 that we met as colleagues in the Department of Sociology at Tulane and these separate interests were joined and brought to fruition in a stimulating and nurturant environment enriched by our many colleagues. To them, we also acknowledge our debt. Finally, this particular project has benefited from the contributions of a number of individuals. The staff of the Government Documents section of Tulane's Howard-Tilton library was ever-helpful and professional in our continual assault on their repository. We thank them for their efforts and apologize for the frequent mess we made. Earlier drafts of the manuscript benefited from the careful readings and suggestions of Beth Rubin, Joe Sheley, Chris Stewart, Lise Diamond-Devine, Larry Powell, and Jed Willard. None of them fully agrees with the end product, so we are necessarily required to absolve them of any further responsibility for this work. So be it!

Introduction:
Poverty, Misery, and Waste

I

> I am at a loss to understand why well-known and generally recognized poverty-breeding conditions, which are both unjust and unnecessary, are tolerated for an instant among a humane, not to say a professedly Christian people. (Hunter 1904, p. viii)

The United States is by far the richest society in the history of the world, and yet the specter of poverty haunts us still. Today, nearly 35 million of our citizens languish in poverty, untouched by (although certainly not unaware of) the opulence around them. The official rate of poverty now stands at 13.5% and has held roughly constant for the better part of the last decade; in fact, the rate is about where it was twenty-five years ago.[1] How poverty can continue to exist in so rich a nation—why it is tolerated at all—has mystified scholars and analysts throughout the twentieth century, as the quotation above attests.

Within the past decade, and for at least the fourth time this century, social scientists, journalists, policy makers, and commentators have re-awakened to poverty amidst our plenty, to destitution amidst abundance. This time around, the mood is unmistakably grim. It seems no longer sufficient to write just about the poor. Today, one writes of the homeless and hungry, the truly disadvantaged, the underclass, the permanently poor—phrases chosen (or so one infers) to underscore the apparent hopelessness, the utter desperation, of today's situation.

Little more than a quarter-century ago, President Johnson declared a war on poverty. The ensuing history has caused many to argue that "the war was lost," that "poverty will always be with us," that "only the poor can help themselves," that "the effort was wasted"—in short, that the war on poverty was misguided and costly, and may have only worsened the problem. Such were the sentiments that helped sweep Ronald Reagan

xv

into the presidency in 1980. In the memorable phrase of the Great Com-
municator himself, "We already fought a war on poverty. Poverty won."

How many Americans accept these notions is anybody's guess. Probably, it is fewer than most would surmise. "The People" rarely speak in the
voice of angels, but neither are they fools. Much that is now being written
about the poverty problem is not so much wrong as it is vacuous and
inexact. The platitudes and clichés being tossed around these days often
contain an element of truth, but eight years of Reaganomics and four
years of Bush have blunted their edge. What seemed incisive criticism a
decade ago reads as mean-spirited apologetics today.

A decade ago, for example, it was not uncommon for analysts to argue
that welfare made poor people welfare dependent and thus that welfare-
state provisions such as Aid to Families with Dependent Children
(AFDC) or general assistance made the poverty problem worse, not
better. We now know that the vast majority of persons who ever go on
welfare stay on welfare only for a year or two, as they weather some
personal or financial crisis, and then return to the labor force as soon as
their circumstances allow it. We also know that the lack of affordable day
care keeps many single parents on welfare even when they would prefer
to be working. We have even learned that many single parents are
essentially forced to remain on welfare so as to maintain their eligibility (and that of their children) for Medicaid benefits, in the absence of
which they would be entirely unable to afford routine health care. The
argument that "welfare perpetuates poverty and dependency" overlooks
a great deal of recent evidence demonstrating the complexities of this
relationship.

In the past decade we have also seen how large-scale economic forces
can conspire to impoverish individuals, families, and even whole communities. It has become more and more difficult to maintain that "poor
people should help themselves" when entire communities are put into
poverty by factory closings and the migration of jobs out of the country,
or when people lose all that they have in the bankruptcy of their local
savings and loan association, or when people are literally wiped out by
uninsured medical expenses or by natural catastrophes. Some are indeed
poor because of indolence and sloth, but many are poor for reasons that
go well beyond their own control.

Certainly, our experience with poverty over the past thirty years has
disabused us of many naive and romantic notions about the poor. As
such, many people are understandably skeptical of any proposed solution, especially if the price is high. And many are likewise doubtful of the
poor's capacity to change, to rise out of poverty and to take a place in
society as independent and productive adults. That such sentiments have
some foundation, however, surely does not imply that everything we

have tried to do in the past three decades to alleviate the poverty problem has been effort wasted. Some of our poverty policies have no doubt been misguided, but some certainly were not. Some fostered dependency and thus worsened the problem, but others did not. There is wisdom to be had in learning which is which, and little but folly in blanket condemnation.

The conclusion that "poverty won" gainsays the many victories against poverty that were registered between the onset of the War on Poverty in 1964 and the world economic crisis precipitated by the Arab oil embargo of 1973. (The scorecard for the era is reviewed in Chapter 2.) The first decade of the War on Poverty saw the overall national poverty rate cut in half. Even greater inroads were made into poverty among the aged and among male-headed black families. These were impressive social accomplishments—ground gained, not lost.[2] We may well have "lost the war," as many have claimed, but it is wrong to deny victory in many of the battles we chose to join.

The weapons of the War on Poverty proved ineffective against the economically troubled decade of the 1970s, a decade when double-digit inflation *and* double-digit unemployment were commonplace (despite their Keynesian impossibility). Thus progress against poverty stagnated in the 1970s, with the national poverty rate hovering around its 1973 level through to 1980 and the election of Ronald Reagan. Reagan came to office intent on dismantling as much of the welfare state as a Democratic Congress would let him get away with; the social welfare spending cutbacks of 1981 and beyond are among his many enduring legacies. Concurrent with these sometimes drastic cutbacks, the national poverty rate began climbing back up (reaching a fifteen-year high in 1983 and remaining roughly at mid-1960s levels ever since), a scourge of homelessness descended upon our cities, and analysts of the poverty scene began writing books about the emergence of a permanent American underclass. Surely these developments are not unrelated.

Did we lose the War on Poverty? Or did we simply give up? The conservative agenda of the Reagan and Bush administrations amounted at least to a cease-fire, if not unconditional surrender. The apparent result of a dozen years of free market economics is not only that there is more poverty than there was in the 1970s but also that today's poverty is much more obdurate and socially destructive. As one learns more and more about what happened in the 1980s, it becomes more obvious that the entire decade was a giant step backward so far as the American poverty problem was concerned.

The bent to be found throughout this volume, perhaps already obvious, is worth stating explicitly. The War on Poverty was not an unalloyed success, but neither was it a total failure. Winning a war against poverty is a worthwhile, even ennobling, national goal—and one within our means.

In the next campaign, we can capitalize on our previous successes and learn from the many failures; we can strike at the poverty problem with better targeting, more efficiency, and less naiveté than before.

II

Those who would struggle against the poverty problem must sooner or later confront the oft-quoted Biblical aphorism, "The poor ye have with you always." This passage is cited in discussions of poverty as though it expressed a profound, inalterable truth, as though it said all that needs to be said on the matter. But Hunter recognized the fallacy in 1904:

> Did not the Lord say, "The poor always ye have with you"? But those who say this fail to distinguish between the poor who are poor because of their own folly and vice, and the poor who are poor as a result of social wrongs. . . . The poor which are always to be with us are, it seems to me, in poverty of their own making. But as surely as this is true, there are also the poor which we must not always have with us. The poor of this latter class are, it seems to me, the mass of the poor; they are bred of miserable and unjust social conditions, which punish the good and the pure, the faithful and industrious, the slothful and vicious, all alike. (pp. 62–63)

As we have already noted (and will note again a half-dozen times in these pages), the rate of poverty was halved between 1964 and 1973. In raw numbers, that was a reduction from about 40 million to about 23 million poor people altogether. Today, the number of the poor is nearly 35 million. The amount and rate of poverty, in short, are not immutably fixed by Biblical truth but rather come and go in response to economic conditions and specific policy interventions. By the same line of reasoning, vast reductions in the amount and rate of poverty are not ruled out by Biblical mandate or social law. Complete eradication of poverty is probably *not* possible since many are poor through "their own folly and vice." But between complete eradication and current conditions there lies a great deal of room for improvement.

There seems to be more concern about poverty expressed today than at any time since the early 1960s. Certainly, more books and articles are being published on the topic than at any time in the recent past. Is this reawakening to be seen simply as a phase in a recurrent cycle of civic activism followed by retrenchment? Why has poverty resurfaced as an urgent social problem now? What accounts for the ebb and flow of our national consciousness of this issue?

Answering these questions would require a different book than we have written, but one thing is clear: the amounts and rates of poverty have little to do with its status as a social issue, a point which we elaborate in the next chapter. That being the case, the explanation for the cycle of interest and lack of interest must lie elsewhere.

Some historians have argued that periods of social activism and quiescence follow generational rhythms on a time scale of decades. The decade of the 1950s—the sleepy years of the Eisenhower era—was a time of relative lack of interest, of the "politics of consensus" and the "end of ideology." As with the cadence of a distant drum, the 1960s and early 1970s witnessed the politics of dissent and the resurrection of ideology, and were accordingly followed by the quiescence and retrenchment of the late 1970s and the so-called "Me Decade" of the 1980s. By this logic, then, we are simply due for another activist phase. But none of this constitutes a satisfactory explanation; rather, it simply restates that which is to be explained.

Perhaps our periodic reawakenings to the poverty in our midst result from cycles of relative deprivation. There are two versions of this thesis sharing a common root, namely, that when significant numbers improve their standards of living, the relative disparity between the "haves" and "have-nots" tends to increase.[3] One possibility, perhaps the less likely, is that the growing disparity evokes compassion or even guilt among the haves; faced with their newfound abundance, people become more charitable towards and concerned about those at the bottom. Alternatively, compassion, guilt, and charity may have nothing to do with it; it may simply be that the growing anger, resentment, and desperation of the "have nots" begin to threaten the social fabric and therefore command a collective response. Increased crime, insurgency, and other social pathologies—even the threat of them—may prompt societal reactions, whether repressive or magnanimous. This, in essence, is the thesis of Piven and Cloward (1971; see also Cloward and Piven 1974), and it seems at least superficially congruent with most of our twentieth century awakenings to poverty, a theme to be explored more fully in Chapter 1.

No matter where we are in the cycle, as a nation we have always expressed a great deal of ambivalence about poverty and about the poor. The Beatitudes enshrine poverty as a blessed condition, but this has not prevented us from looking on the poor in most times and places with anger, repulsion, scorn, and even contempt. More often than not, we blame the poor themselves for their miseries, rather than viewing them as victims of larger and uncontrollable forces (Ryan 1971). From time to time, however, we recognize another, more romantic, even uplifting poverty, epitomized by the Joads, the protagonists of Steinbeck's *The Grapes of Wrath*. Perhaps the difference is only that the Joads are recognizably like the rest of us, clearly the victims of abstract social forces and institutions, and down on their luck. Who among us could possibly deny these decent, hard-working plain folk a bit of assistance? Who would be hard-nosed or mean-spirited in responding to their plight?

Thus we are both repelled by and drawn to the plight of the poor. When faced with an apparently able-bodied adult living off the public trough, our angered response is likely to be, "sober up, take a shower, get a job." Anger fades to concern and sympathy, however, when we learn, for example, that 40% of the poor are children, or that almost 10% of the poor work full-time year-round jobs and an additional 30% work but not full time, or that 12% of the poor are elderly people over age 65. Depending on which part of the poverty population we are looking at, we express anger or sympathy, rejection or guilt. Even in our most hardhearted moments, we find it hard to shake the thought that maybe it is not their fault after all.[4]

Thirty years ago, when we last awakened to the poverty problem and declared war against it, our motives (if not our thinking) appeared clearer than they do today. The Poverty Warriors of the 1960s truly believed that poverty could be eradicated, that enough money spent in just the right ways would inevitably solve the problem, that if we would only supply the opportunities, the poor would avail themselves of them. All this strikes us today as hopelessly naive. The past three decades have made us more realistic and better informed about the dimensions and circumstances of the poverty problem than we have ever been before. But realism need not degenerate into cynicism, nor better information into a hard-bitten, uncaring mood. Being realistic about the poverty problem need not make us any less committed to finding appropriate, workable, humane solutions.

III

We began this book intending to write a lengthy critical essay on the thesis of the emerging underclass, but it has evolved into a book about the urban poverty of the late twentieth century, the poverty of postindustrial America. We found it impossible to say much about the nation's underclass without first locating the underclass within the larger poverty population (Chapter 3); likewise, what we had to say about the poverty situation as a whole itself required a larger historical and economic context (Chapters 1 and 2). The essay we originally intended to write appears here as Chapters 4, 5, and 6; Chapters 1 and 2 provide essential background and historical context; Chapter 3 examines the demographic correlates of poverty; Chapter 7 contains our thoughts about policy directions and future solutions.

In the first chapter we take up issues of definition and measurement. What do we mean by "poverty," and how can we define and assess it? We accordingly review the origins and evolution of the official federal poverty standard and explore the utility of alternative standards. Chapter 2 reviews recent economic and social trends pertinent to the poverty situation—trends in income distribution, employment patterns, family structure, and the like—and also provides an overview of the history of poverty in America from the Great Society to the present day. In Chapter 3 a detailed portrait of today's poverty population is given, organized around particular groups within that population: the working poor, the rural poor, the aged poor, poor women and children, and so on.

Chapter 4 gets us around to the topic with which we began, that of the urban underclass. Although relatively small in numbers, the so-called underclass has recently become the most visible and widely discussed segment of the contemporary poverty population. As might be expected, the term is used by different authors in a variety of ways to demarcate different aspects of the poverty situation, but in the most common rendition, it refers to chronic, concentrated, innercity, minority impoverishment accompanied by extreme social isolation and exceptionally high rates of social pathology of all sorts. The underclass is *not* just the poorest stratum among the poor, but rather that subgroup of the poverty population most resistant to successful intervention.

Various definitions of the underclass, theories about its origins and emergence, and estimates of its size and composition are taken up in Chapter 4. The term itself has become something of a buzzword, often used imprecisely and for mainly polemical purposes. The main (and perhaps only) element common to all definitions and current usage is that the underclass is *chronically* poor. Beyond that, the meaning of the term dissolves into a rather ambiguous mist of causes, symptoms, social and demographic correlates, and behavioral manifestations. The principal problem one encounters in writing about the underclass is that it is never entirely clear what one is writing about. The phrase proves at times to be usefully descriptive, but it is not analytically "clean" or even particularly incisive in many applications.

The distinguishing mark of the underclass (in most presentations) is that its poverty is chronic; thus, the chronicity of poverty is our topic in Chapter 5. Analysts have used the notion of "chronicity" in at least two very different ways. In some versions, it refers to the intergenerational transmission of poverty (the tendency for the children of the poor to remain poor in their own adult lives); in others, the reference is to year-by-year variation (or constancy) in the poverty status of particular persons or households. In the first case, persons are "chronically" poor if they were born to impoverished parents; in the second case, they are "chronically" poor if they remain below the poverty level year in and year out. (These, of course, are not exclusive options.)

That much poverty is *not* chronic is a comparatively recent recognition, a principal result from the Panel Survey of Income Dynamics (PSID) that we exploit heavily in the following pages. We have learned, for example, that there is considerable movement back and forth across the poverty line from year to year. Indeed, if we define the poor as the bottom 20% of the income distribution and then look at family incomes over a five-year period, we find that only about 10% of the population are poor in all five years and that nearly 40% are poor in at least one of the five years. The poverty of many, in short, is not a fixed condition; short-term fluctuations in family economics move large number of persons in and out of poverty on short time scales.

If the chronicity of poverty is the distinguishing characteristic of the underclass, and *if,* as many believe, the underclass has been growing, the seeming implication is that the chronicity of poverty has also been increasing over time. The PSID allows for a straightforward and, as it happens, rather interesting test of this implication, the results of which are also reported in Chapter 5.

Much of the attention being focused on poverty and the underclass these days has derived (at least to all appearances) from a stunning increase in the numbers of homeless people roaming the streets of urban America—a particularly visible and disturbing manifestation of what has been called the "new American poverty." Relatively little was written about the homeless in the poverty analyses of the 1960s and 1970s, although they figured prominently in numerous ethnographies of Skid Row (Bogue 1963; Bahr and Caplow 1974). In the 1980s, in contrast, homelessness came to be recognized as a leading social problem. The sudden visibility and intensity of the homeless problem took many people by surprise, and a vast array of research studies poured forth at once. Chapter 5 concludes with a brief review and summary of the principal themes and findings of these studies, especially as they pertain to an understanding of homelessness as part of the larger poverty problem.

Chapter 6 concerns itself with the inner logic of the urban underclass. Here we consider the various social, economic, and political factors that have conspired to create a more or less permanently impoverished stratum of American society: structural changes in the economy, underemployment and declining labor force participation, subpoverty wages, changes in family composition, and recent developments in education. In the end, we conclude that the underclass is mainly the result of an inadequate demand for labor and of the ensuing and now often chronic joblessness that plagues inner city minority youth. We also examine the forces that have concentrated the underclass geographically in the inner city ghettoes. Finally, we consider some of the more commonly discussed behavioral aspects of underclass existence: drugs, crime, welfare dependency, and related social dysfunctions. Like many others (e.g., Wilson 1987; Currie 1985), we conclude that chronic joblessness lies at the heart of all these worrisome pathologies.

Chapter 7 concludes the book; here our concern is with solutions and with the general drift of our national poverty policies since the demise of the War on Poverty, with particular attention to the Reagan and Bush years. The 1980s were neither kind nor gentle to the poor; to the contrary, much of our current poverty problem seems to have resulted, at least in substantial part, from policy changes initiated since 1981. The program cutbacks and policy directions taken in that period increased the rate of poverty and added to the general miseries of the poor. It is a reasonable national goal to reverse these developments, if not yet in this century then surely soon in the next. We end the book with our thoughts on how this might be accomplished.

IV

Our rekindled concern with poverty and with its underclass component is motivated as much by fear as by compassion. Many are no doubt deeply worried about the lack of opportunity, material deprivation, and family instability experienced by many children in poverty (not to mention adults who also suffer). No one can possibly be comfortable as an entire generation is destroyed. But the concern of many is motivated as much by the escalating violence, crime, and drug abuse that have accompanied the emergence of the urban underclass. Many inner city areas have come to resemble Beirut. Tanks do not yet rumble in the streets, but the rat-a-tat of automatic weapons, wanton violence, and senseless loss of life are now commonplace occurrences. To the average person, these are disturbing and threatening developments; most people understandably want it stopped, as soon as possible, by whatever means necessary. There is no getting around the fact that many of the inner cities have become increasingly nasty places.

It is an easy thought that more police and prisons would solve these problems, but further reflection shows this to be a shortsighted approach. The social contract is, after all, a two-way street. Society may expect, even demand, conformity to its values and social norms but only to the extent that it provides legitimate opportunities for success to the duly obedient. Denied adequate education, access to viable employment, and an income necessary to sustain some reasonable standard of living, what do we expect of the underclass? Blood flows where life is mean.

A heightened police presence in the inner city neighborhoods and a doubling of prison space would in the end only serve to alleviate some of the more troubling symptoms of urban poverty. More police and more prisons will not, in and of themselves, reduce the rate of teenage pregnancy, compensate for the lack of academic motivation, or assist the poor in becoming independent of welfare. Much less will they help feed the hungry or house the homeless. Even less will they address the problems of poor children. As the fundamental nature of today's urban poverty comes into clearer focus, it becomes increasingly apparent that more police and more prisons are not the answer. The social pathologies that have come to characterize the urban underclass go well beyond anything that police and prisons can possibly address.

It may seem an unjustified middle-class bias to use terms such as "undesirable," "socially dysfunctional," or "pathological" to describe the behavioral correlates of underclass existence. To label behaviors such as teenage pregnancy, joblessness, violence, crime, or drug addiction as "pathological" is only to demand conformity to our own narrow moral sensibilities, is it not? The point is well taken but only to an extent. That we should all be more tolerant of diverse lifestyles is inarguable. "Lifestyle," however, implies informed choice, not the absence of alternatives, and although a few may indeed actively choose a life of hunger, homelessness, deprivation, and destitution, their numbers must be small indeed. More to the point, there is no serious question that the behavioral "complex" associated with the urban underclass and often labeled (here and elsewhere) as "pathological" represents a profound barrier to the realization of objectives that are equally valued by all, including the poor: a society free of want, misery, repression, and intimidation. Wilson (1987, p. 6) has criticized liberal analysts of poverty for their reluctance "to discuss openly or, in some instances, even to acknowledge the sharp increase in social pathologies in ghetto communities." Frank discussion of these unfortunate but undeniable facts, Wilson points out, is not racism, is not "blaming the victim," is not stigmatizing, is not even moralistic or judgmental. It is an essential first step towards better understanding.

The problems of the underclass and the problems they in turn pose for society as a whole are deep, diverse, and complex. Neither conservative myopia nor liberal sentimentality will solve them. The principal failings of conservative analyses of poverty have been their unwillingness to recognize larger social and structural determinants and their persistent emphasis on individual imperfection as the cause of poverty. Liberal analysts can in turn be fairly castigated for failing to recognize the pathologies to which Wilson alludes and for simply ignoring (or denying the causal import of) aspects of the problem that are ideologically discomfiting.

The number of the latter is rather large. For example, it is deeply troubling to many liberals that most of the urban underclass is black, and so lengthy treatises are written that gloss over the question of race. It seems unsavory to associate race with poverty, as if this would only feed the prevalent racist stereotype that all the poor are black and all blacks are poor. Neither of these is true, of course: Nationwide, two-thirds of the poor are white, not black, and there is also a large and growing black middle class. At the same time, the concentrated urban poverty that defines the American underclass is principally a minority phenomenon, rates of poverty are much higher among blacks and Hispanics than among whites, and nearly half the nation's black children live in poverty conditions. That these things are true does not imply much of anything about why they are true, which is the more pertinent question. Part of the answer to the contemporary poverty problem must be found in the history of race relations in this country (see Hacker 1992), and it does no good to pretend otherwise.

Much of the pathological behavior now associated with the urban underclass appears to the skeptical eye as an exaggerated caricature of the "do your own thing" mentality so prominent in the 1960s and 1970s. Sexual liberation was very much at the forefront of the movement of that era, and many progressive-thinking people applauded the decline of puritanical sexual strictures. But what then is one to make of the astonishing rates of teenage pregnancy, single motherhood, and illegitimacy in the urban ghettoes? Should we conclude that sexual liberation was perhaps not such a good thing after all? Or perhaps that it was just fine for the white middle class but not for the black urban poor? Neither conclusion seems acceptable, and so, typically, the dilemma is resolved by denying that teen pregnancy, unwed motherhood, and illegitimacy are in any way relevant to the situation and by describing these things merely as symptoms with no causal weight of their own.

Much the same can be said about the plague of drugs that has descended on the inner cities. Surely, there is a causal link to be traced between the innocent "joints" making their way around the peace demonstrations of the 1960s and the "crack" epidemic now threatening the very fabric of urban life. So drug use, like sexual promiscuity, has simply been scuttled off to the bin of epiphenomena, to be treated as a symptom of larger woes. Lives, families, neighborhoods, and entire communities are being destroyed by this unfortunate "symptom." Any realistic analysis must recognize that many of the problems of the inner city are *caused* by drugs and that widespread drug use is a formidable barrier to any workable solution. To conclude otherwise is wishful thinking.

We have written a book about poverty in America, about urban poverty in particular, about possible interventions, and about the need to confront poverty in a rational and constructive manner. As always, it is easier to describe a problem in all its worrisome details than to suggest efficient, workable solutions. We cannot pretend to have all the right answers, but we do hope to have raised most of the right questions. This, however, is for our readers to decide.

Our hope is to have produced a general and largely nontechnical overview of poverty, the underclass, and public policy in the contemporary United States, one accessible to anyone who is curious about the poverty problem. Although we have not forsaken altogether the scholarly niceties of footnotes, references, and tables of data, we have tried to keep them to a minimum. Our principal themes are few and simple.

First, poverty is not by any means monolithic. Among the poor will be found young and old, black and white, men and women. The poor are concentrated in the cities, but rural poverty has not been eliminated. Some of the poor are temporarily poor; others were born poor and have been poor all their adult days. Each subgroup within the poverty population tends to be victimized by different dynamics, saddled with different problems, and in need of different solutions. Poverty is not one problem but many, all sharing a common name.

Second, the so-called underclass, although ambiguously defined and only partially understood, is indeed a new and especially damaging development that cannot be analyzed in traditional terms or dealt with in traditional ways. A critical task for us is therefore to identify how the underclass differs from the larger poverty population and to assess what, if anything, can be done to bring them back into the mainstream. We are not at all sanguine on the point, incidentally. It can be forcefully argued that the situation has degenerated so thoroughly that all hope is lost. We have conjured up some strategies that might nonetheless be attempted before this painful and distressing conclusion is reached.

Third, despite considerable naiveté, mismanagement, and waste, the War on Poverty was not the unmitigated disaster that many have come to believe. Among certain segments of the population, opportunities were expanded, legal access was ensured, and poverty was reduced. Today's poverty policies, unfortunately, tend to overlook, misunderstand, or simply neglect the underlying causes of much of the poverty that remains. Largely cosmetic "fixes" for the more bothersome symptoms of poverty will not serve us well as we prepare for the twenty-first century. If ever there was a time for boldness of vision, it is surely now.

Finally, in the radically altered international political and economic climate of the late twentieth and early twenty-first centuries, we can ill afford to squander our opportunities or to continue policies that abet human misery and waste. The steadily increasing social and economic costs of crime, drugs, illiteracy, joblessness, poor health, urban decay, homelessness, and a host of other poverty-related problems now threaten the viability of our society. We anticipate severe labor shortages over the next decades and understand full well the need for enhanced productivity to compete on the international scene, and yet at the same time we consign an entire class of the population to the very margins of existence and thus essentially guarantee that their net contribution to the social good will be negative. Already, the economic and social price we pay for the poverty in our midst probably exceeds what it will cost to do something about it. This is a madness we can no longer afford. It is not just the poor that need concern us; it is also our dignity as a just and compassionate people.

NOTES

1. Unless otherwise noted, current poverty figures refer to 1990 data, the most recent year available.

2. The allusion here is to Charles Murray's seductive book *Losing Ground* (1984), one of the most widely discussed treatments of the poverty problem to have been published in the 1980s.

3. Even when there is substantial and widespread economic growth, it tends to be uneven, most of all in the past two decades. Although market economies have demonstrated an unparalleled capacity for growth, it is also true that regions, industries, classes, occupations, and social groups benefit quite unevenly from this growth (see Chapter 2, below). Thus, even when the economic pie is growing, the pieces of the pie going to various sectors of the society grow at highly variable rates.

4. At the same time, we have always drawn a distinction between those poor whom we deem "deserving" (e.g., widows, orphans, and the elderly) and those deemed "undeserving" (e.g., unwed mothers, able-bodied adults). While the line between the two has often been murky and clouded by racism and nativism, this distinction has been a critical element in the structuring of programs and entitlements (see Devine and Canak 1986; Katz 1989).

1

The Definition and Measurement of Poverty

Each year the United States Bureau of the Census issues a detailed statistical report on poverty in America, in conjunction with the March administration of the Current Population Survey (see the *Current Population Reports*, Series P-60, annual). These reports provide a count of how many Americans are living in poverty and detailed information on demographic characteristics, educational attainments, work experiences, living arrangements, and other attributes of the poverty population. To illustrate, the 1991 report (the most recent available as of this writing) tells us that in 1990, 33.6 million Americans were poor, amounting to 13.5% of the population.

It is obvious that the Bureau of the Census requires some definition of what constitutes poverty in order to produce these reports. Their definition, indeed, is the official poverty definition employed in all government reports and statistical series and also used by most nongovernmental researchers working in the poverty area. Although enjoying the imprimatur of the federal government, the official definition of poverty contains many arbitrary elements and is therefore not without its faults (or, of course, its utility). Since most of the evidence on poverty available to us employs this official definition, it proves useful to go into some detail on what the definition is and how it was developed.

The intent of this discussion is not to conclude that one definition of poverty is superior to all others or to suggest that the official definition is so deeply flawed as to render it useless for analytic purposes. Any definition of any concept will be more or less useful depending on the specific research tasks at hand. The intent, rather, is to raise some of the many underlying difficulties inherent in the (apparently simple) task of defining poverty and to establish an initial understanding of the principal conceptual issues.

What, then, is the federal government's official definition of poverty? How was this definition developed? What are its strengths and weaknesses? What alternative definitions exist, and what are their comparative advantages? It is obvious that we must understand the definition and

1

measurement of poverty before we can discuss it, measure its incidence, examine its causes, or combat its effects.

At first blush, defining poverty would seem to be a straightforward, even simple, task. Poverty is obviously the lack of something, "a deficiency in necessary properties or desirable qualities" according to the nearest Webster's. Common synonyms include paucity, scarcity, dearth, scantiness, destitution, want, privation, penury, indigence, insufficiency, and meagerness. To be poor is to do without.

The everyday use of the term emphasizes a lack of *material* resources needed to live comfortably or safely. Granting that one may be impoverished in soul, psyche, or spirit as well, we will nonetheless confine ourselves to the material realm and leave these other poverties to the philosophers and moralists who specialize in such matters.

Defining poverty as the lack of necessary material resources is perhaps suitable for ordinary usage and everyday language, but this remains too vague for scientific purposes. To proceed scientifically requires us to spell out exactly (1) what the relevant material resources are, and (2) how much of those resources one needs to enjoy a reasonably safe and comfortable existence.

The first of these issues is readily disposed. In a cash economy such as ours, any mix and level of material goods can be expressed in monetary terms, as the number of dollars of income or wealth necessary to purchase the designated mix. Thus the basket of goods, services, and other commodities required for a "reasonably safe and comfortable existence" can be given a particular dollar value. This does not clarify the *meaning* of poverty, but it does facilitate its measurement.

The more difficult issue, by far, lies in defining a "reasonably safe and comfortable existence" and in deciding on the requisite goods and services that make such an existence possible. Once all this is known, attaching a precise dollar value to it is relatively easy.

ABSOLUTE VERSUS RELATIVE DEFINITIONS

The first decision to be made in defining poverty is whether poverty should be conceptualized as relative or absolute. Can we define some truly basic (absolute) standard of existence such that any and all who fall below that standard are poor? Or must we conceptualize poverty as a condition of *comparative* disadvantage, to be assessed against some relative, shifting, or evolving standard of life? This proves to be a sticky issue.

Consider an absolute conception of poverty. What factors or circumstances should be taken into account in formulating such a conception? A daily nutrient intake of approximately 1500 calories is required to sustain an adult human life over extended periods. Shall we then define the poor as all who fail to achieve this basic nutritional milestone? Probably not, since sustenance of human life clearly requires more than adequate caloric intake; it also requires potable drinking water, adequate shelter from the elements, and so on.

How far through the list of "and so on" should or does one go with one's absolute poverty definition? Does "adequate shelter from the elements" include indoor plumbing or electrical service, for example? A hundred years ago, indoor plumbing was a luxury well beyond the means of most people. Were most people therefore "poor" because they lacked what we now regard as essential? A mere sixty years ago, tens of millions of rural Americans were without electricity. Were they therefore poor? Much of the world's population today still exists without either of these amenities, but in the social context of present-day America, most would consider indoor plumbing and electricity as necessities, not luxuries. One might even argue that in American society today, television sets and automobiles are necessities of life, even though the vast bulk of the world's population continues to exist with neither.

Thus, any realistic, workable definition of poverty must be relative to a society's existing level of economic, social, and cultural development. An absolute standard of poverty appropriate to American society in 1750 and applied to American society today would reveal that almost nobody is now "poor," just as a standard appropriate to the level of development in the middle of the twenty-second century would probably show that today, nearly everyone *is* "poor." We conclude therefore that no sensible definition of poverty can be indifferent to history, society, and culture. No one absolute definition can suffice for all times and places.

At the same time, extremely relativized conceptions of poverty are equally problematic. For example, one can define poverty relative to a society's given distribution of income, considering those in the bottom quintile of the distribution as poor regardless of the absolute level of their incomes. (In this case, we are defining a poverty income *relative* to the average income.) While useful for some purposes, this approach implies by definition that no society can ever eliminate poverty, since in any empirical distribution of income, 20% must lie in the lowest income quintile. By this definition, one-fifth of all people in all societies in all times and places are "poor," neither a useful nor satisfactory conclusion.

In the end, then, a truly workable, satisfactory definition of poverty can be neither entirely absolute nor entirely relative. What is needed is some definition that is sensitive to a given society's level of development but that also demarcates a group of people truly in need according to some objective and nonarbitrary, although socially defined, standard.

Given the obvious difficulties posed in trying to identify absolute

standards of poverty that are nonetheless appropriately sensitive to social, economic, and historical context, some have argued that poverty is
better understood as *subjective deprivation* relative to some pertinent reference group. As in our earlier example, this approach also conceptualizes
poverty as comparative disadvantage, but here the comparison is to other
people or reference groups rather than to a statistical average. In this
approach, people are poor if they think of themselves as poor or if they
are thought of as poor by others. Proponents of this approach see it as
especially useful in a highly affluent society such as ours where only a
small (although still not trivial) minority are so destitute as to be without
agreed on basics such as food and shelter.

Further advantages are thought to be associated with this view of
poverty as relative subjective deprivation. It calls attention to the psychological dimensions of poverty and raises the question of how people come
to define themselves or others as poor. And because in this view poverty
is defined against some reference group or standard, the approach directs
attention to broader income-distributional (or equity) issues.

There are also obvious problems in this approach. It would be a simple
matter to ask respondents in the Current Population Survey whether they
believe themselves to be poor. But what could we infer from their answers? Thinking one is poor and actually *being* poor are not the same
thing. Well-educated, white-collar suburbanites unable to muster the
social ties and $15,000 entry fee for membership in the local country club
might report feeling "poor" even though their incomes were well above
the national average. Alternatively, an uneducated hotel domestic supporting two children on a minimum wage job might not view herself as
poor if her reference group was other inner city residents, many of whom
would certainly be worse off than she (those, for example, who had no job
or other source of income). Compared to neighbors, other family members and friends, she might indeed be *relatively* well off—but still poor.

The problem with the relative deprivation approach to the definition of
poverty is that everyone is deprived relative to someone else, excepting
only the single richest person in the world. The Kennedys are deprived
relative to the Rockefellers. And likewise, everyone is also comparatively
advantaged relative to someone else, excepting only the single poorest
person in the world. A homeless man sleeping in the gutter with a dollar
in his pocket is, after all, better off than another homeless man, sleeping in
the same gutter, but with no money in his pockets at all.

For these more or less obvious reasons, few people are ultimately
satisfied with a purely subjective definition of poverty; most relative
deprivationists would define poverty relative to some objective, quanti-
fiable standard, not relative to people's opinions about who is poor. More
often than not, that standard involves some proportion, usually half, of

the median American family income. Thus, we might wish to consider a family poor if it had to survive on half or less of what the average family survives on.[1] There are many strong advantages to this approach, but it is not the approach taken in the official definition of poverty.

We have so far raised only a few of the complexities involved in defining poverty; many additional issues are discussed in later pages. How, then, does the government manage to come up with an "official" definition? Why, indeed, do we even have (or need) an official definition? It proves useful to address these questions in the broader historical context of attitudes about poverty and the ensuing national policy posture.

POVERTY, POLICY, AND PUBLIC AWARENESS IN THE TWENTIETH CENTURY

As it happens, there was no such thing as an official (federal) poverty standard in the United States until the beginning of the War on Poverty in 1964. This is not to say that people were uninterested in the issue of poverty in earlier times. Quite to the contrary: a trip to any research library will turn up numerous books about poverty in America written at the turn of the twentieth century, and even much earlier.[2] But prior to the War on Poverty, there was no sustained federal policy in place to confront the poverty problem in any systematic way, much less to eliminate the condition, and so there was no reason for the federal government to concern itself with how poverty would be officially defined. In essence, up until 1964, poverty was whatever one could convince others it was.

From time to time throughout American history, and with some regularity as far back as the 1890s, an occasional researcher, journalist, or public official would advance a definition of poverty, gather up isolated bits and pieces of available evidence, and venture a guess as to how many Americans were "poor." In the absence of an agreed-upon national standard, of course, the reliability and validity of these guesses were open to question. Prior to the early 1960s, what we felt we knew about poverty— its incidence, prevalence, sources, dynamics, and consequences—was based largely on isolated ethnographic accounts, many of them dazzling in their insights and revelations, but all of them necessarily limited to a depiction of localized conditions. None of these studies gave firm empirical clues about the poverty situation in the nation at large.

Indeed, from a policy viewpoint, there was no real need to know very much about the national poverty situation because poverty was not defined as a national problem. Many people believed (and many still believe) that poverty results from an insufficiency of effort or from other personal inadequacies; people are poor because they don't want to work, or simply won't work, or because they drink too much, or because they do not make the effort to succeed. In this view, poverty is largely a self-inflicted condition, and there is very little government should or even can do to prevent it.

Michael Katz (1989) reminds us that the origin of the distinction between "deserving" and "undeserving" poor lies in the distinction between neighbors and strangers. Responsibility for the poor "extended to family and community; there it ended" (p. 11). Thus arose the settlement provisions in the poor laws of both England and the United States, whereby legal residence in the community was considered a precondition for alms or other assistance; drifters and migrants—or, as they were known in colonial times, the "wandering poor"—were always someone else's problem.

Efforts in the United States to control the relief rolls by keeping them free of strangers date to the colonial era. In Massachusetts, the chosen mechanism was the process of "warning out." Names of transients, along with information on their former residences, were presented to the colonial courts. Upon judicial review, the person or family could then be "warned out" (that is, told to leave town). Some of the more populous towns actually hired persons to go door to door seeking out and reporting strangers. Up until 1739, when the practice was ended by law, persons were eligible for poor relief if they had not been "warned out" within their first three months of residency; after three months, they were no longer strangers. A corollary process was that of "binding out," whereby transients could be, in essence, indentured to families needing laborers or servants, a colonial-era version, perhaps, of what we now call "workfare." "Binding out" persisted in Massachusetts until 1794 (Wright 1989, Chapter 2).

In a mobile, urbanized society, the distinction between neighbor and stranger has become occluded, but that between the deserving and undeserving poor remains; the "otherness" or "strangeness" of the poor has evolved from geographical to social isolation. Superficially, the distinction is between those who are poor "through their own folly and vice" and those whose poverty results from factors beyond the control of any individual. Thus the aged and the infirm are "deserving," whereas able-bodied males are not. At a much deeper level, as Katz has observed, "the culture of capitalism measures persons, as well as everything else, by their ability to produce wealth and by their success in earning it; it therefore leads naturally to the moral condemnation of those who, for whatever reason, fail to contribute or prosper" (p. 7).

Prior to the twentieth century, to the extent that a possible governmental role in addressing poverty was acknowledged at all, it was local government, not the federal government, that was seen to bear the principal responsibility. And more often than not, even local governments declined to assume stewardship for the poor, preferring to leave interventions in such matters to private charities. To be sure, widows, orphans, and the physically disabled were seen as deserving of sympathy and perhaps even a bit of assistance, but for other poor people, the county workhouse appears to have been the preferred solution. Poverty among able-bodied men seemed to violate the American creed of self-sufficiency, upward mobility, and success; it was assuredly *not* a condition to reward or encourage by generous programs of governmental assistance. The possibility that poverty might be the result of social, economic, or structural forces well beyond anyone's personal control was (and perhaps remains) alien to the thinking of many people. (See Patterson 1986 for an overview and discussion of American attitudes and stereotypes about the poor throughout the nation's history.)

Despite this ambivalence about the poor, severe material deprivation was a highly visible feature of the American social landscape throughout the early years of the twentieth century. In the cities, millions of immigrants were crowded into unsanitary tenements and ghettos, earning pittance wages in the factories, mills, and sweatshops. In the countryside—in Appalachia, in the rural South, indeed throughout the nation—were many additional millions of rural poor, eking out their existence in what can only be called subsistence agriculture, often surviving from year to year with only a few hundred dollars of cash income. While many might well have looked upon the poor with disfavor, or even contempt, very few could possibly have failed to be aware of their existence.

And yet, harsh though material conditions may have been, there was a strong sense of optimism among both poor and nonpoor, an optimism born in the promise of progress, the promise of a better life in the future (Thernstrom 1964). Life in the city tenements was no doubt difficult, often destitute, but it was also dramatically better than the life that immigrants had left behind. Moreover, the nation's rapid development into a powerful industrial and commercial economy seemed to promise an even better future for one's children. There was also an intact sense of community, a feeling that everyone was in the same boat; most of one's neighbors, family, and friends would have been in similar material circumstances, and those who were discernibly better off only provided the evidence that upward mobility was possible. Thus the severe material deprivation that characterized the early years of the century seldom produced a sense of psychological defeat. Poverty may have been everywhere, but so too were the opportunities to rise above it, or so it seemed.

The unprecedented economic growth and increasing personal income generated by the post–World War I boom seemed to confirm these optimistic notions. The "roaring twenties" certainly did not roar equally for everyone; in fact, tens of millions of Americans, especially in the rural areas, benefited little if at all from the postwar economic boom. At the same time, there is no doubt that the postwar affluence was rather widely shared, and this coupled with reduced foreign immigration and a mass exodus from rural America may well have reduced the overall level of poverty.

However much poverty itself may have been reduced in the 1920s, public awareness of the poverty problem seems to have nearly disappeared. With the near-total fadeout of the Progressive movement, the political articulation of the poverty issue fell silent, and the center of concern with poverty shifted from the relatively visible and politicized urban reformers and settlement workers of New York City to the academic ethnographers of the University of Chicago's department of sociology. By the end of the 1920s, poverty was more an academic than a political concern.

The turning point in public awareness of poverty and in the nation's policy response to it was unquestionably the Great Depression, whose effects on these matters are hard to overstate. By the time of the 1932 election, the steadily worsening Depression was already in its fourth year and had left almost no one untouched. The resources of private charities were quickly exhausted, and the already limited capacities of local governments to provide relief were rapidly depleted. With the economy in shambles and with more than a quarter of the labor force out of work, Americans were forced to rethink their ideas about poverty and the proper role of government in responding to it. The Depression made it distressingly obvious that not all poverty resulted from inadequate personal effort or deficiencies of moral character; large-scale, structural social and economic developments could make life difficult for anyone, no matter how willing or able. It was a hard but useful lesson.

Upon taking office, Franklin Roosevelt faced a rising cry for federal intervention to end the Depression or at least contain its effects. His response, of course, was the New Deal, a broad-ranging, multifaceted package of social and economic programs that FDR moved quickly, though cautiously, through Congress and into law. Even in the middle of the worst economic calamity to ever befall the nation, however, policy makers consciously attempted to craft programs that would avoid dependency and preserve self-esteem. Work was preferable to welfare; thus, job creation programs such as the Civilian Conservation Corps and the Works Projects Administration were strongly favored over direct income transfer schemes. Likewise, social insurance tied to labor force participation (in short, unemployment compensation) emerged as the preferred long-term vehicle for income maintenance; direct relief (welfare) remained the province of local government and private charities.[3]

The New Deal successfully contained the worst effects of the Depression, but World War II ended it, and with the Depression over, poverty once again faded from public view. The postwar economic expansion, fueled by the Cold War military build-up, the emergence of widespread consumer credit, the unparalleled generosity of G.I. Bill benefits for education and housing, and the nation's increasingly prominent international economic position allayed any nagging fears that peace would bring a return of prewar economic problems. To the contrary, national prosperity was back and seemed certain to stay, at least for the foreseeable future. Personal incomes rose dramatically, home ownership skyrocketed, and even factory workers could expect to send their children to college. "A chicken in every pot" was no longer the national standard of prosperity. Now, it was two cars in every suburban garage. As John Kenneth Galbraith put it in 1955, poverty had become "nearly an afterthought."

The reality of the 1950s was, of course, significantly different. As in the 1920s, participation in the postwar economic boom was unequally distributed over the population. Many prospered, to be sure, but in readily overlooked sectors of the society—in Appalachia, among ethnic minorities, and among the elderly—the incidence of poverty remained astonishingly high (see Ross, Danziger, and Smolensky 1987). In these groups, destitution was not an afterthought but a continuous fact of life. As Michael Harrington so astutely observed, poverty had not disappeared; it had just become more or less invisible to the public at large. Safely esconced in the burgeoning new suburbs, the "average" American could be largely oblivious to the crushing poverty that continued to exist in the streets of urban ghettos or along the dusty back roads of rural America.

The occasional critic who called attention to these persistent and enduring deviations from the American dream was readily dismissed as a Communist or a crank. Such poverty as might remain was seen as anomalous, isolated, and fleeting, certain to yield to the enduring economic boom.[4] In short, poverty was (and to a certain extent continues to be) at odds with our collective sense of national identity. To be poor was not just to live in want; in a deep sense, it was un-American.

Public consciousness of the poverty problem for most of the last century can thus be easily summarized. Whenever possible, we have tried to deny that poverty existed (excepting those isolated and unimportant pockets that would always remain, as in the oft-quoted Biblical aphorism). When outright denial was not possible, we could attribute the continued persistence of poverty to deficiencies of the poor themselves.

And when events such as the Depression called even this into question, we have sought final solace in economic growth, "the rising tide," as John F. Kennedy put it, "that raises all ships." To the extent that poverty required a "solution," it was to be sought not in income transfer schemes or programs for the poor but through the simple expedient of stoking the American economic engine.

THE WAR ON POVERTY

Today, of course, one is not considered a Communist or a crank in suggesting that poverty might persist even in the face of widespread economic growth and prosperity, that it might result from deficiencies of economic and social structure as well as individual moral failings, and that a solution to the problem might well require targeted, large-scale federal interventions. But all of these are distinctively recent notions so far as public thinking about poverty is concerned, notions that gained widespread currency only in the years after 1964, when Lyndon Johnson announced the War on Poverty in his first State of the Union address.[5]

The origins of the War on Poverty and the subsequent transfiguration of public consciousness about the poor are subject to debate. The usual story, possibly somewhat romanticized in the retelling, begins with Jack Kennedy's campaign for the presidency in 1960. During his primary campaign against Hubert Humphrey, Kennedy campaigned extensively in West Virginia, an early and then-pivotal primary election. In crisscrossing the state, he is said to have been struck by the extreme poverty of Appalachia, something for which his background would never have prepared him. Whether Kennedy's awakening on this issue actually constituted the near-epiphany that certain members of the Kennedy circle claim, the new president did subsequently instruct his Council of Economic Advisors to explore the poverty issue and develop some policy recommendations.

Other writers attach less significance to the West Virginia experience and describe Kennedy's commitment to antipoverty legislation as being somewhat timid and calculated; in this view, the lion's share of the credit for the War on Poverty should go to Johnson, not Kennedy (see, e.g., Lemann 1988, 1991). Still others dismiss these issues of political personality altogether and locate the impetus for the War on Poverty within broader social and structural forces in the United States political economy (Piven and Cloward 1971; Cloward and Piven 1974; Griffin, Devine, and Wallace 1983). There is probably some truth to all these accounts, but in any case, little of tangible significance to the reduction of poverty was accomplished during the Kennedy administration. The initial idea for a War on Poverty may well have been Kennedy's, but it fell to Johnson to transform that idea into a set of specific policies and programs.

As early as 1962, there were a number of signs that a new period of activism and social concern had begun and that something like a War on Poverty might get a sympathetic hearing. The Civil Rights movement had been rejuvenated by the *Brown* desegregation ruling in 1954 and by the strong pro-civil-rights positions taken by both major candidates in the 1960 election. (*Jet* Magazine referred to Kennedy and Nixon during the 1960 campaign as "racially, the two most liberal men ever to run for President.") At the same time, the much-decried political apathy found on American college campuses throughout the 1950s was giving way to a budding student movement. Even in 1962, it was increasingly clear that the nation was at the edge of a new era, a New Frontier.

The year 1962 also witnessed the publication of Michael Harrington's book *The Other America*, a short but moving account of America's poor that is arguably the most important book on poverty ever written. Some—not Harrington himself—attribute inordinate influence to the book, claiming that it alone awakened the nation to poverty. This is doubtlessly an overstatement. Still, the book found a receptive audience (as did Edward R. Murrow's well-known documentary, *The Harvest of Shame*). A review essay by Dwight MacDonald in the January 1963 issue of the *New Yorker* apparently brought *The Other America* to Kennedy's attention and clearly advanced his already developing concern with poverty.

A year later, of course, Kennedy was dead, and poverty became Lyndon Johnson's issue. The War on Poverty was declared in his first State of the Union address in January, 1964. In a matter of weeks, a series of policy proposals had been forwarded to Congress for action, and for the first time since the Great Depression, poverty and its eradication became part of the national political agenda.

In the ensuing legislative discussion of the War on Poverty proposals, the general lack of solid statistical information on poverty in America became painfully obvious. We knew very little about the magnitude and dimensions of the problem. How many Americans in fact lived in poverty? Who were they? How did they become poor? What could be done to help? Not knowing any of these things with any certainty, it was impossible to decide what needed to be done, how much it might cost, or how long it would take. We had declared war against an enemy whose size and forces we could not even estimate. As soon as the War on Poverty was announced, the need for some useable definition of poverty became apparent. This, then, is the context in which the official federal definition of poverty was initially developed.

THE POVERTY THRESHOLD

The origins of the federal poverty standard are fairly well known among poverty researchers (Orshansky 1969; Beeghley 1984; Levitan 1985); indeed, the official standard has been the object of intense scrutiny and debate ever since it was first formulated. Early in 1964, several persons inside and outside LBJ's administration were brought together to begin formulating plans for what would become the Economic Opportunity Act of 1964, the act that launched the War on Poverty. While these legislative plans were being developed, the task of defining poverty was assigned to officials in the Social Security Administration (SSA).

As would be expected, numerous definitional, political, and practical issues were considered, some more germane than others. The choice between absolute and relative definitions of poverty was resolved in favor of an absolute standard. If poverty was to be defined in relative terms, then obviously we would always have some poverty. This seemed to make little sense, and, besides, it was politically unacceptable. If we were going to fight a War on Poverty, then we would have to define the enemy in terms that made victory possible.

How, then, might a suitable baseline poverty level be set? Here, SSA had to steer a difficult course. If the poverty threshold was set too low, many of the truly poor would be defined as nonpoor and hence as ineligible for the very policies and programs intended to end their poverty and achieve their integration into the mainstream. Alternatively, the standard could not be too high since Congress and the electorate would doubtlessly balk at the bill. Finally, the standard could not be overly complex or cumbersome since no one would understand it.

Faced with these constraints, SSA officials determined that the poverty baseline would be expressed as a simple dollar amount representing the annual income a family would require to achieve a minimal but sufficient standard of living. Thereafter, adjustments could be made for differences in family size, living arrangements, and possibly other factors.

A 1955 United States Department of Agriculture (USDA) survey of food consumption had shown that families of three or more persons spent approximately one-third of their income on food. Accordingly, it was determined that the poverty threshold should be set at three times the cost of the food needed by a poor family. So, how much food of what sort does a poor family need?

Now, as it happened, the USDA had for other reasons developed a variety of different food plans. One of these was known as the "emergency temporary low budget diet." This is *not* the same as the so-called "minimum daily adult requirements" diet. The latter is the minimum nutrient intake needed to assure proper bodily functioning over the long term. The former, the "emergency temporary low budget diet," is the minimum nutrient intake necessary to sustain human life over relatively short periods; the USDA estimates that it is nutritionally adequate only for about two months. The diet comprises so many grams of protein and carbohydrates, so much fat, so many milligrams of various vitamins and minerals, and so on.

Once the nutrient components of this emergency diet were determined, USDA shoppers then went to a selection of supermarkets and other food outlets in several major cities, attempting to determine the cheapest possible way to purchase those dietary components. How little is it possible to spend, that is, to obtain foodstuffs containing so many grams of protein and carbohydrates, so much fat, so many milligrams of various vitamins and minerals, and so on? Comparing results across cities, shoppers, and supermarkets, USDA analysts then derived a dollar figure: the minimum amount a family can spend to purchase an "emergency temporary low budget diet." Multiplied by three, that dollar figure then became the official federal poverty line (once adjusted for family size and other factors).[6]

For 1964, these procedures resulted in a poverty threshhold for a nonfarm family of four of $3,169. (By 1990, the four-person poverty standard was up to $13,359.) That is, any family of four with a gross (pretax) cash income at or below this dollar figure was considered poor. Poverty levels were also retrospectively calculated back to 1959. On the basis of these figures, it was determined that 36,055,000 Americans were poor in 1964, some 19% of the total population.

THE PROS AND CONS OF THE POVERTY STANDARD

From its very inception, the federal poverty standard has been widely and continuously criticized. Although not without its defenders, hardly any analyst or commentator on the poverty problem is entirely satisfied with the standard. The sources of dissatisfaction cover a wide range of concerns: (1) the standard is arbitrary; (2) the choice of an absolute rather than a relative definition is inappropriate; (3) the specific baseline from which the standard is derived is inadequate; (4) the reliance on cash-only income in designating households as poor overstates the extent of poverty (income inkind is excluded); (5) the failure to take account of the differing tax statuses of different kinds of income introduces unwarranted inequities; and finally, (6) the use of a single national poverty standard overlooks significant subnational variations. Some of these issues were covered earlier in this chapter; the others are worth exploring briefly here.

Arbitrariness

Some criticize the poverty standard because it contains many arbitrary elements. Why use the "emergency temporary low budget" food plan as the baseline rather than some more nutritionally adequate plan? Why assume that all poor households spend a third of their income on food? Why define poverty in terms of the cost of foodstuffs, rather than, say, the cost of housing or some other essential commodity?

There is no denying these and other arbitrary elements in the official poverty definition. At the same time, there is a certain unavoidable arbitrariness in the definition of *any* concept; thus, any alternative definition of poverty would also be arbitrary in essential respects. The important question to ask about a given definition or measurement is not whether it is arbitrary to some extent (since all are) but whether it can be consistently and reliably applied and whether experts working in the field find it to be useful or generally acceptable. And on these counts, the federal poverty standard fares reasonably well. One must also ask whether there is an obviously better or less arbitrary standard that might be invoked instead. In the case of defining and measuring poverty, there might well be a better alternative, but scholars and policymakers have yet to agree on what it is, despite nearly three decades of looking.

The Baseline

Two general criticisms have been leveled against the chosen foodstuffs baseline from which the poverty standard is derived. The first concerns the apparent nutritional inadequacy of the economy food plan itself. As we have already indicated, that baseline provides sufficient nutrients to sustain human life for about two months, after which the diet becomes progressively less adequate. What, then, should poor families eat after the first two months? If they ate a more nutritionally adequate diet, then their food costs would presumably go up, thus consuming more than the stipulated one-third of their income. It is thus obvious that a higher (more adequate) nutritional standard would result in a correspondingly higher poverty line and therefore in larger numbers of people and households falling below that line (i.e., more poverty).

If one considers the poverty standard as a per-person-per-day food budget, it must be confessed that the standard appears extremely minimal. Consider: In 1990, the poverty line for a family of four was set at $13,359. One third of that figure is the amount available to spend on food, approximately $4,453. Divided among four persons and 365 days in the year, the poverty line allows each poor person to spend $3.05 a day on food, or (assuming three meals per day) about one dollar per meal. One is entitled to ask whether anyone in the modern day and age can feed himself or herself even a minimally adequate diet on these sums. This, of course, is the same as asking whether the federal poverty standard is not overly strict, or in other words, whether many households near but over the standard are not, in fact, objectively impoverished.

A second widely discussed problem with the food baseline concerns the ratio of food to nonfood expenses. As noted, multiplying the food budget by three to obtain a poverty standard stemmed from a 1955 survey showing that families spend about a third of their incomes on food. The one-third figure, however, was an *average* for American families as a whole, not a figure derived specifically from the expense budgets of low-income families. By definition, poor people have less disposable income than other people have, and must therefore spend a higher proportion of their income on their fixed expenses (such as housing, transportation, and the like), leaving a lower proportion to spend on variable expenses such as food. Indeed, recent evidence suggests that more than a third of the nation's poor households spend in excess of 70% of their total income on shelter alone. Once housing and other fixed costs are covered, in short, many poverty households would have much less than a third of the income left with which to eat, and so perhaps a larger multiplier would be appropriate in setting the poverty standard.[7]

The general thrust of both the above criticisms, of course, is that the official poverty standard is set too low and that many households with incomes above the standard nonetheless exist in objectively impoverished conditions. But there are also arguments to be made on the other side, as follows.

Cash Versus In-Kind Income

In-kind income is any benefit received by a person or a household that is not paid out as cash. In the context of poverty, in-kind income usually refers to noncash governmental benefits such as Section 8 housing vouchers (whereby all or a portion of one's rent is paid directly to the landlord by the government) or receipt of medical attention through Medicaid or Medicare (whereby doctors, hospitals, clinics and other health care providers are paid directly by the government). Other governmentally provided in-kind benefits to the poor include food stamps, the distribution of surplus food, and free school lunches for one's children.

In-kind benefits can also come from nongovernmental sources. For instance, employers frequently provide employees with certain fringe benefits in lieu of higher wages. Paid vacation time, sick leave days, and health or disability insurance are standard in-kind benefits received by many working people; in the upper reaches of the occupational structure, free automobiles, lucrative stock options, and sometimes even housing are not uncommon.

Finally, a great deal of in-kind income is entirely privatized. Many people, for example, supplement their diets through hunting, fishing, or gardening; in some sense, their annual incomes should be increased by the exchange value of this additional food. Likewise, many people receive in-kind childcare services, as when a sister or an aunt watches the children while the parents are at work.

Since any household's material well-being can be altered quite dramatically by these sorts of in-kind benefits, the question naturally arises as to how, if at all, in-kind income should be considered when deciding whether any given household is above or below the poverty line. As a matter of fact, in-kind income is not considered at all. Procedurally, the restriction to cash income only simplifies the poverty calculations and to that extent makes sense. Still, numerous critics have pointed out that the exclusion of noncash income serves to understate people's actual standards of living and, therefore, to overstate the number of objectively poor people. The argument, in short, is that many households with cash incomes below the poverty line have sufficient noncash or in-kind income to raise their objective material circumstances out of poverty.

The issue is by no means trivial. Various studies have suggested that the poverty rate would be cut by as much as a third (or in some studies even more than a third) if we included the cash value of federal in-kind benefits as part of a family's annual income. The pertinent calculations are fairly straightforward. The major federal in-kind subsidies to the poor are Medicaid, food stamps, Section 8 housing vouchers, and direct federal subsidies of public housing. (We omit from this list the various income-transfer programs such as AFDC or general assistance because these are *cash* benefits that are included in a household's income when determining whether the household is above or below poverty.) In recent years, total federal expenditures on the four programs just listed have amounted to about $80–90 billion (Executive Office of the President 1992a). With a current poverty population of about 33 million people, the in-kind value of just these four programs works out to about $2,500 for every poor man, woman, and child in the country. A family of four right at the poverty line (1990 cash income of $13,359) would have a *de facto* income of almost $24,000 if they received a proportionate share of federal in-kind benefits and if in-kind benefits were included as part of annual income. Clearly, many families would be lifted over the poverty line by a considerable amount if their in-kind benefits were taken into account.

Others reject this line of reasoning on the grounds that it is both unrealistic and unfair. Consider, for example, the handling of Medicaid, which is, in essence, a health insurance package for the poor whose premiums are paid by the government. Anyone who purchases private health insurance knows that it costs several hundred dollars per month; including the cost of government-provided insurance premiums as a part of income could therefore easily raise a Medicaid recipient's income by several thousand dollars a year. Still, even though recipients' standards of living are improved by virtue of their receiving health care, they have not received any additional disposable income as a result. Thirty-five hundred dollars worth of health insurance is not the same as thirty-five hundred dollars in cash. Cash can be spent on anything one needs—housing, food, clothing, whatever; health insurance benefits cannot be. As Leonard Beeghley (1984) has correctly observed, without Medicaid, the poor would be poor *and* sick, rather than just poor. And likewise, without housing vouchers, many of the poor would be poor *and* homeless; without food stamps, poor *and* hungry. That many of the poor are not hungry, not homeless, and not sick is certainly a commendable social achievement, but it does not make them any less *poor.*

There is also an equity issue raised by these concerns. For the general population, income in kind often is not considered to be true income because it is exempted by the government from taxation (one reason why fringe benefits in lieu of higher wages are so popular). If income in kind received by the poor is to be counted in deciding whether a household is above or below poverty, then by rights income in kind received by the rest of the population should be subject to income taxation. It is certainly unfair to treat income in kind as real income when it is received by the poor but to define it as nonincome for everyone else.

Finally, there is an important sense in which the entire issue is moot, since the available research shows that noncash or in-kind income is *positively* correlated with real cash income; those with the most cash income, in short, also receive the most income in kind (Noto 1981; Burstein 1983; Surrey and McDaniel 1985). Taking income in kind into account would therefore *increase,* not decrease, the disparity in material resources between the poor and the remainder of the population.

Taxable and Nontaxable Income

A household is considered to be poor if its *pretax* annual income falls below a certain level. In terms of economic well-being, however, the spendable or posttax income is more relevant. Since some cash income is exempt from taxation, the result is an apparently inequitable situation where one family can be below the poverty line and yet have *more* spendable income than another family that is above the poverty line.

Consider, as an example, a family of four (the Smiths) whose 1964 wages amounted to $3,174, or $5 more than the 1964 poverty line (=

$3,169 for a family of four). Since the Smiths' pretax income is above the line, they are not considered poor and are not eligible for poverty programs. However, in 1964, the Smiths would have incurred an effective tax liability of about 4%, or $127, reducing their after-tax income to $3047, a below-poverty figure. Imagine now a second family of four (the Joneses) with a 1964 income of $3165, just beneath the poverty line, but with this income derived from Mr. Jones' tax-exempt disability benefit. In this hypothetical case, the Joneses are considered poor (and eligible for certain poverty programs) while the Smiths are not, even though the Smiths' spendable income is $118 *less*. Thus the treatment of untaxed income can create obvious inequities in the poverty-program system.

A Single National Standard

Finally, numerous critics have pointed out that the cost of living is substantially different in various cities and regions of the country; in particular, the cost of living is generally higher in the large central cities where the poor tend to be concentrated. There is also considerable variation from city to city; it costs more to live in New York, Washington, or San Francisco than in Indianapolis, St. Louis, or New Orleans. A single baseline poverty figure applied throughout the country obviously fails to account for these often substantial cost-of-living differences. The direction of the bias is presumably to *understate* the extent of poverty in higher-cost cities, and to *overstate* the extent of poverty in lower-cost cities. And since many federal programs allocate funds based on the percentage of poor people in a specific city, the result is possibly large inequities in the distribution of federal poverty dollars.

RECONSIDERING THE POVERTY THRESHOLD

Given all these difficulties, why have we retained the poverty index? The answer proves fairly simple. First, many of the criticisms leveled at the official definition would apply with equal force to *any* definition. And clearly, there must be *some* definition before research or programs can go forward. Second, admitting all the flaws in the official standard, no one has yet come up with anything agreeably or substantially better. Third, whatever the flaws, the existing baseline has at least provided us with a reasonably consistent and sensitive standard used by pretty much everybody working in the poverty area. Finally, and perhaps most importantly, we must remember that the poverty threshold is only an *indicator* of poverty that proves more or less useful given the purposes at hand. If we avoid reification (in this case, treating the indicator as the thing itself), the official poverty standard—warts and all—proves to be an extremely useful tool.

DATA ON POVERTY

We have already stressed that definitions of poverty will be more or less useful depending on the analytic or policy purposes at hand. We thus draw upon more than one definition in the following chapters, although for obvious reasons we stick with the official definition whenever possible. There are also various kinds of data on poverty that prove more or less informative depending on the uses to which they are put. The three general sorts of data we employ here are *cross-sectional* data, *time-series* data, and *panel* data. Metaphorically, these correspond to a snapshot, a slide show, and a motion picture.

Much of what we would like to know about poverty can be answered with observations taken at a single point in time—in short, with a snapshot. For example, what percentage of the United States population is below the poverty line in a particular year? This kind of information is usually referred to as cross-sectional and is especially useful when attempting to compare across units of analysis. For example, we might want to know what American city has the highest incidence of poverty, and so we would compare poverty rates across cities for some specified year.

There are, of course, occasions when a snapshot does not give us what we want. Cross-sectional data are static, and sometimes we need to know about trends, about how some indicator varies over time. In this case, we need a series of snapshots (a slide show), or, in short, *longitudinal* information. The accumulation of a temporally ordered sequence of cross-sectional observations is called a "time series," the obvious value of which is that it allows us to examine how things change over time. For example, we might want to know whether poverty in the United States increased from 1989 to 1990.

For some questions, neither a snapshot nor a slide show will suffice; only a motion picture will provide the necessary data. For example, we can tell from our annual poverty "slides" that there were more than 31 million poor people in the United States in both 1989 and 1990. But was it the same 31 million people in both years? (That is, were all the poor people of 1990 also poor in 1989, or was there movement back and forth across the poverty line during those years?) This question is critical because it bears on the chronicity of poverty, an issue we explore in Chapter 5, and the only way to answer it is to follow the same people from one year to the next so that the flows into and out of poverty can be documented. Repeated observation of the same sample of people over time is called a *panel survey*. One extremely important such survey is the Panel Study of Income Dynamics (PSID), an ongoing, national, federally funded project conducted by the Institute For Social Research at the University of Michigan that has followed a sample of 5,000 American families for more than twenty years. As a source of information on the dynamics of poverty, it is literally without peer and is therefore heavily exploited in the following pages.

As is obvious, subsequent chapters in this volume present a *collage* of snapshots, slide shows, and motion pictures, each with poverty in America as the focal point and central theme. As background to the remainder, the next chapter considers the number of the poor, the poverty trends over time, and the changing composition of the poverty population.

NOTES

1. Unlike the approach using income quintiles discussed earlier in the text, this approach does not constrain a given percentage of the population to be in poverty. By definition of the median, half of any distribution must fall below the median value of the distribution, but there is no constraint on how far below the median any case has to fall. If the median United States family income is, say, $30,000, then by the logic of this approach, families with incomes less than $15,000 would be considered poor. There is no statistical reason that requires any actual family's income to fall beneath that value. In contrast, the bottom quintile of any distribution necessarily contains 20% of the total cases. So defining poverty as a proportion of the median income is more reasonable than defining it in terms of percentiles in a larger income distribution.

2. "Critics began noticing poverty on a large scale in the United States as long ago as the early 1800s. Observations about the paradox of poverty, the belief that poverty is out of place in a country as rich as ours, were first made in 1822" (Shenkman 1988, p. 160). Notable works on poverty in America of the eighteenth, nineteenth, and early twentieth century include Hunter (1904), Patterson (1986), and Jones (1992).

3. Aid to Dependent Children (ADC, later to become Aid to Families with Dependent Children, or AFDC), now the nation's largest and most visible relief program, was not enacted until 1935, when it was passed as a relatively minor provision of the Social Security Act. The intention of its designers was dramatically different from what the program later became. Congress initially intended ADC as a relatively small "safety net" for women with children who required temporary assistance in the face of sudden familial or economic dislocation such as the death of a spouse. In the 1930s, women with children but no spouses were rarely divorced, abandoned, or never married; they were mostly widows. In basic design and intent, then, ADC was intended as relief to young widows whose children were not yet old enough to fend for themselves.

4. The Galbraith book cited earlier, *The Affluent Society* (1955), is a case in point. Although Galbraith's book was not indifferent to the residual pockets of poverty amidst plenty, his unbridled optimism and sense of the problem's transience and curability are striking.

5. We do not intend to romanticize or overestimate the depth and breadth of the transformation in public thinking about the poor that was occasioned by the War on Poverty. Throughout LBJ's tenure as President, there was a large and increasingly vocal opposition to the premises, logic, and goals of his Great Society program. In retrospect, the seemingly boundless optimism of the early 1960s was naive; mistakes were made, money wasted, and opportunities squandered. All this aside, it is also clear that LBJ's initiatives had a widespread and relatively rapid effect on how people viewed the poverty problem.

6. Originally, there were also adjustments made for sex of the family head, number of minor children, and farm-nonfarm residence. The initial idea was that subsequent revisions of the poverty line would be based on changes in the price of foodstuffs. Minor modifications of these protocols were approved in 1969 and again in 1980. Among the changes: (1) the sex of the family head was no longer considered relevant; (2) the farm-nonfarm distinction was abolished; and (3) annual revisions to the poverty standard were tied to changes in the overall Consumer Price Index (CPI) rather than to the changing price of specific food items.

7. More recent survey information provided by the USDA's Economic Research Services division suggests that the average American family now spends about *one-fourth* of its income on food. If this were adopted as the standard, the corresponding poverty line would be about 33% higher than it is, and the number officially designated as poor would increase by many millions.

2

Poverty Then and Now: What's Different, What's the Same?

Concerns about poverty in America date at least to the early nineteenth century. In 1822, the Society for the Prevention of Pauperism remarked, "Our territory is so expansive, its soil so prolific," that poverty should be "foreign to our country" (Shenkman 1988, p. 160). As a topic of social concern, in short, poverty has been on the American agenda for nearly as long as we have been an independent nation. And yet in the 1980s, a number of authors began writing about the "new" American poverty, suggesting that something fundamental had changed in the extent, circumstances, social distribution, or consequences of poverty in the postindustrial era. What, if anything, distinguishes the poverty of today from that of previous times? What is different? What is the same? It has now been nearly thirty years since the advent of an official poverty threshold; our purpose here is thus to provide a three-decade overview of continuities and changes in the overall poverty situation.

TRENDS IN THE POVERTY THRESHOLD, 1959–1990

We begin with the history of the official poverty threshold itself. Figure 2.1 shows how the threshold has changed over time in then-*current* dollars; Figure 2.2 converts the series to constant (1990) dollars. In then-current dollars, the poverty threshold has risen dramatically, from $2,973 dollars in 1959 to $13,359 in 1990 (for an average family of four persons), a 450% increase. This, of course, does *not* mean that the average poor person of 1990 is four and a half times better off than in 1959, but rather that inflation has reduced the value of the 1990 dollar to less than a quarter of its 1959 value. Once converted to constant dollars (as in Figure 2.2), the poverty standard has not changed at all; indeed, the trend line is remarkably flat (in itself not surprising since the poverty threshold is adjusted for inflation annually). In terms of what an income can purchase, in other words, the poverty-level income of today is identical to that of

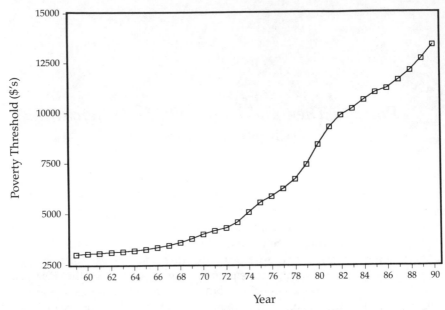

Figure 2.1. Poverty threshold for a family of four, 1959–1990 (current dollars).

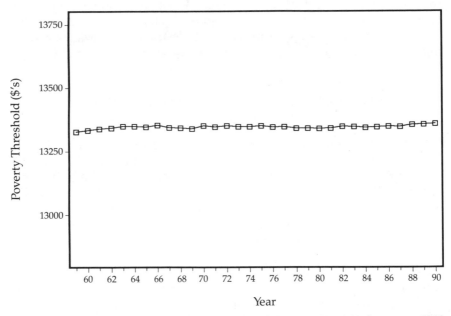

Figure 2.2. Poverty threshold for a family of four, 1959–1990 (constant 1990 dollars).

three decades past. In absolute purchasing power, today's poor are just as poor as the poor have always been.

Since 1959, of course, real family incomes (adjusted for inflation) for the U.S. population as a whole have increased considerably; in fact, they have nearly doubled.[1] Measured against the median family income as a standard, in other words, the *relative* position of the poor has deteriorated. This is shown graphically in Figure 2.3, which depicts the poverty threshold as a percentage of the median family income over time. In 1959, the poverty threshold amounted to more than half (about 55%) of the median family income, a percentage that steadily declined through about 1970 and that has hovered right around 40% since (reaching an absolute low of 37.0% in 1989). Relative to the average American income, in short, today's poor are substantially *worse* off than they were thirty years ago.

The data in Figure 2.3 lend themselves to interesting calculations. In 1990, the poverty threshold for a family of four was $13,359, and with that as the standard, the poverty rate stood at 13.5%. In the same year, the median American family income was $35,353. If we were to define poverty as a percentage of the median family income and use the 1959 value as the standard, then the 1990 four-person poverty threshold would have been (.55 x $35,353 =) $19,444, or more than $5,000 higher than the actual threshold. All told, there were about 8 million American households, comprising well more than 20 million persons, whose 1990 incomes fell between $13,359 (the actual 1990 poverty standard) and $19,444 (what the 1990 standard would be under the above assumptions). Adopting the 1959 standard, in short, would give us a poverty count in excess of 50 million, as opposed to the 33.5 million counted with the official 1990 definition. If nothing else, these calculations illustrate that a large stratum of the American population lives distressingly close to the poverty standard, if not quite at or below it. They also show that relatively modest changes in the poverty standard produce relatively large changes in the size of the poverty population.

Summarizing briefly, the data so far considered show that (1) today's poverty income will purchase just about the same basket of goods and services that the 1959 poverty income would have purchased; however, (2) the overall American standard of living as a whole has improved significantly over the past three decades; therefore, (3) compared to average standards of living, the position of the poor has worsened. A person right at the poverty line in 1959, in other words, was quite a bit closer to the average standard of living than a poor person is today. This is only a roundabout way of saying that the gap in living standards between the poor and the middle class has widened (see U.S. Bureau of the Census 1991a, 1991b, 1991c; and Mishel and Simon 1988).

One can also consider the poverty threshold against prevailing ideas

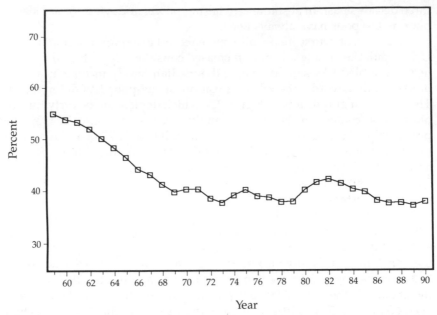

Figure 2.3. The poverty threshold (4-person family) as a percent of median family income, 1959–1990.

about how much money people need to live in the United States. The Gallup organization has periodically asked national samples of adult Americans what they think is "the smallest amount of money a family of four needs each week to get along in this community."[2] Interestingly, year in and year out, the official poverty threshold amounts to only 60–70% of this subjective minimum income. In 1959, for example, the average nationwide response to Gallup's question was $79 per week, or about $4,100 per year. The four-person poverty line in 1959 was $2,973, or only 72% of what the average American felt was the minimum necessary income.

Figure 2.4 expresses the annual poverty threshold as a proportion of Gallup's average estimated minimum cost of living from 1959 to 1985. As already noted, what the average American thinks of as the minimum necessary income is always considerably higher than the official federal poverty standard (the general public, in short, is more generous in these matters than the government). Note too that the poverty threshold has tended to fall relative to the estimated minimum, especially during the late 1960s. Through the mid-1960s, the official poverty standard constituted 70–75% of the estimated minimum; from the mid-1960s through the early 1970s, this proportion steadily fell; from 1977 on, it has tended to increase. Still, all fluctuations are within a fairly narrow range (58–75%).

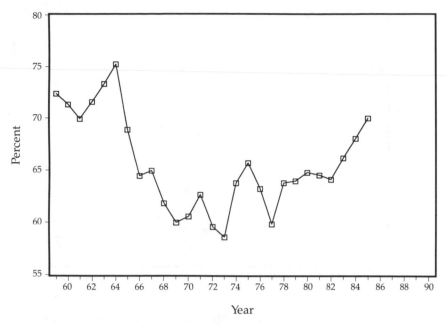

Figure 2.4. Poverty threshold (4-person family) as a percent of the estimated minimum cost of living reported to the Gallup Poll, 1959–1985.

Clearly, were we to define poverty according to responses to Gallup's question, we would again have much more poverty than the official standard demarcates.

TRENDS IN POVERTY, 1959–1990

Over the past thirty years, the actual number of Americans living below the official poverty line has varied from a low of about 23 million in 1973 to a high of nearly 40 million in 1960 (Figure 2.5). Year-to-year fluctuations in the number of the poor can be quite substantial. These annual changes, which often amount to several million persons, result mainly from macroeconomic conditions that affect the unemployment rate. During periods of general economic growth (the 1960s and postrecession 1980s), the rate of employment increases and the number of the poor goes down. Alternatively, during recessionary times, unemployment and therefore poverty tend to increase. Other factors also influence the general rate of poverty, as we shall see in later chapters, but the rate of employment is probably the most critical.

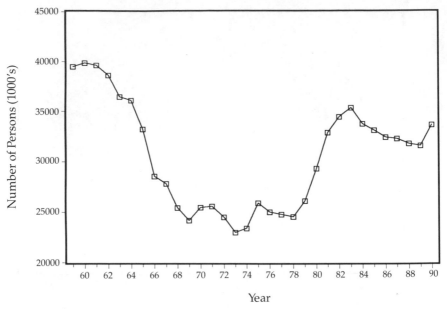

Figure 2.5. Number of persons below the official poverty line, 1959–1990 (in thousands)

Decade by decade, the overall pattern is reasonably clearcut. The number of the poor declined steadily throughout the 1960s, from 40 million poor at the beginning of the decade to about 25 million poor at the end. The sharpest declines occurred after the onset of the War on Poverty in 1964. Throughout the 1970s (often referred to as the "Decade of Inflation"), the number in poverty fluctuated right around the 25 million mark, with no obvious trend in either direction. Then, starting in 1979, the number of the poor began to increase, reaching the 35 million mark in 1983. Throughout the rest of the 1980s the number of American poor slowly declined, reaching a low of 31.5 million in 1989. With the 1990 recession, however, the number of poor increased by almost 2 million persons and has continued to increase since.

The 1983 figure is of historical significance because it represents the largest number of persons in poverty ever recorded since the beginning of the War on Poverty in 1964 (that is, until 1991). In five years, the gains of the previous two decades were totally erased as some 10 million persons were added to the poverty count. In these respects, the 1980s can only be described as a giant step backward. One obvious but essential thing that is "new" about poverty today, in short, is that there is a lot more of it than there used to be twenty years ago.

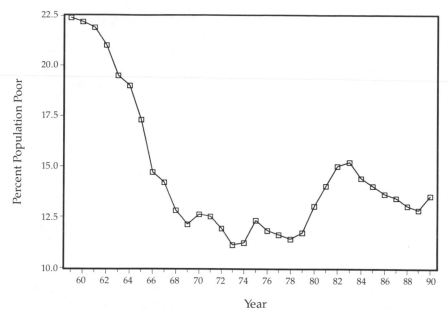

Figure 2.6. Percent of population below the official poverty line, 1959–1990.

For comparative purposes, most observers prefer to look at the poverty *rate* (the percentage of the total population living at or below the poverty line) rather than the raw numbers. This is a common method of standardization that allows more meaningful comparisons across years, localities, and subpopulations. The thirty-year trend in the poverty rate is shown in Figure 2.6. As can be seen, the highest poverty rates—in excess of 20% of the population—preceded the War on Poverty. From the early 1960s through 1973, the rate of poverty in America was halved (falling from 22.2% to 11.1%). From 1973 through the end of the decade, no further progress was made, and beginning about 1980, the rate began to increase, reaching a post-1965 peak of 15.2% in 1983 and remaining at mid-1960s levels since. Thus the secular trends in the poverty rate are much the same as the trends in the total numbers; overall, the pattern is one of considerable progress in the 1960s, stagnation in the 1970s, and significant deterioration in the 1980s.

From 1983 through to the end of the decade, then, nearly 35 million Americans lived at or below the official poverty standard each year. It is hard to appreciate just how large a number 35 million is. The number of the poor in the United States, for example, is approximately equal to the total combined population of the nation's forty largest cities, is larger than the population of Canada (by about ten million), and is twice the combined populations of the seven nations of Central America. There are four times more poor people than there are college students, six times more poor people than Jewish people, twenty times more poor people than there are writers, artists, entertainers, and athletes combined. There are more poor people in the United States than there are seconds in a year.

THE WAR ON POVERTY: SUCCESS OR FAILURE?

As already noted, the poverty rate reached its all-time low of 11.1% in 1973, having dropped by half from the rates that prevailed in the early 1960s. Since 1973, no further progress has been made, and since 1978 some significant regression has occurred. What, if anything, can be inferred from these trends about the successes or failures of the War on Poverty?

The arrested progress of the 1970s and the backsliding of the 1980s have prompted many critics to conclude that the War on Poverty was an expensive failure at best and an unmitigated disaster at worst (see, for instance, Murray 1984; Anderson 1978; Gilder 1981). These critics argue that the rapid increases in social welfare spending of the 1960s and 1970s fostered indolence and dependency among the poor by rewarding promiscuity and destroying all sense of familial and work obligations. At the same time, the post-1965 "welfare explosion" is said to have consumed resources that might otherwise have been used for productive investment and to have resulted in today's massive federal deficits. In their extreme form, these attacks depict the welfare programs first launched in the War on Poverty as the root of all contemporary evil.

It would be pointless to deny the overall lack of progress against poverty since 1973 or to gloss over the inefficiencies and outright waste that plagued and continue to plague many poverty policies and programs. Unlike Harrington (1984), we do not believe that every War on Poverty program worked as it was intended. At the same time, the conservatives' blanket condemnation of the War on Poverty programs is, we think, motivated more by ideology than evidence. The successes, failures, and legacy of the War on Poverty are pursued in a number of other works, but some basic observations are in order here.[3]

First, the initial decade of the War on Poverty saw the poverty rate cut in half. This certainly would not qualify as a total victory, and not all of the decline in the poverty rate can be unambiguously attributed to the War on Poverty itself. Nonetheless, halving the rate of poverty must qualify as a commendable and important achievement by any standard. Secondly, it is surely no coincidence that progress against poverty ended in 1973. To the contrary, the economic dislocations resulting from the events of that year wreaked havoc on all the advanced industrial economies, ours certainly included. Given the rates of inflation and the levels of unemployment following 1973, even holding the line against poverty would have to be counted as some accomplishment. Finally, we also do not think it coincidental that the rate of poverty began to increase just as the Reagan Administration was beginning to engineer large cutbacks in welfare spending. Much of what Reagan tried to do in 1981 was exactly what conservative critics had been urging, with an *increase* in poverty as the apparent result.

Indeed, the history of the past three decades would seem to suggest that the rate of poverty declines when spending on welfare programs increases (1964–1973), except when general economic conditions are extremely troubled (1973–1980), and that the rate of poverty increases when welfare spending is cut (1980 to date). Admittedly, this conclusion oversimplifies a complex reality, but it is closer to the truth than the conclusion that "we already fought a war on poverty. Poverty won." A more accurate conclusion, perhaps, is that we surrendered just as the tide was beginning to turn.

RECENT TRENDS IN THE MACROECONOMY: INCOME AND INCOME DISTRIBUTION

Realistically, the rate of poverty and other aspects of the poverty problem must be considered in light of larger trends in the macroeconomy. Despite a few relatively prosperous "boom" years, the United States has experienced very little economic growth since 1973; such growth as has occurred has tended to be extremely uneven. Obviously, the overall rate of growth puts strict limits on how much progress against poverty can be made.

John Kennedy referred to economic growth as "the rising tide that lifts all ships," a memorable phrase, perhaps, but demonstrably false. All ships do not rise when the economic tide comes in, and all ships do not fall when the tide goes out. In general, as we have already noted, poverty tends to decline when the economy is healthy and growing, especially when unemployment ebbs, but this pattern admits of many exceptions.

The era subsequent to the first Arab oil embargo witnessed two major recessions, first in 1974–75 and again in 1982–83, these being the most unsettling economic periods since the Great Depression. Both were accompanied by increases in the number of the poor (Figure 2.5). More characteristic of the overall era, however, was the pattern of limited, uneven, "stop-start" economic growth (as opposed to the more or less continuous growth that prevailed from the end of World War II through the early 1970s). Overall economic sluggishness has created what amounts to a zero-sum distributional struggle, where gains among some are inevitably offset by losses among others (Thurow 1980). Moreover, the sectoral and geographical unevenness of recent growth patterns has resulted in heightened market-based inequalities; were it not for governmental transfer payments, significantly more poverty would exist since market forces have become increasingly inegalitarian (see Devine 1983; Devine and Canak 1986).

Evidence on the recent trends in income distribution illustrates the effects of these increasingly inegalitarian economic forces (Table 2.1). Throughout the twentieth century the distribution of income has been highly skewed, with the most affluent fifth of the population commanding more than 40% of the total income (Kolko 1962; Williamson and Lindert 1980). Between 1973 and 1990, the income share going to the most affluent fifth increased (from 41.1% of total income to 44.3%, an increase of 7.8%). And likewise, the share going to the poorest fifth declined (from 5.5% to 4.6%, a loss of 16.4%). The higher one goes in the income distribution, the sharper these trends become; the income share going to the most affluent 5% increased from 15.5% to 17.4% (an increase of more than 11%). Overall, between 1973 and 1990, approximately 3.0% of total national income was redistributed from the least affluent three-fifths of the population to the most affluent fifth, with the lion's share going to the richest 5%.[4]

One commonly used measure of the overall degree of income inequality is the Gini index, which increased by 11.2% during the period under discussion, reaching an all-time postwar high of .401 in 1989, with a slight fall to .396 in 1990. Roughly, the Gini index can be interpreted as the proportion of the total income that would have to be shifted around in order to achieve a completely equal distribution. In 1990, this would have required the transfer of nearly 40% of the total national income from the more affluent to the less. (It is worth a note, if only in passing, that the degree of income inequality, as indexed by the Gini coefficient, is higher in the United States than in most other advanced industrial nations. It is also worth noting that the distribution of *household* income is more highly skewed than the *families-only* data we have been discussing.)[5]

Granted, the distributional trends reviewed here are generally modest. Levy (1988, p. 2) has reviewed these same materials and concludes, "income inequality is very large, but it has remained relatively constant since World War II." The key word here is "relatively." It would obviously be mistaken to conclude that the past decade has witnessed a wholesale transformation of the income structure, but it would be equally mistaken

Table 2.1. The Distribution of National Family Income by Income Fifths, 1973–1990

| Income Group | Percent Share Received | | Rate of Change |
	1973	1990	1973–90
Lowest fifth	5.5	4.6	−16.4%
Second lowest fifth	11.9	10.8	−9.2
Middle fifth	17.5	16.6	−5.4
Fourth fifth	24.0	23.8	−0.8
Top fifth	41.1	44.3	+7.8
Top 5%	15.5	17.4	+12.3
Gini index of concentration	.356	.396	+11.2
N (×1000) =	55,053	66,322	

Sources: U.S. Bureau of the Census 1988a, 1991b.

to deny the general drift. As a nation, we are becoming less equal, not more. The share of the pie going to the affluent is growing; increased impoverishment among the nonaffluent is the inevitable consequence.

Also, statistically modest trends in income and income distribution can have dramatically large consequences for those at the bottom. A thousand dollar income gain means relatively little to a person earning $80,000 a year, and likewise, the most affluent fifth of the population has probably barely noticed its marginally increasing share of the total income. A thousand dollar income loss, on the other hand, can mean a great deal to a family below the poverty line—it can spell the difference, for example, between mere poverty and outright destitution. The marginally decreasing share of the total income going to the poorest fifth of the population, in short, has no doubt been vastly more consequential than the marginally increasing share going to those at the top.

EMPLOYMENT PATTERNS

Dramatic international shifts in investment, production, and employment lie at the base of these increasingly inegalitarian income trends. Structural forces have accelerated already substantial postindustrial developments. Viewed with optimism, these developments are associated with the much celebrated stock market boom, the information and computer revolutions, and the rebirth of leaner, more efficient, and more competitive American firms. A less sanguine frame of reference calls attention to the downside manifestations of these trends: the decline of American smokestack industries, massive public and private indebtedness, unprecedented industrial concentration, an increasing dependence on foreign credit, and immense trade deficits (see, e.g., Blumberg 1980; Thurow 1980, 1992; Bluestone and Harrison 1982; Harrison and Bluestone 1988).

All these developments have wrought profound changes in the US labor market. Jobs in the manufacturing sector have steadily disappeared, having been replaced by jobs in services (hence, the emerging "service economy"). While some view this as a benign, even commendable development, the decline of the manufacturing sector has meant the loss of hundreds of thousands of unskilled and semiskilled blue-collar jobs—jobs that traditionally sustained entire families and that provided entry-level positions to the relatively uneducated and to minorities who thereby gained a solid foothold in the labor market and a chance to move up. For the poor and near poor, the repercussions of the "service economy" have not been benign; they have been ruinous.

The service economy and its presumed benefits have received wide-spread publicity as the inevitable consequence of postindustrialism and the information revolution; the very phrase evokes images of software designers, materials engineers, and international commodities brokers. In fact, very few of the newly created service-sector jobs are in "high-tech" occupations requiring highly educated, technologically sophisticated, and therefore well-paid labor; most of them involve minimum wage retail sales positions, clerical work, and domestic services. A recent report from the Economic Policy Institute (a Washington think tank) concludes, "the two lowest paying industries—retail trade and services (business, personal, and health)—accounted for 84% of all job growth from 1979 to 1987" (see Mishel and Simon 1988; also see Harrison and Bluestone 1988).

The Economic Policy Institute report (Mishel and Simon 1988, pp. 19–23) also makes it clear that an increasing percentage of the workforce has become marginalized. Between 1973 and 1987, the temporary help industry quadrupled its share of the labor force, growing from 0.3% to 1.2% of the total employment. Likewise, the percentage of part-time workers who would prefer full-time work (the "involuntary" part-time employed) escalated from about a third of the part-time labor force (33.7%) to more than half (53.5%) (also see Tilly 1991). Fewer and fewer workers receive once-customary fringe benefits; thus as many as 37,000,000 Americans are now without health insurance of any sort. Episodes of unemployment, on average, tend to be longer and more frequent in the late 1980s than at any other time in the post-World War II era. Whatever the indicator—hours, pay, or benefits—workers seem worse off today than in prior postwar decades.

What all of this has meant for the poor and near-poor is that the labor force has become a less and less plausible route to economic independence and upward mobility. Factory jobs at decent wage rates with fringe benefits have been replaced by unbenefited minimum wage jobs with little possibility of advancement. Historically, factory jobs even at the lowest skill levels were adequate to support a family and a modest but respectable standard of living, and one could always "bid up" to better jobs as seniority accrued. None of this can be said of minimum wage work cooking hamburgers at MacDonald's or making beds at the Holiday Inn. Poor people know well what policy makers in Washington too easily forget—that the minimum wage is "chump change."

THE MINIMUM WAGE

The federal minimum wage was raised to $3.35 an hour in 1981 and remained at that level through 1990, when an act of Congress raised the minimum to $3.85 with a further increase to $4.25 taking effect in 1991. (A slightly more generous plan was vetoed by President Bush.) Prior to this recent increase (which is to say, throughout the decade of the 1980s), the actual purchasing value of the minimum wage steadily declined; the nominal wage in 1989 ($3.35 per hour) was worth only $2.31 in 1980 dollars, the lowest figure in three decades. The peak value was registered in 1968, when the minimum wage was worth $3.79 (in 1980 dollars). From 1968 to 1989, the buying power of the minimum wage eroded by 40%; in the 1980s alone, its value declined by 24%.

The recent increase in the minimum wage actually restores very little of this lost buying power. Assuming *no* inflation, the congressionally proposed (and vetoed) minimum of $4.55 an hour would only be worth $2.94 in constant 1980 dollars; the enacted minimum is worth substantially less. What today's minimum wage will buy is equivalent to the value of the minimum wage in the mid-1950s and is well below the purchasing power of the minimum wage in 1980 (which was worth $4.92 in constant 1990 dollars). Throughout the 1980s, in other words, the economic position of those working at the minimum wage steadily worsened, a reality that the recent increase alters only slightly.

It is useful to compare the minimum wage to the federal poverty line. In 1990, a full-time worker (forty hours a week, fifty weeks a year) laboring at the minimum wage would have had gross earnings equal to 58% of the four-person poverty level; that worker's family would have fallen short of the official poverty threshold by over $5000. A worker putting in fewer than 40 hours a week or working fewer than fifty weeks a year would be in still more straitened circumstances, of course. According to the Economic Policy Institute (1988, p. 41), there were over 2 million persons who worked full time at the minimum wage as recently as 1987.

Alternatively, one might imagine a 1990 family of four where both parents were working the entire year at the minimum wage, one full time (i.e., forty hours per week) and the other half time. The gross earnings of that family would fall *below* the poverty threshold by $1800. These calculations are not purely academic: in 1990, 49.8% of all heads of poverty families worked at least part of the year, and 15.2% worked year round, full time.[6]

The new minimum wage annualizes to a gross income less than three-fifths of the four-person poverty standard. What we call the "minimum" wage is in fact a subpoverty wage—not a living wage by any realistic standard. The inadequacy of the minimum wage becomes even more apparent when one realizes that today's minimum wage would have to be $6.00 an hour (in today's dollars) to have the purchasing power of the minimum wage in 1968 and that it would have to be $6.68 an hour before the annualized gross minimum wage earnings would equal the four-person poverty level. And yet the modest recent increase from $3.35 to $4.25 per hour involved an intense and protracted political struggle.

Conservative critics of federal poverty policy, such as Charles Murray and George Gilder, condemn governmental welfare programs because they are thought to destroy the motivation to work, foster dependency, and promote indolence. The plausibility of these arguments must be reconsidered in light of the work disincentives of a minimum wage that does not raise even a full-time, year-round worker above the family poverty level. How much incentive is there to work for one's livelihood at $4.25 an hour? How many young, inner-city men and women are motivated to take up drug dealing or other crimes as the only available alternative to employment at this wage level? These are not idle questions; to the contrary, they may well lie at the heart of the contemporary poverty problem.

FAMILY, WORK AND INCOME

The broad economic and distributional trends reviewed to this point have caused increasing numbers of families to rely on multiple earners to "make ends meet" (Table 2.2). Real family incomes have been effectively constant since 1973, even as the average number of earners per family has increased. Thus putting more members into the paid labor force is how many families have managed to "break even" in the face of generally unfavorable economic trends. In the absence of these additional earners, real family incomes would be well below their 1973 levels and many more families would be beneath poverty than actually are.

Table 2.2. Trends in Median Family Income and Work Experience, 1963–1990

Year	Median Family Income 1990 Dollars	Percent of Families With Two+ Workers	Married Female Labor Force Participation[a]
1963	$26,666	48.3%	22.5
1967	31,042	52.9	26.5
1969	33,617	54.0	28.5
1973	35,429	53.9	32.7
1977	34,514	54.5	39.4
1979	35,255	57.0	43.3
1983	32,356	54.7	49.9
1987	35,601	57.3	56.8
1990	35,353	58.2	--

Notes:
[a] With children under six years.
Sources: See Table 2.1.

Between 1973 and 1987, the percentage of families with multiple wage earners increased from approximately half to three-fifths. Increasing labor force participation among married women with children under six accounts for the bulk of the overall increase; today, nearly three-fifths of mothers with preschoolers work in the paid labor force. It was once customary to refer to working women as "secondary" earners, but as these trends amply suggest, the incomes of second and third earners are rarely superfluous to overall family well-being. As we have already said, these "secondary" earners—and only they—have kept total family incomes even with their 1973 levels.

Actually, this last conclusion is overly sanguine in that it focuses on the incomes of second and third earners and ignores the costs. A family with preschoolers and both adults at work obviously requires day care services, a cost that would not be incurred if only one of the adults worked.[7] Second earners also incur added commuting expenses and the like. Families where all adults work are also likely to eat away from home more often and may even find it necessary to purchase housekeeping services. If one discounted family incomes by the costs incurred in having all adults in the family at work, the *net* incomes of these families would obviously be less. This suggests that despite the appearance of constancy, *effective* family incomes have probably eroded somewhat since 1973.

One might also consider families that are not intact, where there is only one adult present in the household. Lacking the option to deploy additional earners as a means of staying even, these households must inevitably fall behind. It is hardly a surprise that poverty is much more widespread in one-earner households, especially if that single earner is a woman (whose average earnings are only 60–70% of the earnings of a comparable male), or a minority (of whom much the same may be said), or both. Many have pointed with alarm to the exceptional rate of poverty in households headed by single black mothers. Given the well-known effects of race and gender on employment and earnings and the inability of single-adult households to deploy second or third earners, however, a high rate of poverty among single black mothers is inevitable.[8]

POVERTY AND WELFARE

Stark images of welfare mothers buying steak with their food stamps, widely publicized (although empirically infrequent) cases of welfare fraud, and a generalized concern that lots of undeserving and unneedy people are getting a free ride off welfare have made it easy to overlook the many positive achievements of our antipoverty efforts. As we have already seen, poverty has not by any means been eliminated. Given the macroeconomic trends reviewed here, the structural forces that have served to exacerbate inequalities, and the consequently increasing size of the population at risk of poverty, total victory is probably out of the question; as we have already said, even to have held the line against poverty over recent decades was a significant achievement. But there is very little doubt that our many social welfare programs *have* managed to reduce certain forms of poverty among certain population groups. Sadly, the failures seem to be much better known than the successes.

First things first: most of the dollars spent by the federal government on social welfare programs are *not* spent on the poor, an essential point to keep in mind when hearing that "welfare" is now the single largest item in the federal budget. More than half of the total federal social welfare expenditure ($350 billion of the total $580 billion in 1990) was paid out in Social Security and Medicare benefits to the aged and their survivors. Also included under social welfare expenditures are all veterans' programs, federal and railroad worker retirement programs, workmen's compensation and unemployment benefits, Department of Defense health and medical programs, federally sponsored medical research, federal aid to education, and so on (see Executive Office of the President 1992a, b).

In 1990, expenditures on programs targeted mainly or exclusively to the poor amounted only to about $121 billion, roughly 20% of total social welfare expenditures. The much-decried upward spiral in social welfare spending that occurred in the 1960s and early 1970s was due primarily to escalating Social Security payments (now indexed to the cost of living) and to the rapidly increasing costs of health care, pensions, education,

and other (often middle-class) entitlement programs, and only secondarily to increased spending on the poor. In fact, in real (constant)
dollars, spending on the poor has declined since at least 1981, when the
Reagan administration narrowed the scope, number, and size of federal
antipoverty programs.

That said, it nevertheless remains true that federal spending has substantially reduced poverty in many cases. Were it not for the various
federal programs, the incidence of poverty would be much worse than it
is, and many additional millions would fall below the poverty line. For
instance, in 1990, 4.8 million families above the poverty level received
means-tested cash assistance in the form of Aid to Families With Dependent Children (AFDC), Supplementary Security Income (SSI), or other
public assistance. Without this aid, more than 17 million additional persons would have fallen below the poverty threshold. And 1990 was not an
unusual year in this regard. Throughout most of the 1980s, more than 6
million above-poverty households received federal income supplements
that kept them out of poverty (see U.S. Bureau of the Census 1989b,
p. 348).

The most substantial progress against poverty has occurred among the
nation's elderly. At the inception of the War on Poverty, the rate of
poverty among those sixty-five and older was 35.2%—higher than the
rate for any other age group and a national disgrace. Increases in Social
Security coverage and benefits, the introduction of Medicare, expanded
pension programs, and the indexing of Social Security payment levels to
the Consumer Price Index have turned this situation completely around;
today, the poverty rate among the elderly is *lower* than in any other age
group. The turnaround in the economic well-being of the elderly as a class
has been a spectacular success, by far the most stunning achievement of
the War on Poverty, and a telling lesson in what can be accomplished by
increased welfare spending.

Another impressive success is to be found in the very substantial
reduction of poverty among intact, male-headed black families. Overall,
the rate of poverty among blacks remains extremely high, about three
times the rate for whites. Still, in 1959, 43.2% of the married couple
families headed by nonwhite males were below poverty. By 1966, that
figure had been cut to 27.0%, and by 1990, the figure for black male-
headed families stood at 12.6%—still more than twice the rate for white
male-headed households but slightly less than the poverty rate for the
population as a whole (U.S. Bureau of the Census 1968, p. 5; 1989a, p. 69;
1991c, table 4). That much remains to be done in reducing poverty among
the black population does not gainsay the importance of what has already
been accomplished.

These success stories sustain broader generalizations. Historically, the impoverishment of the older population was the result of inadequate to nonexistent levels of income replacement upon retirement. Private pension plans were relatively rare and Social Security payments were miserly. Worse, these already inadequate income streams were essentially fixed and therefore steadily fell behind the cost of living. The solution to the problem of poverty among the aged was thus obvious: they needed more generous Social Security payments that increased automatically when the cost of living went up. In short, we solved this part of the poverty problem by *throwing money at it*. And we did this with little or no concern about fostering dependency or encouraging indolence among the aged. Most elderly people today are in fact highly or entirely dependent on their monthly check from the government, but the "welfare dependency" of the aged is rarely a source of concern.

The declining rate of poverty among intact black households seems to have resulted largely from the partial breakdown of educational and occupational discrimination against blacks and other minorities. This has in turn resulted in the formation of a fairly large, stable, and growing black middle class, another positive legacy of the War on Poverty that is frequently overlooked.

To be sure, part of the success so far recounted is due to what is called "creaming," that is, taking on the easiest cases first (in this case, solving the poverty problem for those groups in the population whose poverty is most amenable to solution). Since we *expect* the aged and the retired to be idle, we never had to worry about the work disincentives that might be created by increased Social Security payments. We solved their problems easily—we gave them more money. And likewise, poor but intact minority households are not incapacitated by the burdens of single earners, broken families, and the like. Given better opportunities, they find it possible to succeed.

Unfortunately, much of the poverty that remains seems rather more complex, more resistant to remediation, more expensive to solve—in a word, more obdurate. All this is *least* true of the working poor. Here as among the aged, we need not worry about the motivation to work; all we need is to ensure that their employment earns them a livable (nonpoverty) wage, for example, by raising the minimum wage, expanding employer job credits, or increasing the earned income tax credit (Devine and Wright 1990). But much of today's poverty results from far more than a simple lack of funds or overt discrimination against minorities; it results from a tangled web of structural, social, and psychological factors that will not yield easily or cheaply to intervention. Equalizing the structure of opportunity, granting more open access to education, employment, and training, and providing programs of assistance to help individuals and families through hard times are all certainly desirable, but they may not be sufficient in the face of an inadequate demand for labor, increasing family disorganization, drug abuse, and a host of related barriers.

THE "NEW AMERICAN POVERTY"

In recent years, analysts across the ideological spectrum have begun writing about the "new" American poverty, thus suggesting that the poverty of the 1980s is very different from the poverty of ten, twenty or thirty years ago (e.g., Harrington 1984, 1988; Murray 1984; Wilson 1987; Haveman 1988a, b). What is this "new" poverty? What makes it any different?

The late Michael Harrington (1984) viewed the "new" poverty largely in qualitative terms, labeling it as more profound, difficult, and tenacious than the poverty of the past, a point with which hardly anyone seems to disagree despite their otherwise substantially different understandings of the dynamics and etiology of the poverty problem. Neo-conservatives such as Charles Murray (1984) have joined with liberal analysts such as Ken Auletta (1983) and William J. Wilson (1985) in identifying the "new" poverty as the poverty of the emergent *underclass,* an entrenched and (in the opinion of many) largely intractable form of minority poverty characterized by dependency, chronicity, antisocial behavior, and geographical concentration.

When writing about social change, exaggeration comes easily. Aspects of social structure change slowly when they change at all, and so claims about the "new" should always be viewed with some caution. There certainly *seems* to be much that is different about the poverty of today, and the notion of an emerging underclass *seems* a seductive explanation of the changes. But in fact, much that has been said about the "new" poverty was equally true of the old.

Harrington (1984, 1988) depicts the poverty of the underclass as having resulted from a number of new structural and social forces that have emerged over the past two decades, but he also acknowledges that much of the so-called new poverty is not altogether new: for example, rural poverty or the poverty of minority groups, which are familiar and long-standing. For Harrington, the "new poverty" refers to such groups within the poverty population as the working poor, children, welfare mothers, undocumented workers, and the homeless, but each of these groups has *always* been found among the poor, although perhaps not in today's numbers or concentration.

Similarly, Haveman (1988a) contrasts "old" and "new" inequalities (as measured by earnings differences and poverty rates). Those most disadvantaged by the old inequalities, as Haveman depicts them, were the elderly, blacks, and women. The new inequalities, in turn, are said to center more on the young (primarily black and Hispanic youth), single-parent families (meaning, of course, mostly women with dependent children), and elderly blacks. The relative disappearance of the elderly from the ranks of the poor is a genuine change, as we have already acknowledged, but otherwise, one is more impressed by the similarities between Haveman's "old" and "new" inequalities than by the differences.

Harrington, Haveman, and other analysts have stressed three critical points in their discussions of the emerging "new poverty," each well taken and worthy of emphasis here. First, increased educational and employment opportunities and the partial dismantling of racial and sexual discrimination in these spheres have allowed a substantial number of blacks and other minorities (especially those living in male-headed households) and many educated single women a chance to escape from poverty. Secondly, expanded retirement benefits and coverage have greatly reduced poverty among the aged. Finally, structural changes in the political economy have simultaneously tended to concentrate poverty among other demographic groups. Those now clustered at the bottom tend to be children and women heading their own households. But even here, as we shall see, the changes that have occurred are more variations on a theme than wholesale transformations.

Our point is that in a number of important respects, the so-called "new" poverty is not appreciably different from the old. Poverty in America has always been concentrated among minorities and women; this was true at the onset of the War on Poverty and remains true today. Likewise, poverty then and now is largely a plague of the uneducated and the unskilled. At least some people throughout our history will have been found to labor at subpoverty wages and thus to constitute the "working poor." At least some poor people at all times and places will have found minimally acceptable housing beyond their reach and would thus constitute the "homeless poor." Even the antisocial behavior now commonly associated with the "new" underclass—crime, family instability, teenage pregnancy, illegitimacy, alcohol and drug use, welfare dependence—has always been disproportionate among the poor (Jones 1992). In many respects, the notion of a "new" American poverty is very misleading.

Consider, for examples, three purported trends in the poverty situation that have been much discussed in recent years: the feminization of poverty, the growing poverty of children, and the poverty of the working poor. Table 2.3 compares the situation in 1959 to 1990 in the rates of poverty for various demographic subgroups. The trends mentioned above would naturally lead one to expect increasing rates of impoverishment among women, children, and the employed, but in fact the rate of poverty has *declined* substantially for all three groups. What has tended to change for

Table 2.3. Poverty Rates for Various Demographic Subgroups: 1959 and 1990

	1959		1990	
Demographic Group	Rate	Percent of All Poor[a]	Rate	Percent of All Poor[a]
All persons	22.4%	—	13.5%	—
Number of poor		39,490,000		33,585,000
White	18.1	72.1	10.7	66.5
Nonwhite (Black)[b]	54.6	27.5	31.9	29.3
Hispanic[c]	e	e	28.1	17.9
Persons in families	20.8	87.5	12.0	75.1
Male-headed households	15.7	70.1[f]	7.1	37.7
White	13.2	e	6.2	30.4
Nonwhite/Black	43.2	e	12.6	6.6
Hispanic	e	e	17.5	8.9
Female-headed households[d]	49.4	17.8	37.2	37.5
White	40.2	10.7	29.8	18.2
Black	70.6	6.1	50.6	17.9
Hispanic	e	e	53.0	6.3
Unrelated individuals	47.4	13.0	20.7	22.2
Male	37.1	4.0	16.9	8.5
White	33.9	3.0	14.9	6.2
Nonwhite (Black)	51.0	1.0	29.3	2.0
Hispanic	e	e	29.4	1.2
Female	54.1	9.0	24.0	13.7
White	52.3	7.7	21.6	10.8
Nonwhite (Black)	67.9	1.3	42.0	2.4
Hispanic	e	e	42.0	1.1
Elderly (65+ years)	35.9	10.9	12.2	10.9
White	33.8	9.4	10.1	8.1
Nonwhite (Black)	59.0	1.5	33.8	2.6
Hispanic	e	e	22.5	.7
Children (< 18)	27.3	44.4	20.6	40.0
White	20.1	28.4	15.9	24.5
Nonwhite (Black)	63.8	14.3	44.8	13.5
Hispanic	e	e	38.4	8.5
In male-headed households	21.7	32.4	10.9g	16.5
White	17.0	22.5	9.5g	12.5
Nonwhite (Black)	58.0	9.9	19.8g	2.8
Hispanic	e	e	e	e
In female-headed households	72.6	10.3	53.4	21.9
White	66.6	5.9	45.9	10.7
Nonwhite (Black)	82.7	4.4	64.7	10.5
Hispanic	e	e	68.4	3.9
Working poor				
Year round, Full time[h]	9.4i	36.9i	2.5j	4.8
< Yr. round, Full time	26.9i	32.6i	12.6j	17.8

Notes:

a Nonexclusive.

b Nonwhite for 1959; black for 1990.

c Persons of Hispanic origin may be of any race.

d Based on estimated number of persons in such families.

e Data not available.

f No spouse present.

g 1987 year data, related children in other (non-female-headed) households.

h Working full time, 50–52 weeks.

i Pertains to families and family members only.

j Pertains to persons 16+ years of age.

Sources: U.S. Bureau of the Census 1968, 1969, 1989a, 1991c.

each group is their rate of poverty *relative* to other groups and therefore their relative proportions within the poverty population.

First, the working poor: in 1959, the rate of poverty among the year-round, full time gainfully employed was 9.4%; in that same year, more than a third (36.9%) of the poor were members of families in which someone was employed full time. Slightly less than an additional third of the poor (32.6%) lived in families where someone was also working, but at less than full-time. Despite the increasingly voiced concern about the "new" working poor, the rate of poverty among the year-round, full-time employed had declined to 2.5% in 1990, and their proportion in the poverty population had declined to less than 5%. In 1959, the rate of poverty among the full time employed was about two-fifths the rate experienced by the American population as a whole (9.4% to 22.4%), whereas in 1990, the rate among the full-time employed had dropped to a fifth of the national rate (2.5% to 13.5%). The poverty situation among those employed full-time has actually improved significantly over the past three decades, by whatever indicator one chooses.

The picture for women and children is somewhat more occluded, but the essentials are nonetheless clear.[9] In 1959, the poverty rate among single women without children was 54.1%, and in 1990, 24.0%—a large and obvious decline. The rate among households headed by women was 49.4% in 1959 and 37.2% in 1990, a substantial reduction, not an increase. In 1959, 27.3% of all children under age 18 were below poverty; by 1990, the rate of poverty within this group had declined to 20.6%, a relatively small change but opposite to the postulated direction.

Simplifying slightly, what has happened in the past three decades is that the rate of poverty has declined considerably for the nation at large and has also declined in every important demographic subgroup. The *rate* of decline, however, has differed appreciably from one group to the next, so that the *proportional* representation of each group in the larger poverty population has changed. Thus, the rate of poverty among female-headed households declined, as we have already noted, from 49.4% in 1959 to 37.2% in 1990. But this is a substantially smaller decline than that registered in the population as a whole, so the proportion of the poor living in female-headed households has dramatically increased, from 17.8% to 37.5% over the past three decades. Among single women, likewise, the rate of poverty has declined, but their proportion among the poor has increased, from 9% in 1959 to 13.7% in 1990. All told, the proportion of women among the poor has nearly doubled over the past thirty years. As is thus apparent, the "feminization of poverty" does not refer to an increasing rate of poverty among women, but rather to an increasing proportion of women among the poor. And likewise with many of the other trends that are postulated as having created the "new" American poverty of today.

The overall trends in poverty revealed in Table 2.3 provide some basis for optimism, since the rate of poverty has declined everywhere since 1959. Unfortunately, the compositional changes to which we have just alluded provide the other and less optimistic part of the story. Critical demographic and familial changes have occurred in American society over the past three decades, with evident consequences for the poverty situation. Nowhere is this more apparent than in the number of persons, especially children, living in female-headed households.

Despite a reduced *rate* of poverty among female-headed households and among the children living in such households, the actual number of families headed by women and the number of their children have both substantially increased over the past decades. The result is that in 1990, the number of poor persons living in female-headed households stood at 12.5 million people, compared to only about 7 million thirty years earlier. In 1959, persons living in female-headed households comprised less than one in five of the poor; today, it is nearly two in five.

The pattern for children is similar. In 1959, the poverty rate for children in households headed by women was 72.6%. Although the *rate* of poverty in this group dropped to 53.4% in 1990, the earlier figure represented about 4 million children, and the latter figure more than 7 million, and the proportion of the poor who were children living in female-headed households accordingly grew from 10.3% to 21.9%. As with the feminization of poverty, the "increasing poverty of children" does *not* refer to an increasing rate of poverty among children (in female-headed households), but rather to an increasing proportion of these children among the poor. These, of course, are assuredly not the same thing, although confusion on the point is widespread.

CONCLUSIONS

When all is said and done, much of the so-called new poverty proves to be quite familiar, but there remains a certain heuristic utility in the concept. The "new poverty" notion nicely captures the altered demographic configuration of poverty and demands that we consider the shifting structural, economic and psycho-social forces that have produced these changes. Also, the concept alerts us that poverty is not at all monolithic. Rather, the faces of the poor are many, and they have changed over time.

Much of the "old" poverty was as chronic as the "new" poverty is said to be. One would hardly characterize the intergenerational deprivation of rural Mississippi or Appalachia as otherwise. The "new" poverty, however, at least seems to be more deeply entrenched, more tightly concentrated in the central cities, and more pathological. This is the poverty of the underclass that we take up in detail in later chapters.

The poverty of decades past seems to have been less deeply rooted, less self-destructive, and less socially catastrophic than the poverty of today. It was seemingly more tractable and arose more from the lack of opportunity than from the lack of determination to succeed in socially acceptable terms. The labor market and familial dislocations associated with the old poverty were more understandable, if no less invidious, than the forces at work today. The old poverty seemed more temporary, more amenable to intervention, and less likely lead to personal and social devastation.

The poverty that existed at the dawn of the War on Poverty was concentrated among three major groups: the aged, minorities, and women. In the three decades since, rates of poverty have declined significantly in all three groups. One cannot help but think that in the past thirty years, we have managed to solve the easier half of the poverty problem, with the far more difficult half remaining. The components, etiology, and dynamics of this "more difficult half" of the American poverty problem are thus the topics to which we turn next.

NOTES

1. The median family income level, adjusted for inflation, increased quite regularly from 1959 to 1973, but has largely stagnated since. Moreover, the post-1973 pattern of stability is largely attributable to an increase in the average number of earners per family (see U.S. Bureau of the Census 1988a, 1991b).

2. The raw data for this presentation can be found in *The Gallup Report* Gallup Organization (1985). Gallup asks people how much money a family needs each *week* to get by; we have multiplied the average response by 52 to convert to an annual income. Also, Gallup has not asked the question in every year; we have interpolated through the missing years with a standard linear interpolation, a crude but serviceable approximation. Since the responses to the Gallup question are in then-current dollars, we have used the then-current-dollar poverty figures for the presentation.

3. For readers interested in more comprehensive evaluations of the War on Poverty, we recommend Haveman (1977), Danziger and Weinberg (1986), Patterson (1986), Levitan (1985), and Shapiro and Greenstein (1988).

4. According to Blau (1992, Ch. 3), this upward transfer of income was an explicit priority of Ronald Reagan's economic policies.

5. The U.S. Bureau of the Census defines a household as "all persons who occupy a housing unit" while the term family refers to "groups of two persons or more . . . related by birth, marriage, or adoption and residing togethre" (1991b, p. 228).

6. According to census data, fewer than a third (29.9%) of impoverished families did not have anyone working, and more than two-thirds of these families without earners were single female-headed households (U.S. Bureau of the Census 1991c, table 19).

7. Fewer than a third (30.6%) of working mothers with children under six have their children taken care of in their own home, which is likely to be the least costly arrangement. The plurality (40.2%) take their children for care to some other home (about half these cases involve relatives; the other half do not). About one in seven (14.8%) utilize group care centers, and in the remaining cases, the mother cares for the child while she is working (see U.S. Bureau of the Census 1986, table 626).

8. In actuality, the rate of poverty among Hispanic female-headed households marginally exceeds the rate for black female-headed households. Numerically, however, the former are only a third of the size of the latter.

9. Unless otherwise noted, all data discussed in this section are taken from the U.S. Bureau of the Census (1968, 1969; 1989a, 1991c).

3

The Contemporary Demography of Poverty

Words are seductive; they simplify complex realities. To speak, for example, of "the" homeless is to suggest a unitary character to "the" homelessness problem and to depict "the" homeless as a single, undifferentiated group. In point of fact, of course, there are many different kinds of homeless people, each with their own problems, resources and needs. The needs of young, mentally ill, black homeless women with children are obviously very different from the needs of elderly, white, alcoholic homeless men; and likewise, as Smith (1985) has so astutely observed, homelessness is "not one problem but many."

So too with poverty and "the" poverty problem. "The" poor do not comprise a homogeneous group and poverty is not a single, unitary problem. Rather, there are many different kinds of poor people and many different forms of poverty. In this chapter, we begin the process of parceling out the various components of the poverty population so as to get closer and closer to that portion that concerns us in the remainder of the book, the urban underclass. We thus begin with those components of the poverty population that do not figure in current discussions of the underclass: specifically, the working poor, the rural poor, the elderly, and impoverished children.

The particular groups we examine in this and later chapters are not totally exhaustive of the poverty population although they do encompass the vast majority. Neither are these subgroups wholly exclusive; often there is overlap among them. We have chosen subgroups for discussion on the basis of certain shared characteristics that are related to the dynamics of poverty within each subgroup. As is true of any crude typology, however, we recognize (and will occasionally make reference to) critical variation that exists within each subpopulation we examine.

THE WORKING POOR

Most of the poor (about three-quarters) live in families, that is to say, as groups of individuals related by blood or marriage. A small proportion

(2.7% of the total) live in what the Census Bureau terms an "unrelated subfamily," that is, as "a group of related persons whose members are not related to the person maintaining the household in which the subfamily lives" (U.S. Bureau of the Census 1991c, p. 8). These two groups combined comprise about 26 million persons living in about 7.4 million poor households. The remainder of the poor, about 7 million poor people, live as unrelated individuals, that is, by themselves.

Of the many myths and stereotypes that corrupt our understanding of the poor, none is so damaging as the belief that the poor are poor by choice, that they lack the motivation to work, that they are poor through "their own folly and vice." (See Ryan 1971 for a discussion and critique of this view.) All this is doubtlessly true of some poor people—indeed, of many. But the principal function of this viewpoint is to get the rest of us off the hook. Edelman (1964) has suggested that if the poor are indeed poor because of their indolence, then the rest of us must be nonpoor because of our hard work and thrift. Conversely, if the poor were to be poor despite "hard work and thrift," then the difference between them and us would only be a matter of luck. That the poor *must* lack motivation and industriousness is thus implicit in the values of middle-class society.

However convenient the "lazy, shiftless bums" theory might be, it is surely misleading since almost three-fifths (59.6%) of the poverty households that existed in the United States in 1990 had at least one household member who worked at least part of the year. In 1.3 million poor families, or almost a fifth of all poverty households (17.9%), there was more than one worker. Similarly, more than half (53%) of the single (unrelated individual) poor worked at least part of the year. All told, in 1990, approximately 61% of the nation's poor worked or lived in households where someone worked.

Just over half of the poor (50.8%) are outside the prime labor force participation ages, that is, are less than 18 or more than 65. (Poverty among children and the elderly is discussed at greater length later in this chapter.) Among poor persons within the prime age ranges, the rate of labor force participation is obviously very high; the overwhelming problem here is *not* that they lack motivation but that they are not able to work as much or as frequently as they need or would like. These, of course, are the part-time and seasonally employed, and they comprise the largest share of the working poor. At the same time, almost 6 million poor Americans in 1990 lived in families where someone worked full time all year round. Here the major problem is not insufficient hours but inadequate wages.

David Ellwood's pathbreaking book *Poor Support* (1988) examines the plight of the working poor in great detail. In testimony before Congress, Ellwood observed that the working poor are "primarily two-parent families. They are mostly white, typically with two or three children. Roughly half live in small towns and rural areas, half live in the cities and suburbs. The majority are high school graduates. In short, they do not fit the stereotypes at all."[1] He further notes that poverty among the working population increased during the late 1970s and early 1980s to the point where more than one of every eight full-time, full-year, male workers earned too little to support a family of four above the poverty line. The problem is particularly acute among young families.

In a similar vein, Robert Greenstein of the Center on Budget and Policy Priorities, Marian Wright Edelman of the Children's Defense Fund, and others have reported in testimony before Congress that in the 1978–1987 decade, more than 3 million children, the majority of whom lived in working households, became impoverished, so that at present 8 million poor children (two of every three) live in a household where someone works. The rate of poverty among two-parent families has increased faster than the rate among single-parent families. Finally, during the same decade, the number of working poor increased by almost 2 million. Among full-time, year-round workers, the increase was 43%.[2]

Table 3.1 presents evidence on the work experience of impoverished American family householders from 1959 to 1990, first for all poor households then separately for female-headed poor households. The latter are treated separately because the rate of poverty among households headed by women exceeds the overall rate by more than a factor of three (34.4% vs. 10.7%). These data confirm, first, that the fortunes of the working poor closely reflect labor market adjustments to cyclical and secular macroeconomic changes. In addition, however, changes in family structure, specifically the increasing number and proportion of female-headed families, and the labor market experiences of women heading these households, are vital determinants of the size of the working poor population.

The overall number of the working poor ebbs and flows in direct response to cyclic fluctuation in the demand for labor. When demand is high (as evidenced by the aggregate unemployment rate of 3.5%, circa 1969), the proportion of persons working part of the year or not at all due to an inability to find work is quite low. Alternatively, a slackening in the demand for labor, as evidenced by the 1977 and 1987 figures, results in fewer hours and numbers of weeks worked as well as higher rates of unemployment.

This cyclicity is especially pronounced among female householders. Between 1969 and 1990, the number of impoverished female householders more than doubled (from 1.83 to 3.77 million). In so doing, this group increased from a bit more than a third (36.9%) of all working poor households to slightly more than half (53.1%). Thus fluctuations in the demand for labor disproportionately affect the labor force experiences of

Table 3.1. Work Experience of Impoverished Civilian Family Householders, 1959–1990

	1959	1969	1977	1987	1990[d]
Total impoverished households					
Number (1000s)	8158	4947	5290	7022	7098
Percent					
Aggregate poverty	22.4	12.1	11.6	13.5	13.5
Unemployment rate	5.5	3.5	7.1	6.2	5.4
BLS U-7 unemployed[a]	—	5.4	9.8	9.3	NA
Who worked at all	68.9	54.8	48.5	47.2	49.1
Worked 50–52 Wks	37.3	26.2	20.2	19.0	
Full-time	32.1	21.6	17.2	32.4	15.0[e]
Worked < 50 weeks	31.6	28.6	28.4	28.2	34.1
Main reason for working less than 50 weeks					
Can't find work	14.7	7.2	11.3	12.9	2.1
Ill or disabled			3.8	3.0	3.4
Keeping house			8.1	6.5	7.1
Going to school	—	—	—	1.4	5.0[f]
Other	16.9[b]	21.5[b]	5.1	4.4	—
Main reason for not working at all					
Can't find work	1.2	.7	3.9	5.9	3.7
Ill or disabled	9.7	15.4	14.3	12.4	9.6
Keeping house	11.2	15.2	21.7	21.7	21.6
Going to school	.1	1.0	2.2	3.0	3.8[f]
Retired	—	—	7.7	8.8	2.0
Other	8.9[c]	12.8[c]	1.6	1.1	—
Female householders					
Number (1000s)	1916	1825	2610	3636	3768
Percent					
Of total poor	23.5	36.9	49.3	51.8	53.1
In poverty	35.0	38.2	36.2	38.3	33.4
Unemployed	5.9	4.7	8.2	6.2	
Worked at all	42.9	42.7	35.9	39.3	43.1
Worked 50–52 weeks	15.8	12.6	7.8	11.9	
Full-time	10.9	26.3	22.1	23.3	8.0[e]
Worked < 50 weeks	27.1	30.1	28.1	27.4	35.1
Main reason for working less than 50 weeks					
Can't find work	4.9	3.5	7.7	9.4	1.1
Ill or disabled			2.4	2.6	13.3
Keeping house			15.8	11.0	12.1
Going to school			1.5	1.5	5.1[f]
Other	22.3[b]	26.5[b]	.6	2.9	—
Main reason for not working at all					
Can't find work	1.5	1.4	5.0	6.1	2.8
Ill or disabled	5.4	11.3	10.4	10.6	8.2
Keeping house	47.5	41.1	43.5	37.0	35.6
Going to school	.4	1.1	3.2	3.4	4.7[f]
Retired	—	—	1.0	2.9	.3
Other	2.3[c]	2.4[c]	.9	.7	—

women; this is surely no surprise. Simultaneously, a slack labor market results in less full-time and full-year employment and prompts increased rates of unemployment across the board.[3]

How is one to explain these fluctuations in the size and composition of the working poor? In years when the aggregate demand for labor is high, labor force participation among the poor is also relatively high; and in years when demand slackens, labor force participation slackens. Are we to assume that laziness ebbs and flows in just the right manner to produce this pattern? Is it not more plausible to conclude that the work effort of the poor responds to the *opportunities* for work presented in the larger economy? Clearly, the aggregate work effort of the poor derives more from social-structural and economic factors than from individual deficiencies of effort or motivation.

What, then, can be said about recent "opportunities for work" afforded the poor? One salient fact has surfaced in a Senate Democratic Policy Committee Report of 1988. That report showed that only one in ten of the private sector jobs created in the 1980s was in industries with above average earnings; eight of ten new jobs have been created in low paying services and retail trades.

Data from the Department of Labor add important details to the portrait of the working poor (see U.S. Department of Labor 1988, 1989). In 1987, the average earnings of all nonsupervisory workers on private nonagricultural payrolls, converted to an hourly wage rate, were $8.98; the median hourly wage of workers actually paid on an hourly basis was $6.47.[4] The average hours worked per week by these workers was 34.8. Simple multiplication yields an average gross weekly salary of $312.50 for private, nonagricultural, nonsupervisory workers and $225.16 for those actually paid on an hourly basis. Dividing the 1987 four-person poverty threshold ($11,611) by 52 yields a weekly poverty level of $223.28; that, in other words, was the weekly wage necessary for an earner to have stayed above the four person poverty line. Thus the average weekly wage paid to private, nonagricultural, nonsupervisory workers was only about 140%

Notes:
[a] Total full-time jobseekers plus ½ part-time jobseekers plus ½ persons on involuntary part-time schedules plus discouraged workers as a percent of the civilian labor force less ½ the part-time labor force (see BLS 1988, p. 734).
[b] Undifferentiated sum of listed reasons.
[c] Includes retired.
[d] 1990 data not strictly comparable to earlier years.
[e] Year-round, full-time
[f] School or other
Sources: U.S. Bureau of the Census 1969, p. 53; 1970, p. 60; 1979, p. 8; 1989, p. 91; 1991, pp. 15, 98, 103; U.S. Department of Labor 1988.

of the poverty line, and that paid to hourly wage-rate workers was virtually equivalent to the poverty line.[5]

Table 3.2 shows median weekly earnings of full-time wage and salary workers in a variety of occupations for 1987. As is obvious, there are many occupations whose average weekly wage fell short of the standard necessary to stay above the four-person poverty threshold. These data, to emphasize, are for full-time workers only and therefore they do not reflect the state of impoverishment among part-time workers, which is obviously much worse.

Table 3.2 gives a convenient portrayal of the occupations of the working poor and near-poor. There were, for example, 2,750,000 retail sales workers whose median weekly earnings did not exceed the poverty standard for a family of four, 336,000 bank tellers, 142,000 private child care workers, 146,000 servants and cleaners, 188,000 bartenders, 1,200,000 health service workers, over a half-million waiters and waitresses, 711,000 sewing machine operators, and 570,000 farm workers. The predominance of traditionally female occupations on this list is unmistakable. Many of the women working in these jobs are married to men with substantially higher earnings, but increasingly the women head their own households and support themselves and their children on their own wages. The low wages typically paid to women workers are a principal reason for the feminization of poverty discussed earlier.

Although the average income earned in most occupations exceeded the four-person poverty threshold, it was often not by very much. Many of the jobs with earnings sufficient to stay above poverty still afforded very little economic security; many who were not technically beneath the poverty line could very easily have become so in the face of the merest misfortune: a brief period of unemployment, a costly illness, or some other family catastrophe. Further compounding the difficulties of low-wage workers is that they are also the least likely to receive fringe benefits, particularly employer-provided health insurance.[6]

Column 4 in Table 3.2 depicts average earnings as a proportion of the "earnings necessary to escape poverty" (computed by dividing the four-person poverty threshold by the 44 weeks that the average American worker worked in 1987). "Earnings necessary to escape poverty" were roughly 120% of the official (1987) four-person poverty line. Using this standard as the baseline, we see that workers in a number of additional occupations were at "risk" of poverty (or, what amounts to the same thing, near-poor): 1.3 million janitors, almost a million freight and stock handlers, and millions of service workers.

Column 5 depicts median earnings as a proportion of the minimum income that people felt was necessary to support a family (as measured in the Gallup polls). Adjusted for inflation, this figure was $319 and constituted 143% of the official four-person poverty line. With this as the standard, we find that the median wages of secretaries, bookkeepers, licensed practical nurses (LPNs), butchers, and roofers were also insufficient.

Table 3.3 examines the average earnings of full-time workers by familial and demographic characteristics. In general, what is true of the poor is also true of the working poor—women, minorities, and the young are at highest risk. Special attention should be paid to the earnings of multiple-earner households, which are of course much higher than those of single-earner households. We call attention to this point only to stress that a rising divorce rate has left more and more households without the "fall-back" of additional earners to enhance family incomes; this, like the low average wages paid to women workers, is a principal factor in the feminization of poverty discussed previously.

Who, then, are the working poor? First, they are part-time and seasonal workers whose annual hours of work are insufficient to keep them above poverty. Secondly, they are full-time workers in minimum wage or near-minimum-wage occupations, principally semiskilled and unskilled workers in nonunionized sectors of the economy. Finally, they are disproportionately women, minorities, the young, and single-earner households. All of them evidence, by their labor force behavior alone, a willingness to work; that they remain poor despite this willingness is a large-scale social and economic problem, not a personal deficiency. Indeed, the United States stands alone among the advanced industrial societies in having a sizable percentage of its working people beneath the poverty threshold; elsewhere in the industrialized world, the notion of the "working poor" has become nearly an anachronism.

A few final comments on the working poor are in order. First, given the low wages, insufficient hours and lack of fringe benefits that are characteristic of many jobs, coupled with relatively generous welfare benefits of various sorts, many people will find that they are better off not working. Consider the situation of a poor woman with children who is eligible for Aid to Families With Dependent Children (AFDC). In the more generous states, that woman will receive (1) a monthly cash payment of several hundred dollars, (2) Medicaid benefits (whose worth is easily a few hundred dollars a month), (3) food stamps, (4) possibly a Section 8 housing voucher that can be used in lieu of rent, and (5), at least in some states, subsidized day care for her children. If her alternative to all this is working, say, 25 hours a week at the minimum wage, then the overwhelmingly rational decision is not to work. As the late Michael Harrington observed, this women would have to hate her children to take the job rather than stay on AFDC.

In our state, Louisiana, the monthly AFDC payment is a pittance, but

Table 3.2. Median Weekly Earnings of Full-Time Wage and Salary Workers by Select Occupations As a Proportion of Family Poverty Indices, 1987

Occupation	Number (1000s)	Median Weekly Earnings[a]	As Proportion of		
			Poverty Threshold[b]	Necessary Earnings[c]	Gallup Index[d]
All occupations	80836	$373	1.67	1.41	1.17
Private nonsupervisory	10216	$313	1.40	1.19	.98
Executive, admin. and managerial		$530	2.41	2.01	1.66
Public admin.	431	$542	2.43	2.05	1.70
Financial mgrs.	434	$623	2.79	2.36	1.95
Property mgrs.	248	$420	1.88	1.59	1.32
Accountants	1090	$492	2.21	1.86	1.54
Professional	10678	$518	2.32	1.96	1.62
Aerospace engineers	106	$757	3.39	2.87	2.37
Chemists	121	$631	2.83	2.39	1.98
Elem. sch. teachers	1173	$462	2.07	1.75	1.45
Lawyers	338	$813	3.65	3.08	2.55
Registered nurses	1125	$482	2.16	1.83	1.51
Technical	2797	$429	1.92	1.63	1.34
Computer progrs.	474	$543	2.43	2.06	1.70
LPNs	294	$316	1.42	1.20	.99
Sales	7657	$376	1.69	1.42	1.18
Real estate	356	$479	2.15	1.81	1.50
Sales workers	2747	$222	1.00	.84	.70
Admin. support	14226	$308	1.38	1.17	.97
Secretaries	3285	$301	1.35	1.14	.94
Bookkeepers	1311	$299	1.34	1.13	.94
Bank tellers	336	$234	1.05	.89	.73
Services, private household and protective	8314	$234	1.05	.89	.73

Occupation					
Child care workers	142	$ 94	.42	.36	.29
Police	88	$607	2.72	2.30	1.90
Servants and cleaners	146	$161	.72	.61	.50
Services, other	6326	$217	.97	.82	.68
Bartenders	188	$223	1.00	.84	.70
Health services	1279	$226	1.01	.86	.71
Janitors/cleaners	1327	$258	1.16	.98	.81
Waiters/waitresses	550	$190	.85	.72	.60
Precision products	10992	$419	1.88	1.59	1.31
Butchers	230	$326	1.46	1.23	1.02
Carpenters	901	$365	1.64	1.38	1.14
Machinists	458	$443	1.99	1.68	1.39
Mechanics	3812	$424	1.90	1.61	1.33
Roofers	112	$339	1.52	1.28	1.06
Machine operators	4858	$284	1.27	1.08	.89
Lathe	57	$419	1.88	1.59	1.31
Textile sewing	711	$186	.83	.70	.58
Typesetters	54	$316	1.42	1.20	.99
Welders	517	$378	1.70	1.43	1.18
Transport	3799	$382	1.71	1.45	1.20
Freight/stock handlers	986	$279	1.25	1.06	.87
Farm workers	570	$197	.88	.75	.62

Notes:

a Based on multiplication of average hourly earnings of nonsupervisory workers on private nonagricultural payrolls ($8.98) by the average weekly hours worked (34.8).

b Weekly four-person poverty threshold = $223.00. Derived by dividing the official (1987) four-person poverty threshold ($11,611) by 52 weeks of calendar year.

c "Earnings to escape poverty threshold" = $264.00. Derived by dividing the 1987 four-person poverty threshold ($11,611) by 44 weeks (the actual average of weeks worked).

d Gallup Index = $319.00. Based on 1985 national sample response (i.e., $302) to question: "What is the smallest amount of money a family of four needs to get along in this community?" adjusted by rate of inflation for 1986 and 1987.

Source: U.S. Department of Labor 1988, Table B-31.

Table 3.3. Median Weekly Earnings of Full-Time Workers by Familial and Demographic Characteristics as a Proportion of Family Poverty Indices, 1987

Family Type (By Head of Household)	Number (1000s)	Median Weekly Earnings	As Proportion of		
			Poverty Threshold[a]	Necessary Earnings[b]	Gallup Index[c]
Total families[d]					
Married couple	33844	$637	2.86	2.41	2.00
1 earner	12668	$405	1.82	1.53	1.27
Husband	9640	$477	2.14	1.81	1.50
Wife	2272	$230	1.03	.87	.72
2+ earners	21176	$776	3.48	2.94	2.43
Husband and wife	14955	$741	3.32	2.81	2.32
Female-headed	6963	$317	1.42	1.20	.99
Hshldr earner only	3675	$263	1.18	1.00	.82
Male-headed	1926	$478	2.14	1.81	1.50
1 earner only	1144	$353	1.58	1.34	1.11
Whites					
Married couple	30095	$647	2.90	2.45	2.03
1 earner	11385	$416	1.87	1.58	1.30
Husband	8784	$485	2.17	1.84	1.52
Wife	1946	$231	1.04	.88	.72
2+ earners	18710	$785	3.52	2.97	2.46
Husband and wife	13232	$748	3.35	2.83	2.34
Female-headed	4959	$329	1.48	1.25	1.03
Male-headed	1501	$492	2.21	1.86	1.54

Blacks					
Married couple	2768	$529	2.37	2.00	1.66
1 earner	924	$289	1.30	1.09	.91
Husband	581	$335	1.50	1.27	1.05
Wife	264	$215	.96	.81	.67
2+ earners	1843	$675	3.03	2.56	2.12
Husband and wife	1318	$646	2.90	2.47	2.03
Female-headed	1822	$284	1.27	1.08	.89
Male-headed	352	$383	1.72	1.45	1.20
Age					
16–24 years old	12252	$242	1.09	.92	.76
25–34 years old	26383	$373	1.67	1.41	1.17
35–44 years old	20568	$435	1.95	1.65	1.36
45–54 years old	12957	$429	1.92	1.63	1.34
55–64 years old	7776	$405	1.82	1.53	1.27
65+ years	899	$310	1.39	1.17	.97
Race & Sex[e]					
White	69358	$383	1.72	1.45	1.20
Men	41150	$450	2.02	1.70	1.41
Women	28208	$307	1.38	1.16	.96
Black	9050	$301	1.35	1.14	.94
Men	4679	$326	1.46	1.23	1.02
Women	4371	$275	1.23	1.04	.86
Union Affiliation					
Union members	15670	$465	2.09	1.76	1.46
Non-union	63269	$342	1.53	1.30	1.07

Notes:
[a] See note a, Table 3.1.
[b] See note b, Table 3.1.
[c] See note c, Table 3.1.
[d] Excludes families without wage or salary earners and those in which householder is self-employed.
[e] Workers sixteen years and over.
Source: U.S. Department of Labor 1988, Tables B-29, B-32.

59

AFDC makes one automatically eligible for Medicaid benefits. The value of the Medicaid benefit *alone* exceeds the wage paid in most of the service jobs in the local economy. Indeed, private medical insurance is now so expensive, and employment-related health insurance so rarely offered to working women, that many women in Louisiana and elsewhere find they *must* remain on AFDC specifically in order to retain their Medicaid benefits. (Allowing employers and employees to "buy in" to Medicaid would be one way to avoid this perverse pattern.)

Does the welfare system sketched above pose a "work disincentive," as many have claimed? *Of course!* The critics are unquestionably correct in their assessment of this problem, but they err when they suggest that we solve it by dismantling the welfare system or by cutting back on welfare benefits. When welfare is more attractive than work, the solution is not to make welfare less attractive but rather to *make work more attractive*. The essential first step would be an ample supply of employment opportunities with customary fringe benefits, ample hours, and decent wages. Why do we even expect people to work when the earnings from many jobs will not suffice to keep a family out of poverty? When the critics demand that people get off the welfare rolls and into jobs, they should understand that under current conditions they are asking poor people to make an economically irrational decision.

Many of the nation's poor do not receive welfare. Table 3.4 reveals that only 41.8% of the poor received cash assistance through such means-tested programs as AFDC, and that only 48.8% and 52.0% of the poor resided in households receiving food stamps and Medicaid. Altogether 71.6%, or 24 million, of the nation's poor lived in households that received some form of means-tested assistance in 1990. Alternatively, 28.4%, over 9 million impoverished persons, lived in households that received no such assistance.

Interestingly, many nonpoor persons also receive such benefits. In fact, almost 30 million nonpoor Americans received some form of means-tested assistance, suggesting that were it not for critical programs such as AFDC and Medicaid, tens of millions of the nation's near poor would be pushed beneath the poverty threshold. As the data in Table 3.4 indicate, many of these persons would be children living in female-headed households.

A final note: In the nether reaches of the labor force, the distinction between working and not working is often dim. Many poor people work in off-the-books casual jobs or present themselves daily at the day labor outlets. How much labor of this general sort gets reflected in official statistics is anybody's guess. Many homeless poor will wash dishes in a restaurant in exchange for a meal or sweep up after closing in a small business in exchange for a place to sleep for the night. Other homeless

Table 3.4. Program Participation, Percent Persons by Income Status in House-holds Receiving Assistance, 1990

Type of Assistance Program/ Demographic Subgroup	Participating All Income Levels		Participating Below Poverty	
	Percent	Number[a]	Percent	Number[a]
Means-Tested Assistance, all persons	21.4	53,249	71.6	24,031
Related children < 18				
In married couple families	15.3	25,802	78.0	3,828
Related children < 18				
In female-headed families, nsp[b]	68.6	9,464	93.7	6,903
MTA excl. school lunches, all persons	17.4	43,275	64.0	21,505
Related children < 18				
In married couple families	14.5	6,961	60.9	2,990
Related children < 18				
In female-headed families, nsp[b]	59.1	8,145	87.1	6,415
MTA cash assistance, all persons	10.1	25,156	41.8	14,040
Related children < 18				
In married couple families	6.3	3,017	28.4	1,393
Related children < 18				
In female-headed families, nsp[b]	44.1	6,085	69.5	5,117
Food stamps, all persons	9.2	22,790	48.8	16,375
Related children < 18				
In married couple families	7.7	3,675	47.3	2,320
Related children < 18				
In female-headed families, nsp[b]	46.9	6,474	76.9	5,659
Medicaid, all persons	13.4	33,347	52.0	17,469
Related children < 18				
In married couple families	11.1	5,341	46.8	2,295
Related children < 18				
In female-headed families, nsp[b]	51.4	7,089	78.2	5,758
Public/subsidized housing, all persons	4.1	10,138	19.9	6,667
Related children < 18				
In married couple families	1.9	904	10.3	505
Related children < 18				
In female-headed families, nsp[b]	22.7	3,130	36.1	2,655

Notes:
[a] In thousands.
[b] nsp, no spouse present.
Source: U.S. Bureau of the Census 1991c, Table E.

people spend long, arduous hours seven days a week scavenging aluminum cans from trash cans or off the streets. Whether any of the above persons would be considered "employed" in official labor force statistics is unlikely, but there is no denying that they support themselves, at least in substantial part, through their own labor. Our point is that the proportion of the poor who in fact work to support themselves is no doubt higher than reflected in official employment statistics.

THE RURAL POOR

The poverty of the underclass is largely urban poverty, but rural poverty has not disappeared from the American scene. Unfortunately, any discussion of the rural poor is complicated by the frequent changes the federal government makes in its city-size categories and designations. In the thirty years since the government first began to keep systematic data on poverty, the city-size nomenclature has shifted from nonfarm/farm to urban/rural and then again to metropolitan/nonmetropolitan. These changing designations (and the associated changes in definition and record keeping) attempt to capture evolving qualitative differences in the meanings of terms such as "urban" and rural" in an era of widespread urbanization, but they also greatly complicate comparisons over time.

The labels farm, rural, and nonmetropolitan overlap to some degree, but they are not identical. Specifically, the farm population is defined as persons living in rural territories who derive some specified minimum of their income from the sale of agricultural products.[7] The "rural" category consists of the farm population plus other nonfarm persons residing in nonurban areas.[8] Finally, "nonmetropolitan" refers to all persons outside of metropolitan statistical areas (MSAs); it includes the farm population plus the rural population plus the populations of small cities and towns.[9]

These changing designations reflect the changing reality of our nation's economy and demography. Over time, the locus and activities of the United States population have shifted from rural areas and agricultural pursuits to an urbanized industrial life. Even more recently, we find evidence of important postindustrial economic transformations and accompanying population shifts within large-scale urban (metropolitan) areas. Recent censuses document the movement out of central cities into suburban and exurban regions.

Rural (Farm) Poverty:

As the rural population of the United States has decreased, so has the incidence of rural poverty. In 1990, only about 2% of the nations population remained in rural America,[10] and of that small percentage only about half were economically dependent on agriculture, the remainder being employed in a variety of nonfarm activities: factories, lumbering, mines, and so on.

Not surprisingly, the economic fortunes of those who remain dependent on farming fluctuate dramatically with the vicissitudes of agricultural markets.[11] Farm income also remains highly sensitive to interest
rates. Consequently, farm poverty rates have historically been much
higher (and more volatile) than the nonfarm rates, although that has
become less true in the past two decades.

The rate of farm poverty dropped dramatically from more than 50% in
1959 to about 11% in 1990. Even as late as 1967, the farm poverty rate was
routinely twice that of the nonfarm rate; these days, the rates are very
similar. This 75–80% reduction in farm poverty between 1959 and 1990,
however, does not reflect a major turnaround in the economics of the
family farm so much as a continuous replacement of small-scale, economically marginal family farming operations by large-scale agribusiness
enterprises. In fact, the size of the farm population shrank from more than
15 million in 1959 to less than 5 million in 1990, even as the rate of
agricultural productivity dramatically increased. Unable to "make it" in
farming, 10 million people left altogether, and half of those who remain
are employed in nonfarm pursuits. Thus, the rate of poverty within the
remaining farm population has plummeted.

Many have lamented the decline of the family farm. In the more
romanticized versions, honest, hardworking yeomen have been driven
off the land by uncaring market forces and unscrupulous agribusiness
operators. The rate of farm poverty in 1959—a bit more than half—
should suffice to dispel this notion. In fact, for most of the twentieth
century, "family farming" was barely more than subsistence agriculture,
characterized by hard work, long days, and deep economic privation.
Many family farmers of the 1930s–1950s were not "driven off" their land
into "alienated" factory labor; for many, it was a positive, conscious
choice that was accompanied by remarkable improvements in the family's standard of living (see Jones 1992; Lemann 1991).

The net result of the trends of the last three decades is that farm poverty
now accounts for only 1.6% of all poverty in the United States as compared to 20.3% of the poverty total in 1959. More concretely, there were
534,000 farm poor in 1990, nearly all of them living in families. On
average, farm families are somewhat larger than American families as a
whole (3.59 vs. 3.19 persons).[12] In general, the average family cash incomes of both the farming poor and nonpoor lag behind their nonfarm
counterparts. For those on the farm, these figures are $5,214 and $31,560
respectively; among nonfarming families the corresponding figures are
$5,868 and $36,680.

Some other facts about the farm poor: Among the 616,000 farm poor are
220,000 children under the age of eighteen (36% of the total) and 65,000
senior citizens (11% of the total). Only 6% of the farm poor are black. At

Table 3.5. Poverty Rates (Percentage), Farm vs. Nonfarm, 1959–1990

	1959	1967	1977	1987	1990
Farm	50.5	25.9	17.1	12.6	11.2
Nonfarm	19.6	13.5	11.3	13.5	13.6

Sources: U.S. Bureau of the Census 1969, 1979, 1989a, 1991c.

the same time, the incidence of poverty among black farmers is 33.9%; the corresponding rate for white farmers is 12.1%. Less than 5% of the farm poor live in female-headed households, and only 2.6% of the farm poor are children living in such households. These figures represent a sharp contrast with the nonfarm poor, of whom 37.7% live in female-headed households and 22% are children living in female-headed households.

Nonmetropolitan Area Poverty

Although the farm population has diminished to 2% of the population, 22.4% of the United States population—more than 56 million people— live in nonmetropolitan areas: in the small cities and towns and rural areas (U.S. Bureau of the Census 1989a, pp. 27–28). Since the 1970 Census, the population of nonmetropolitan areas has grown by almost 20% so as to comprise slightly more than a fifth of the national population. Despite this population growth, or perhaps because of it, the nonmetropolitan areas have a higher than average poverty rate of 16.3%, and they contain about 27% of the nation's total poverty population.

Poverty in the nonmetropolitan population is confounded by racial and regional factors. First, the South is overrepresented: 44% of the non-metropolitan population resides in the South as compared to 34% of the overall U.S. population. Thus, some nonmetropolitan poverty is linked more to region than to city size. Within the South, the nonmetropolitan population is disproportionately black. In the nation as a whole, blacks comprise 12.4% of the total population, 9.4% of the nonmetropolitan population, and 29.3% of the poverty population. In the South, blacks comprise 20.3% of the nonmetropolitan population and 41.3% of the nonmetropolitan poor. In fact, 96.8% of all poor nonmetropolitan blacks live in the South. Outside of the South, the nonmetropolitan population is 96.3% white. Thus, as numerous authors have observed, small town and rural poverty outside the South is almost exclusively a white phenomenon. Whites comprise 92% of the nonsouthern nonmetropolitan poverty population.

The age-dependent populations—children and the elderly—comprise approximately half of the poor in nonmetropolitan areas. Out of a total of 9.1 million nonmetropolitan poor, 3.4 million are children and an additional 1.3 million are elderly. The incidence of poverty among these two groups is 22.9% and 16.1% respectively. The former rate runs about 10% ahead of the age-specific national rate, and the latter exceeds the age-specific national rate by almost a third.

As shown in Table 3.6, the overall poverty rate in nonmetropolitan areas exceeds the metropolitan area rate. This is true for blacks, Hispanics, and whites. Except for the Northeast section of the country, it is also true regionally. However, in the Midwest and West the nonmetropolitan poverty rate exceeds the metropolitan rate by only one or two percentage points, whereas the difference in the South is almost 50%. Despite generally dwindling differences between the South and non-South over time, the South continues to fare more poorly in many socioeconomic categories, and in the rate of poverty in the small town and rural areas, the disparity exceeds 50%: 20.5% in the South vs. 13.0% elsewhere. Overall, blacks comprise slightly less than a quarter (23.6%) of all nonmetropolitan poverty. In the South, however, the figure is 41.3%

Although the incidence of nonmetropolitan poverty in the South exceeds the rate in other non-metropolitan areas, a comparison of mean family sizes and incomes of southern vs. nonsouthern nonmetropolitan poor families shows negligible differences. The family size difference amounts to .17 persons (poor southern families in the small towns and rural areas are slightly larger), and the income difference amounts to $127 a year. Perhaps contrary to expectation, the mean family income of the black poor in nonmetropolitan areas is higher than the corresponding figure for poor whites. This difference is particularly pronounced in the South, where it exceeds $550, but this advantage is offset by the slightly higher average size of southern nonmetropolitan poor black families (.5 persons).

THE ELDERLY POOR

Historically, poverty rates among the elderly have exceeded those in the general population, often by a factor of two (Figure 3.1). Indeed, widespread economic privation among the elderly was a principal motive for the War on Poverty of the early 1960s. At that time, private pension plans were relatively rare and exceedingly ungenerous, especially for nonunion workers outside the white-collar ranks. Further, a large proportion of retirees were not covered by Social Security, and many who were covered found that their Social Security checks were often insufficient to stay above the poverty level.

The rate of poverty among the elderly exceeded the overall poverty

Table 3.6. Poverty Rates (Percentage), Nonmetropolitan, Metropolitan, Suburban, Central City, and Poverty Areas: 1990

	Nonmetro Areas	Metro Areas	Metropolitan Areas Noncentral Cities	Central Cities	Poverty Areas
All persons	16.3	12.7	19.0	8.7	33.3
White	13.5	9.9	14.3	7.6	26.7
Black	40.8	30.1	33.8	22.2	43.7
Hispanic	32.0	27.8	31.7	22.8	42.0
Region					
Northeast	10.3	11.6	21.6	5.9	36.2
Midwest	13.2	12.2	21.4	6.2	35.9
South	20.5	13.9	18.0	11.3	31.4
West	14.8	12.7	15.9	10.5	33.2

Source: U.S. Bureau of the Census 1991c, Tables 8 and 9.

rate until 1982 (Figures 3.1 and 3.2). Through the end of the 1960s, the elderly rate was routinely twice the overall rate. The disparity narrowed steadily throughout the 1970s and closed entirely in 1982; since that year, the poverty rate among the elderly has been less than the overall rate.

As we have already said, this massive reduction of poverty among the

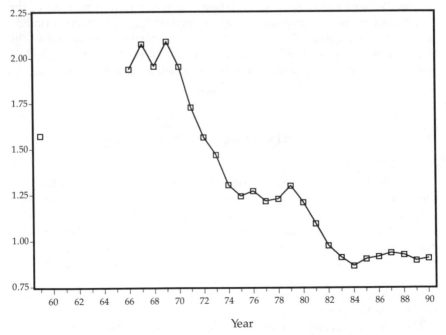

Year

Figure 3.1. Ratio of percent of elderly poor to percent of all poor, 1959–1990.

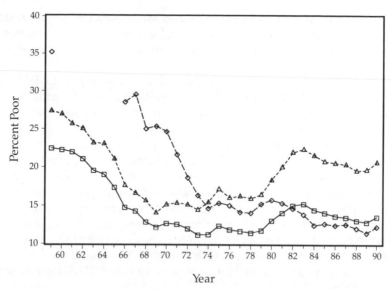

Year

□ Total U.S. Population   △ Children Under 18   ◇ Persons 65+ Years

Figure 3.2. Incidence of poverty among general population, children, and the elderly, percent, 1959–1990.

aged is one of the great success stories of postwar American social history, and it was accomplished almost exclusively by legislative and executive mandate and by an enormous infusion of federal monies. Obviously touched by the desperate circumstances of many of the elderly, a succession of Congresses and presidents responded with a variety of programs designed to reduce poverty among the aged, including Medicare, the Supplemental Security Income (SSI) program, expanded eligibility for social security, several large increases in benefit levels, and, perhaps most importantly, the pegging of social security payment levels to changes in the cost of living. The price for all this has, of course, been steep. In 1990,

Table 3.7. Poverty Rates (Percentage) among the Elderly, 1959–1990

	1959	1967	1977	1987	1990
Total poverty rate	22.4	14.2	11.6	13.5	13.5
Rate among persons 65+	35.2	29.5	14.1	12.2	12.2
White	33.1	27.7	11.9	10.1	10.1
Black	62.5	53.3	36.3	33.9	33.8
Male	38.1a	23.7	10.5	8.5	7.6
Female	64.2a	33.9	16.7	14.9	15.4
Ratio: Elderly/Total	1.57	2.08	1.22	.90	.90

Note:
[a] Combines two-person families with head 65 years old and over plus unrelated individuals 65 years old and older
Sources: U.S. Bureau of the Census 1968, 1979, 1989a, 1991c.

federal expenditures on Social Security and Medicare alone approximated $300 billion. From this two lessons can be learned. First, the reduction of poverty among any group is not cheap; secondly, no price is too high when the goal is worthy.

Selected trends in poverty among the elderly are shown in Table 3.7. Between 1959 and 1990, the rate of poverty among the elderly was reduced by almost two-thirds (compared to a one-third reduction in the overall rate). Notwithstanding this progress or the size of the federal expenditure on programs for the elderly, approximately one in eight of the nation's senior citizens continues to live below the poverty line—a total of 3.6 million elderly poor. Moreover, various subpopulations among the elderly experience substantially higher rates of impoverishment than the aggregate figure indicates. Poverty is notably more widespread among elderly women (15.4%) than among elderly men (7.6%), and older blacks are more than three times as likely to be in poverty (33.8%) as older whites (10.1%). Thus, the rate is highest of all among elderly black women, among whom the incidence of poverty is 38% (U.S. Bureau of the Census 1991b, p. 24).

POVERTY AMONG CHILDREN

If the recent trends in poverty among the aged are a great achievement, the poverty rate among children is an ongoing national disgrace. The child poverty rate has exceeded the overall rate for as long as data have been gathered on the subject; the disgrace is that this disparity has become larger, not smaller, in recent decades (see Table 3.8, Figures 3.2 and 3.3). Today, the rate of poverty among children is higher than the rate in any other age group of the population. One child in five lives below the poverty line, and conversely, 40% of the poor are children. Figure 3.2 shows the trend in child poverty since 1959. Between 1959 and 1970, the child poverty rate declined precipitously (as did the poverty rate in the nation as a whole). In the 1970s, the child poverty rate crept slowly upward and then jumped dramatically upward in the early years of the 1980s. The 1990 figure, 20.5%, remains beneath the 1959 figure (26.9%) but substantially exceeds the 15% rates characteristic of the early 1970s. Table 3.8 provides more information regarding trends in child poverty and differences across racial/ethnic and family groups. In general, these data indicate that some substantial progress was achieved in the lowering of juvenile poverty rates during the 1960s and early 1970s. Since the mid- to late 1970s, however, the situation has either stagnated—as for instance has occurred with children living in families headed by minority women—or, it has gotten even worse (e.g., for children living in families headed by whites).

Two "risk factors" for poverty are especially salient among children: race and female headship. In 1990, the poverty rate among "related" white children was 15.1%, and among black children, nearly three times that (44.2%). Among Hispanic children the rate was 37.7%.[13] Thus, nearly half of all black children and two-fifths of all Hispanic children in the nation live in poverty. Absent fathers also make children poor. As we have just indicated, the overall child poverty rate in 1990 was 20.5%. Among children living in households headed by women, the poverty rate was 53.4%. Among children living in households headed by black and Hispanic women, the incidence of poverty was 64.7% and 68.3% respectively.

The exceptional poverty rate among children in female-headed households is principally a result of three factors, two of which were mentioned

Table 3.8. Poverty Rates (Percentage) Among Related Children under 18, 1959–1990

	1959	1967	1977	1987	1990
Total poverty rate	22.4	14.2	11.6	13.5	13.5
Rate for related children under 18	26.9	16.3	16.0	20.0	20.5
White	20.6	11.3	11.4	15.0	15.1
Black[a]	63.8	47.4	41.6	45.1	44.2
Hispanic	—	—	28.0	39.3	37.7
Ratio: children/total	1.22	1.17	1.40	1.51	1.53
Rate in families					
with male heads[b]	22.4	11.5	8.5	10.9	10.2
White	17.4	8.7	7.1	9.5	9.2
Black	58.0	35.3	19.9	19.8	18.1
Hispanic	—	—	17.9	28.3	26.5
Rate in families					
With female heads	72.2	54.3	50.3	54.7	53.4
White	64.6	42.1	40.3	45.8	45.9
Black	82.7	72.4	65.7	68.3	64.7
Hispanic	—	—	68.6	70.1	68.3

Notes:
[a] Nonwhite in 1959, thereafter black
[b] For 1987, refers to all non-female headed (nsp) families; for 1990, married couple families
Sources: U.S. Bureau of the Census 1968, 1979, 1989a, 1991c.

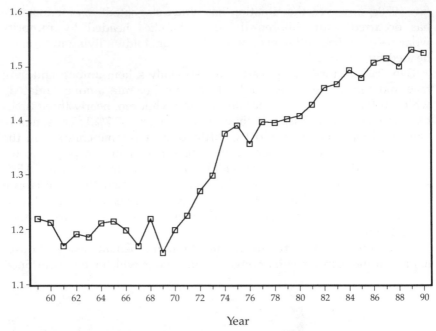

Figure 3.3. Ration of percent of children poor to percent of all poor, 1959–1990.

in our discussion of the working poor. First, wages paid to women average only about 60% of the wages paid to men. Second, female-headed households do not have the option of putting additional earners in the labor force to increase the overall family income. A third factor in the poverty of female-headed households is nonpayment of child support by absent fathers. Many of the women with children who are heading their own households were never married to the children's father; fewer than 4% of the unmarried fathers of these children pay any child support. Indeed, only about a third of the mothers who *have* been married receive child support payments from their former husbands (Hamilton and Wright 1986, p. 190).

Many commentators on the poverty situation bemoan the irresponsibility of young women who become pregnant and then find that they cannot adequately support their child. Getting pregnant, however, is not something that young women do on their own; the active complicity of a male partner is essential. Wilson and many other analysts include the high rate of female headship as part of the "tangle of pathology" that marks the urban underclass, but is profoundly erroneous to ascribe this problem to women alone. The irresponsibility of men as much as that of women is implicated in the high rate of poverty among children living in female-headed households.

In 1990, there were more than 13 million children living below the poverty line in the United States. These children spend their critical formative years without the benefit of an adequate income and all that an adequate income implies: sufficient nutrition, medical care, housing, education, and so on. Considering the deficits with which they begin life, we should not be surprised that so many of them become the impoverished adults of the next generation.

Children are poor because their parents are poor; no one sees them as responsible for their own plight. By the same token, child poverty cannot be eliminated except by eliminating poverty among their parents, which is tantamount to eliminating poverty altogether, and one is entitled to wonder whether the will to do this exists. Hubert Humphrey was fond of saying that the mark of civilization is found in how children are treated. The rate of poverty among American children is a sad testament indeed.

SUMMARY

All social problems lend themselves to stereotyping, and poverty is no exception. When we think of "the poor," we seldom think of the elderly poor, and yet the elderly comprise nearly 11% of the category. Neither do we think of impoverished children, who comprise 40% of the category, nor poor working adults, who comprise about half of the remainder. That three-quarters of the poverty population are either outside the prime labor force participation years or in fact working comes as a great surprise to many, and yet this is perhaps the most salient fact about poverty in the United States today.

Table 3.9 summarizes a great deal of information about the contemporary American poverty population. The first column shows raw numbers, the second column shows poverty rates for each subgroup, and the third shows the distribution of the poor across these same subgroups. The table shows, for example, that there were 33.6 million poor people in the United States in 1990, 13.2 million of them related children. The rate of poverty among children is 20.5% (meaning that slightly more than 20% of all children are poor); in turn, children comprise almost 40% of the poverty population (i.e., 39.5% of all poor people are related children). Similarly, 8.1 million of the nation's poor are adults (25 or more years old) who have not completed high school. Among all adults not having completed high school, about one in four (23.6%) is impoverished. These

8.1 million persons constitute a fourth (24.1%) of the nation's poor and account for a half (50.0%) of the poverty population twenty-five or more years old.

Much of the confusion about the nature of poverty in America results from failing to distinguish between the second and third columns of Table 3.9. Many people, for instance, think of poverty as a black problem. It is true that the rate of poverty among African-Americans is about three times higher than the rate among whites, but since there are so many more whites than blacks to begin with, the large majority of the poor (nearly two-thirds) are white. We also tend to think of poverty as a big city problem, and this too is both true and false. As we have noted, the overall poverty rate is higher *outside* the metropolitan areas (16.3%) than inside them (12.7%), but since nearly three-quarters of the population lives inside metropolitan areas, some 73% of all poor people are also found in those areas.

The poverty of greatest concern these days—and that which occupies our attention in the next section of this book—is the poverty of the urban underclass. As we see in the following chapter, there is little or no consensus among analysts and commentators on exactly what the "urban underclass" is, but it is fairly obvious what the underclass is not: it does not include the working poor, the nonmetropolitan poor, the elderly, or children. We can thus use the data contained in Table 3.9 and the analyses reported above to put some crude empirical limits on the size of the underclass population. Since the categories shown in the table overlap, our estimate cannot be exact, but even the rough order of magnitude proves revealing.

There were, all told, 33.6 million persons below poverty in 1990. Subtracting 13.3 million poor children and 3.7 million elderly poor leaves us with a population of 16.6 million poor adults in the prime labor force years. Of these, 8.6 million had at least some work experience during the year, which leaves 8.0 million poor adults who did not work at all in 1990. (About 100,000 of the 8.7 million workers reported in Table 3.9 were below the age of eighteen.) Of these, we can assume that 27% (or approximately 2.5 million) lived outside the metropolitan areas, which would reduce the remainder to 5.5 million. If we restricted the notion of "urban" to the central cities only (which is consistent with the vernacular usage of the term "urban underclass"), then 57.6% of the remaining poor would be "nonurban," and we would be left with about 3.17 million as the maximum possible size of the urban underclass population, which is less than a tenth of the total poverty population. That is to say, if by "urban underclass" poverty we are referring to poor, nonworking, prime-age adults in the central cities, then better than 90% of the poverty that exists in America today is of some other sort. It is, however, the conditions and

Table 3.9. The Demographics of Poverty: Examining Trends[a]

Characteristic	Number (1000s)	Percent with Characteristic Who Are Poor	Percent of all Poor
All impoverished persons	33,585	13.5	100.0
Related children under 18	13,251	20.5	39.5
White	7,696	15.1	22.9
Black	4,412	44.2	13.1
Hispanic[b]	2,750	37.7	8.2
Aged (persons 65+ years)	3,658	12.2	10.9
White	2,707	10.1	8.1
Black	860	33.8	2.6
Hispanic	245	22.5	.7
Race/origins			
White	22,326	10.7	66.5
Black	9,837	31.9	29.3
Hispanic	6,006	28.1	17.9
Residence			
Farm	534	11.2	1.6
Nonfarm	33,051	13.6	98.4
In metro areas	24,510	12.7	73.0
In central cities	14,254	19.0	42.4
Outside central cities	10,255	8.7	30.5
In Nonmetro areas	9,075	16.3	27.0
In poverty areas[c]	12,547	33.3	37.4
Region			
Northeast	5,794	11.4	17.3
Midwest	7,458	12.4	22.2
South	13,456	15.8	40.1
West	6,877	13.0	20.4
Family composition			
All families	7,098	10.7	79.0[d]
White	4,622	8.1	65.1[e]
Black	2,193	29.3	30.9[e]
Hispanic	1,244	25.0	17.5[e]
Married couple families	2,981	5.7	42.0[e]
White	2,386	5.1	33.6[e]
Black	448	12.6	6.3[e]
Hispanic	605	17.5	8.5[e]
Female householder, nsp[f]	3,768	33.4	53.1[c]
White	2,010	26.8	28.3[e]
Black	1,648	48.1	23.2[e]
Hispanic	573	48.3	8.0[e]
Male householder, nsp[f]	349	12.0	4.9[e]
White	226	9.9	3.2[e]
Black	96	20.4	1.4[e]
Hispanic	66	19.4	.9[e]
Persons in families w/ female head, nsp[f]	12,578	37.2	37.5
White	6,210	29.8	18.5
Black	6,005	50.6	17.9
Hispanic	2,115	53.0	6.3
Unrelated individuals	7,446	20.7	22.2
Male	2,857	16.9	8.5
Female	4,589	24.0	13.7

continued

Table 3.9. continued

Characteristic	Number (1000s)	Percent with Characteristic Who Are Poor	Percent of all Poor
Persons 16+ having work			
Experience in 1990	8,675	6.5	43.0g
White	6,394	5.6	31.7g
Black	1,988	14.4	9.9g
Hispanic	1,487	15.0	7.4g
Full-time, 50–52 weeks	2,038	2.5	10.1g
White	1,514	2.2	7.5g
Black	450	5.5	2.2g
Hispanic	418	7.2	2.1g
Persons 16+ having no work experience in 1990	12,523	22.1	62.1g
White	8,295	17.7	41.2g
Black	3,672	47.9	18.2g
Hispanic	1,883	40.1	9.3g
Main reason for not working			
Ill or disabled	2,945	35.6	14.6g
Keeping house	4,051	22.8	20.1g
Attending school/other	2,092	27.1	10.4g
Retired	2,570	12.1	12.8g
Unable to find work	866	51.3	4.3g
Persons 25+, educational attainment			
< H.S. completion	8,092	23.6	50.0h
White	5,576	20.3	34.4h
Black	2,246	39.5	13.9h
Hispanic	1,738	31.8	10.7h
Male	2,932	18.1	18.1h
Female	5,160	28.6	31.9h
Completed H.S./no college	5,457	8.9	33.7h
White	3,851	7.2	23.8h
Black	1,434	22.2	8.9h
Hispanic	458	13.9	2.8h
Male	1,916	7.0	11.8h
Female	3,541	10.4	21.9h
Some college	1,676	5.8	10.4h
White	1,181	4.7	7.3h
Black	420	14.0	2.6h
Hispanic	121	8.8	.7h
Male	568	4.1	3.5h
Female	1,111	7.2	6.9h
Completed college	961	2.8	5.9h
White	732	2.4	4.5h
Black	136	6.9	.8h
Hispanic	75	6.9	.5h
Male	456	2.5	2.8h
Female	505	3.2	3.1h

Notes:
a Unless otherwise noted, figures pertain to 1990 and are from U.S. Bureau of the Census, 1991, CPR, Series P-60, #175.
b Persons of Hispanic origin may be of either race.
c Defined as census tracts with 20%-plus poor population based on the 1980 census.
d Percentage of total poor living within family units (25,232/33,585).
e Percentage of poor families only.
f nsp, no spouse present.
g Percentage of all poor persons 18+ years ($N = 20,154$).
h Percentage of all poor persons 25+ years ($N = 16,189$).

behaviors of the other 10% that are uppermost in people's minds when they worry about the poverty problem.

NOTES

1. House of Representatives 1989, p. 55.
2. House of Representatives 1989, p. 78.
3. Since 1969 involuntary part-time employment has accounted for an ever-increasing share of jobs in the United States as employers restructure work in an effort to cut wage and benefit costs (see Tilly 1991, pp. 10–18).
4. Comparable comprehensive data for years since 1987 are not yet available as of late 1992.
5. Further, the divisor of 52 weeks is somewhat unrealistic, as most workers do not work and are not paid for 52 weeks. According to census statistics, the mean (average) number of weeks worked by the 129 million Americans working in 1987 was 44. If we substitute 44 as the divisor, the more realistic weekly wage needed to stay above poverty would rise to $263.89, a figure that lies between the actual average weekly earnings of private, nonsupervisory, nonagricultural workers and those paid to hourly workers.
6. Only slightly more than 60% of the workforce receives group health insurance. For executives, managers, and unionized blue-collar workers the figure is near 80%. For service workers and those employed in retail trade, however, the coverage is only 34% and 38% respectively (1986 data; U.S. Bureau of the Census 1989b, table 671). In all, there are approximately 37,000,000 Americans without health insurance of any kind.
7. This is the Current Population Survey definition in use in the late 1980s (U.S. Bureau of the Census 1988c). In the early 1960s, the definition of "farm population" used a lower dollar value for the minimum income derived from farming and also involved a consideration of the acreage in production.
8. Not surprisingly, the definition of "urban" has also changed over time. In essence, the Census Bureau has used the criterion of an area with a concentrated minimum population of 2,500 for some time. For a more exact definition and discussion of changes over time, see U.S. Bureau of the Census (1975, p. 2).
9. Prior to January, 1980, MSAs were known as standard metropolitan statistical areas (SMSAs). Despite the name change, the definition itself did not appreciably change. As per the 1980 Census of Population, Volume 2, "Subject Reports" (U.S. Bureau of the Census 1985), the general concept refers to an area having a high level of economic and social integration characterized by a concentrated population nucleus surrounded by adjacent communities. SMAs have "one or more central counties containing the areas's main population concentration; an urbanized area of at least 50,000 inhabitants" (p. A-3) (see also U.S. Bureau of the Census 1975, p. 3).
10. Each census between 1940 and 1970 showed an absolute decline in the size of the rural population; in the 1980 census, however, the rural population increased by 5.6 million. Most of this is exurban development rather than a return to

the farm. Throughout the 1970s and '80s, the number of farms, farmers, and farm employees has continued its decline.

11. To illustrate, in 1986 the farm poverty rate was 19.6%, well above the nonfarm rate. One year later, in 1987, the farm poverty rate was 12.6%, slightly below the nonfarm rate.

12. Data on family size and those in the next two paragraphs pertaining to the farm poor are for 1987.

13. Inclusion of nonrelated children raises the incidence of juvenile poverty by one-half to one percent depending on the specific category. Inasmuch as the Bureau of the Census provides less comprehensive information on nonrelated children, we have chosen to report on related children in family units.

4

Who and What Is the Urban Underclass?

The term "underclass" entered the vocabulary of public policy debate in the early 1980s and has since been appropriated by various authors who use the term in different and often inconsistent ways. It is of some interest to consider the term strictly from the viewpoint of class terminology. Although there is no standardized vocabulary of social class, many authors speak of an upper class, a middle class, a working class, and a lower class, with further differentiation at times within these categories. In many presentations, the upper class comprises the wealthy and powerful, the middle class refers to white-collar workers, the working class refers to manual workers, and the lower class is the same as the poor. In this framework, the "underclass" would therefore be that class of the population "under" or beneath the lower class. But "under" or "beneath" in what sense or along what dimension? No one uses the term to refer simply to the poorest of the poor, or to the least educated, or to those in the least prestigious occupations, and so the "underness" of the underclass is not defined by any of the usual criteria of social class placement.

Realistically, there is no single dimension that will serve to identify the underclass (or such, in any case, is one of the conclusions of this chapter). In most applications, the term apparently refers to the intersection of a number of defining characteristics—some structural, some behavioral, some attitudinal, and some ecological. Further, no subset of these characteristics is either a necessary or a sufficient condition for membership in the class. In general, the underclass comprises those persons who are at the bottom of the economic and social barrel, but most would include the urban criminal and drug-dealing elements within the underclass even though their incomes are frequently substantial. Actual poverty, it appears, is not the condition of membership in the underclass but rather whether the person operates within the urban poverty environment. Perhaps the necessary economic criterion is that the person either be poor or derive his or her income from victimizing the poor. And yet there are many people who victimize or exploit the poor for their own personal gain who are not considered part of the underclass—for example, owners of businesses in central city poverty areas and absentee landlords who rent to the poor.

We perhaps come closer to the meaning of the term underclass when we introduce notions of social merit or worth. Americans have always found it necessary to distinguish between the "deserving" and the "undeserving" poor: the former, victims of circumstance or unfavorable economic trends who deserve sympathy and assistance; the latter, the lazy and shiftless who could "do better" for themselves if they wanted and who therefore merit contempt. But even this does not quite get us where we want to go. The net social value of most of the "undeserving" poor is zero; they contribute nothing to the collective good but are by and large harmless. The underclass, perhaps, is that subgroup within the undeserving poor whose overall social value is negative—not the foolish and besotted so much as the brutal and wicked, those persons whose activities threaten the very fabric of urban social life. The difference between the undeserving poor and the underclass perhaps is this: our attitude towards the former is one of ridicule and disdain; our attitude towards the latter is one of fear, even hatred. In this version, what the underclass is "beneath" is contempt.

Most commentators on the underclass define the phenomenon inductively, pointing to contributing factors such as chronic poverty, welfare dependency, dysfunctional behaviors, or social isolation, without an explicit discussion or understanding of how these factors combine to create a class. While often informative, this path proves ultimately unsatisfactory because it resolves largely by fiat fundamental issues of definition and causation that should be approached empirically. If we are ever to solve the problems of the underclass, we will first need some understanding of what the class is and how it has been created; it is not enough to say that the underclass is everything about the urban poor that we don't like.

In many respects, the current situation mirrors that of the larger debate over poverty that took place twenty-five or thirty years ago, when an array of social scientists, journalists, and policy makers argued over how poverty would be defined (Chapter 1). The definition that eventually emerged was, of course, arbitrary, but it did facilitate research, experimentation, understanding, and intervention. This is not to suggest that we should arbitrarily adopt a definition of the underclass, or that any definition will suffice. Our point, rather, is that the lack of a working consensus on what the underclass is has led to a great deal of confusion.

The material covered in the present chapter clarifies but does not resolve the issue of how to define the underclass. When all is said and done, the notion of an "underclass" is less a concept than a metaphor, and metaphors (unlike concepts) do not admit of precise definition. This is not to say that metaphors are without use, however, even in social science. To say that rainfall over the past six hours has averaged 1.3 inches per hour is a well-defined and very precise statement; to say that it is raining cats and dogs is wonderfully imprecise but for most human purposes says all that needs to be said. And so too with the underclass. There is a widespread and not inaccurate perception that many of the central cities are "going to hell in a hand-basket." A not-bad definition of the underclass is that they are the bearers of the basket.

UNDERCLASS AND LUMPEN-PROLETARIAT

Historically, our understanding of social classes and class dynamics has been informed by the writings of Karl Marx and it proves useful to review Marx's thinking with an eye to defining the underclass. Presumably, a Marxian-based class analysis would begin by viewing the underclass as either the lowest stratum of the working class or as the contemporary lumpen-proletariat. According to Marx (see *Capital*, Vol. 3, 1967, pp. 788–94), the accumulation of capital inevitably leads to an expansion of the "surplus" (or economically redundant) labor force, comprised of at least four principal segments. "Floating, latent, and stagnant" persons (p. 794)—the first three segments—are marginalized members of the working class who form the "reserve army" of workers. The fourth segment—the lumpen-proletariat—remains outside the labor force (and thus the working class) and consists of social deviants, misfits, criminals, and other dregs of society.

Marx portrayed the lumpen-proletariat as an economic threat to the working class and as a reactionary, even retrograde, political force. He was openly contemptuous of their political capacity and leanings and was convinced that they would be enemies of the working class in the ultimate class struggle. Still, Marx identified the existence of a lumpen-proletariat as a consequence of capital accumulation—the human victims of the capitalist economic system.

There are obviously some descriptive similarities between Marx's lumpen-proletariat and the contemporary underclass: economic redundancy, political disorganization, and criminal and deviant behavior. There is also merit in locating the source of the problem at the structural level, specifically in the logic and organization of the economy. Thus, the problem of the underclass is not reduced to a discussion of individualistic factors such as the lack of effective "coping strategies" or other personal deficiencies of outlook or motivation. Finally, it is useful to remember that the "surplus population" is not monolithic; it is internally differentiated between those who are marginalized but who retain some attachment to the labor force and society and those who lie entirely outside of social institutions. This recognition of both mainstream and deviant elements within the surplus population (or underclass) is an important insight to which we return later.

Still, there are problems in trying to apply a Marxian framework to the contemporary underclass. Granted, the past decades have seen a severe erosion in the number of semi- and unskilled jobs (e.g., Wilson 1985; Kasarda 1985); this has reduced labor force attachment in some sectors and completely severed the connection in others. But in what realistic sense could it be said that the result has been a "reserve army" of labor? In classical Marxism, the function of the economically redundant population is to depress the price of labor, but it is altogether obvious that displaced semiskilled and unskilled workers cannot help to control the wages of engineers or computer technicians. If today's underclass is to be seen as a "reserve army," then it must be asked, just what are they "on reserve" to do?

Neo-Marxian analysts such as James O'Connor (1973) have replaced the Marxian notion of "surplus labor" with that of "surplus population" and have explicitly disavowed any significant labor force function for the group. In Marx's time, of course, issues of education or skill were largely immaterial; nearly all workers were uneducated, largely unskilled, and therefore essentially interchangeable. In the highly segmented and technically sophisticated labor market that now exists, few if any opportunities are available to those without requisite skills, and so the unskilled cease to function as an industrial reserve army. Instead, they come to comprise a dependent surplus population that necessitates increasing social expenses (the cost of "containment," as O'Connor has it) to be borne by the state and its taxpayers. This, then, is one source of the "fiscal crisis of the state," namely, the ever-increasing expenditures necessary to contain the surplus population.

O'Connor's emendation usefully calls attention to the larger social and economic processes through which people are wasted—pushed out of viable economic roles or never economically integrated at all—and through which an underclass might be created. Surely, the loss of semi- and unskilled jobs in the central cities, and the ensuing joblessness, are critical developments of the past decades (e.g., Ellwood 1986; Jencks and Peterson 1991), a point to which we also return later in this chapter.

Perhaps the chief virtue of Marxian and neo-Marxian conceptions is that they focus attention on large-scale social and economic processes. Much of the contemporary concern with the underclass, in contrast, is focused on individual factors and deficiencies. It is an interesting and pertinent question why one particular individual develops a "deviant" value system or engages in antisocial behaviors while another person— similar to the first in demographic characteristics, family structure, educational background, and employment opportunities—conforms to more socially acceptable standards. Such a question is best explored in psychological and social-psychological terms. But psychology alone fails when we turn to whole neighborhoods and communities where thousands or tens of thousands of individuals exhibit underclass outlooks and behaviors.

To our thinking, contemporary discussions of the underclass have overemphasized the role of the individual. While often recognizing that nonindividual factors such as the family, peer group, neighborhood, economic structure, and patterns of migration are critical causal elements, few accounts integrate these elements in a serious fashion (Wilson's work is the clear exception, as we shall see). As we elaborate in the following pages, an adequate definition and understanding of the underclass requires some attention to (1) structural and economic factors, (2) social-psychological components, (3) behavioral phenomena and (4) spatial-ecological factors. None of these considered in isolation from the others proves sufficient.

THE UNDERCLASS AND THE NEW URBAN REALITY

In the nearly three decades since we declared a national War on Poverty, numerous market and demographic forces have introduced new inequalities that have offset the poverty reduction effects of antipoverty and income-transfer programs. As we showed in Chapter 2, the result is a higher degree of income inequality and polarization today than has existed at any time since the Second World War (Haveman 1988a, 1988b; Mishel and Simon 1988).

Increasing economic inequality is worrisome. More troubling still is the evidence that many of our nation's urban areas are in the midst of a profound and deleterious transformation. Once the centers of culture and civilization, the cities have increasingly become hollow shells, abandoned by the working and middle classes and now home to a qualitatively different syndrome of entrenched and chronic poverty, social disorganization, deviance and lawlessness, anomie and social isolation, homelessness, rampant drug abuse, welfare dependency, and on through a long list. This new urban poverty is concentrated in certain extremely low-income central city neighborhoods, is predominantly black in its composition, and is corrosive of the social fabric (Katz 1989, Ch. 4). This is the poverty of the underclass.

The notion of a "new urban reality" is derived from the work of Peterson (1985) and is meant to express the recent and often dramatic structural, economic, demographic, and ecological changes that have swept over the postindustrial metropolis. To many, the idea of "postin-dustrialism" connotes high technology, gleaming steel and glass office towers, and reclaimed brownstones, lofts, and storefronts now housing the upscale and the trendy. These effusions ignore the consequences of postindustrialism for those without the skills needed to contribute to a postindustrial society. Among these consequences, or so we argue in this chapter and the next, is the emergence of the new urban poverty, the urban underclass.

The poverty of industrial society was by and large tractable, at least in principle. The key virtue of industrial society, after all, is industriousness, something available to nearly all (although, to be sure, never evident in all). Success in industrial society required one to possess the proper attitude and certain minimal skills. Success in the emergent postindustrial society requires one to possess certain higher order intellectual skills that are *not* equally available to all; those without the requisite skills find that the jobs remaining to them are not adequate to support a family or to sustain a minimally acceptable standard of living. They thus drift away from the mainstream of society and into the underclass, becoming further and further isolated, more and more indifferent to the norms and values that otherwise bind society into a coherent whole. What is therefore new about the poverty of urban postindustrial society is its relative destruc-tiveness, intractability, and hopelessness.

DEFINING THE UNDERCLASS

Is the underclass an economic, social, psychological, or ecological con-struct? Does the underclass consist of positions, people, values or be-haviors? Is the term itself meant to be solely descriptive and analytic, or does it also carry intended moral and ideological overtones? That the term has been used in all these ways is a source of great confusion; researchers have yet to agree fully on what the underclass is, and they continue to debate on whether there is a "better" (more descriptive, less pejorative) term that adequately describes the phenomenon.

Amidst the definitional confusion are four common themes stressed by most (but not all) authors: economics, social psychology, behavior, and spatial concentration. Let us take these up in turn.

First is the *economic* dimension (Glasgow 1980; Wilson 1987; Allen and Farley 1986; Murray 1984; Ruggles and Marton 1986; Cook and Curtin 1987). Everyone agrees that the underclass has something to do with poverty and more specifically with poverty of a very distinctive sort. Since the first studies of family income dynamics were published in the 1970s, it has become customary to distinguish between *chronic* and *epi-*

sodic poverty. One of the central findings from those studies was that much American poverty is in fact not of the chronic variety; rather, persons and families move in and out of poverty on short time scales owing to short-term fluctuations in family economic and demographic circumstances (Bane and Ellwood 1983; Ruggles and Marton 1986). The chronically poor, in contrast, are those who are poor year after year, generation after generation, and it is this chronic poverty, in most accounts, that defines the economic aspect of the underclass.

The chronically poor are a definite minority within the larger poverty population, although there is evidence that chronic poverty is increasing (Devine, Plunkett, and Wright 1992). Analysis of longitudinal data from the Panel Study of Income Dynamics (PSID) clearly indicates that most American poverty is relatively short term, caused mainly by family dislocation and dissolution and only secondarily by labor market experiences *per se* (Duncan et al. 1984). In fact, the PSID data show that although nearly a quarter of all American families were below the poverty line in at least one year between 1969 and 1978, only 3% were below the poverty line in eight or more of those ten years. (More recent data on the increasing chronicity of poverty in the United States are presented below in Chapter 5.)

Glasgow's (1980) in-depth treatment of the underclass is one among many that emphasizes the economic dimension. In Glasgow's definition, the underclass is "a permanently entrapped population of poor persons, unused and unwanted, accumulated in various parts of the country" (1980, p. 3). Rejecting both the "culture of poverty" thesis associated with the work of Oscar Lewis (1966) and the highly individualized explanations of conservative and neoconservative theorists (Gilder 1981; Murray 1984; Wilson and Herrnstein 1985), Glasgow identifies the underclass as a relatively new group of impoverished black Americans trapped in intergenerational poverty by chronic unemployment, underemployment, welfare dependency, racism, and other institutional barriers that prevent upward mobility. In explicitly rejecting a normative definition, Glasgow stresses that his use of the term "underclass" is not intended to "connote moral or ethical unworthiness, nor . . . have any pejorative meaning (p. 8)."[1] Rather, the emphasis is on the workings of an economic structure that yields low to nonexistent life chances for a large and growing stratum of the population.

It is not sufficient, however, to define the underclass simply as the chronically poor. Chronic poverty falls disproportionally on households headed by blacks, females, the elderly, and those living in rural areas and in the South (Duncan et al. 1984, pp. 50–51). No one, so far as we know, includes the elderly poor among the underclass, and almost everyone looks on the underclass principally as an urban development. Also, as we have already suggested, many elements within the urban underclass (criminals, pimps, drug dealers, and the like) often have substantial incomes, although they have come overwhelmingly from impoverished central city backgrounds. Still, we get respectably close to the common sense understanding of what the underclass is if we say that it results from entrenched, chronic urban poverty.

In addition to chronic poverty, the underclass can also be characterized along various *social-psychological* dimensions (Auletta 1983; Long and Vaillant 1984; Murray 1984; Cook and Curtin 1987). The underclass rejects many of the norms and values of the larger society. Among underclass youth, achievement motivation is low, education is undervalued, and conventional means of success and upward mobility are scorned. There is widespread alienation from society and its institutions, estrangement, social isolation, and hopelessness, the sense that a better life is simply not attainable through legitimate means. Society itself comes to be seen as an alien and hostile institution; conventional norms of civility, reciprocity, and respect come to hold no sway. The technical term for all this is anomie—the absence of a shared normative structure that otherwise governs social interaction. In the absence of normative constraints, the culture of the underclass thus comes to resemble the Hobbesian "war of all against all," with every individual a predator maximizing personal advantage at the expense of those who venture near.

Analysts who stress these social-psychological aspects of the underclass are sometimes criticized for "blaming the victim" or, what amounts to the same thing, for suggesting that the problems of the underclass would dissipate if they would only adhere to middle-class norms and values. Certainly it would be wrong to focus on underclass values without acknowledging their many structural roots. One need not spend a great deal of time in a poor, central city public high school classroom to understand that the experience is not conducive to high achievement motivation or to a belief that educational success will pay off in the future and is therefore worth the effort. In many of the central cities, rates of unemployment among young nonwhite men now routinely exceed 40 or 50%; the half or so lucky enough to have a job will usually be laboring at the minimum wage. This situation provides fertile ground for hostility, estrangement, and hopelessness to flourish. Processes as diverse as urban renewal and the siting of the interstate highway system have conspired to bulldoze many former low-income neighborhoods to the ground or to cut them up into isolated enclaves. A sense of neighborhood or community is difficult to sustain when the neighborhoods and communities of the poor have themselves been destroyed. And it is very hard to maintain a belief in the efficacy of society's institutions when drug deals are being conducted on every other corner, when crime and violence are rampant, when the crackle of gunfire is part of one's everyday experience. To say that the underclass has rejected many of society's norms and values is not to deny that they have done so for good reasons. Much less is it to say that they are personally to blame for many of these developments.

Beyond the economics and social psychology of the underclass lies an important *behavioral* dimension, and this is the component that has everybody worried. Just being poor and hopeless or anomic is not sufficient; rather, the poverty, hopelessness, and anomie must translate into antisocial, "deviant," dysfunctional, or threatening behaviors: criminal activity, drug and alcohol abuse, welfare dependency, joblessness, teenage pregnancy, and so on (Glasgow 1980; Auletta 1983; Murray 1984; Wilson 1987). Wilson (1987) refers bluntly to this behavioral complex as a "tangle of pathologies" that has profoundly eroded the quality of urban life; certainly, this "tangle" lies at the heart of common sense understandings of what the underclass is and why something needs to be done about it.

The behavioral dimension of the underclass is stressed most insistently by Auletta (1983). While recognizing that poverty is a correlate of the underclass phenomenon, he also observes that:

> the underclass need not be poor—street criminals, for instance, usually are not. Which brings us to a second characteristic that usually distinguishes the underclass: *behavior*. Whatever the cause—whether it is the fault of the people themselves or of society, whether poverty is a cause or effect—most students of poverty believe that the underclass suffers from *behavioral* as well as income deficiencies. The underclass usually operates outside the generally accepted boundaries of society. They are often set apart, they say, by their 'deviant' or antisocial behavior, by their bad habits, not just by their poverty." (Auletta 1983, pp. 27–28, emphasis in original)

Although largely descriptive, Auletta's behavioral approach is useful because it provides a rationale for classifying the underclass into distinct subgroups. Auletta is thus among the first to recognize the heterogeneity of the underclass population, in contrast to the more popular monolithic description.[2] (This acknowledgment of the diversity of the underclass is echoed and elaborated by Ellwood 1987, Wilson 1987 and others.) Specifically, Auletta identifies four distinct subgroups of the underclass population: passive long-term welfare recipients; hostile (i.e., violent) street criminals, who are often school dropouts and drug addicts or dealers; nonviolent hustlers (pimps, con artists) who earn their living in the underground economy; and the "traumatized," consisting of "drunks, drifters, homeless shopping-bag ladies and released mental patients who frequently roam or collapse on city streets" (1983, p. iv).

Many other authors have also treated the underclass as multidimensional, among them Danziger (1989), Ellwood (1986, 1987), Ellwood and

Bane (1984), Bane and Ellwood (1983), Sawhill (1987), Ricketts and Sawhill (1986), and Wilson (1985, 1987). Ellwood's (1987) depiction of the underclass is representative; he sees the class as a relatively small subset of the nation's urban poor, primarily consisting of minorities who are concentrated and caught in the pathology of the ghetto (see also Katz 1989). As such, this group suffers from geographic, economic, and social isolation.

> What one sees in America's ghettos is concentration, as poor people are crowded together; isolation, as middle class families move out; deprivation, as children grow up poor; inferior education, as central city schools decay; and limited opportunity, as low-skill jobs evaporate or move out of the city. Crime and drugs add additional elements. Children living in this environment see few role models, limited opportunity, a poor educational system, intimidating yet respected criminals, and a decaying infrastructure. At best, such children are left with despair. They see no opportunity of joining the mainstream they see in abundance on television. They have little reason to believe that something they do can change their lives, since all their friends are poor. Virtually none have jobs. Frankly, if pathologies did not develop in an environment as horrendous as this, it would be a modern miracle. (Ellwood 1987, pp. 49–50)

Auletta's typology, his depiction of the lives of various members of the manpower training group he observed, Ellwood's emphasis on concentration, and other ethnographies of urban ghetto life (Liebow 1967; Anderson 1978, 1990) suggest that an adequate definition of the underclass must encompass not only the perpetrators of underclass behavior, but also their direct victims, that is, the nondeviant poor (children, the elderly, the infirm, the working poor) who live amidst the deteriorated urban conditions associated with underclass life. After all, poor, anomic, socially isolated criminals, alcoholics, addicts, and other deviants (and their victims) have existed throughout history; what makes the contemporary situation different is the *ecological* dimension of the underclass— the increasing spatial concentration of all the above dimensions into certain tightly defined central city neighborhoods.

The ecological dimension of the underclass is most explicitly discussed by Wilson (1987) and focuses attention on the increasing density of the economic, social-psychological, and behavioral components (see also Ricketts and Sawhill 1986; Danziger and Gottschalk 1987; Ellwood 1987). The basic theory is that there is some critical "density" or concentration of the other components at which a given neighborhood ceases being just a poverty area with lots of problems and becomes a true underclass enclave.

The analogy with nuclear fission is presumably intentional: at some critical density, the central neighborhood explodes and shock waves propagate outward into adjacent neighborhoods, which in turn explode until the chain reaction finally stops at impenetrable (or policable) social or physical boundaries, with little but devastation and human rubble left behind. This is similar to what is sometimes called the "contagion theory of neighborhood decline," although these days, the image of nuclear explosion seems more apt than that of a fatal but slowing spreading infection.

The theme of social isolation and spatial concentration is central to Wilson's analysis of the underclass. Stating that the underclass is a "heterogeneous grouping of inner-city families and individuals whose behavior contrasts sharply with that of mainstream America" (1987, p. 7), Wilson rejects present-day racism as a critical explanatory principle, arguing that the underclass constitutes a polarized entity within the black community itself (see also Wilson 1978).

Paradoxically, Wilson argues that the significant gains many black Americans have achieved in education, occupational standing, and income in the last quarter-century are partly responsible for the emergence of the underclass. During that quarter-century, an era when longstanding legal barriers to full citizenship were removed (as evidenced by the Civil Rights Act of 1964, the Voting Rights Act of 1965, and numerous other Great Society programs), many African-Americans experienced historically unparalleled rates of upward mobility and newly won access to higher education, the white-collar and professional occupational ranks, and better housing opportunities. At the same time, many blacks and other minorities were unable to take advantage of these new opportunities and continue to suffer disadvantage in income, education, occupational attainment, and other valued opportunities and rewards. Thus, the result of new opportunity has been a heightened degree of class polarization within the black community.

As black Americans have experienced increased upward social mobility, many have also become geographically mobile, leaving the central city black communities for better, more affluent, and more stable neighborhoods elsewhere. Thus ghetto communities that once housed black professionals, teachers, skilled craftspersons, shopkeepers, and gainfully employed industrial workers have experienced an exodus of these and other upwardly mobile African-Americans. Two interrelated consequences follow from this exodus. The first is the virtual destruction of many local indigenous institutions—black churches, voluntary associations, locally owned businesses, and the like—that would otherwise exercise the social control necessary for the normal functioning of any healthy community. The second is simply the increasing concentration of the poor, especially the chronically impoverished minority poor, in inner city neighborhoods.

Building on the work of Kasarda (1985), Wilson further argues that this situation has been exacerbated by major structural shifts in the global economy. Transformations in the occupational structure have resulted in the loss of many thousands of unskilled and semiskilled jobs. This loss has primarily affected minority and immigrant groups who have historically relied on entry-level industrial positions with low educational requirements. The net result, as we have already suggested, is increasing class polarization within the black community, in that one segment has achieved substantial mobility while the other remains trapped in deeper, more concentrated impoverishment in the ghetto.[3] And it is this latter group that experiences exceptional rates of unemployment, low rates of labor force participation, high levels of school separation, drug abuse, crime, out-of-wedlock births, welfare dependency, and all the other aberrant manifestations of underclass life.

Associated changes in the economics and demographics of housing have also contributed to the simultaneous exodus of middle-class blacks and the increased concentration of the minority poor in central city neighborhoods. An increasingly restrictive housing market, often exacerbated by shortsighted federal policies (see Rubin, Wright, and Devine 1992), has served to fuel gentrification, restrict the low-income housing stock, and thus further concentrate the poor, especially the minority poor, in central city areas.

Two additional, interrelated elements are central to Wilson's account of the underclass. The first concerns the historic consequences of racism, a factor that Wilson clearly downplays relative to other analysts (see, e.g., Glasgow 1980; Hacker 1992) but that he recognizes (following Lieberson 1980) as an important and distinctive aspect of the black urban experience. The second factor concerns the extremely adverse labor market opportunities faced by urban black males, the effect this has on their capacity to function as family providers, and the consequent high rate of female-headed households in the ghetto.

In sum, Wilson rejects any attempt to view the underclass phenomenon as singular in cause or effect. Rather, he posits "complex sociological antecedents that range from demographic changes to problems of economic organization" (1985, p. 134). Following this lead, we also argue that all four of the components we have discussed are essential in understanding "the" underclass, although some analysts (for example, Jencks 1989) have (with justifiable reason) abandoned any single definition and have simply postulated that there is an economic underclass, a moral underclass, an educational underclass, and an ecological underclass. We prefer a definition of "the" underclass as *persons living in urban, central city neighborhoods or communities with high and increasing rates of poverty, espe-cially chronic poverty, high and increasing levels of social isolation, hopelessness, and anomie, and high levels of characteristically antisocial or dysfunctional behavior patterns.* No one factor is sufficient to create an underclass; all must be simultaneously present.

In our view, therefore, it is more appropriate to speak of underclass *neighborhoods* than of underclass *individuals;* so far as individuals are concerned, the only criterion for class membership is that they live in underclass neighborhoods as we have defined them. This definition implies that stable, industrious, working-class black families or even relatively affluent black businessmen or professionals who live in underclass neighborhoods are to be included among the membership of the class. In our definition, then, the underclass consists of impoverished, antisocial, anomic individuals and also their victims elsewhere in the same under-class urban neighborhoods. In other words, as we understand it, the underclass should not be thought of as a "thing" to which people belong but as a set of social-structural conditions that define the terms of exis-tence in a geographical location.

Central to our perspective is the role of the neighborhood as the relevant spatial-ecological unit. The neighborhood is both a physical site and an integrative sociocultural context. The neighborhood forms the immediate arena of extended social interaction in which mediating groups contribute to a material, ideational, cognitive, and affective frame-work that simultaneously offers both constraint and opportunity. This framework of which the neighborhood is a part constitutes the critical cultural mechanism by which individuals process and subsequently translate broader social currents and conditions into individual re-sponses. It is the neighborhood in which structures such as peer and reference groups operate in conjunction with (or in opposition to) more formal organizations such as churches and schools to produce either social integration or isolation.

What has happened to the neighborhoods of the poor in the past few decades? Is there any evidence to suggest, as our viewpoint demands, that these neighborhoods have been characterized by increasingly con-centrated poverty and social dysfunction? A statistical examination of the 33,585,000 of the nation's poor in 1990 reveals that 12,547,000 of them (or 37.4%) live in so-called "poverty areas," which are defined as census areas with a poverty rate of 20% or higher. Within the poverty areas themselves, so defined, the poverty rate is 33.3%, or about two and one-half times the overall national rate.[4] Focussing further just on the central cities, we find 14,254,000 impoverished persons, or 42% of the nation's poor. More than half of these urban poor persons (52%, or 7,404,000 people) live in census poverty areas. In the central city poverty areas, the overall poverty rate is

38.4%, or nearly three times the national figure. These figures show the degree to which poverty is currently concentrated in certain run-down inner city areas (although they do not address the question of recent trends).

Submerged within these figures are rather dramatic racial disparities. About a quarter (26.6%) of impoverished whites lived in poverty areas in 1990; about three-fifths (61.7%) of the nation's black poor lived in poverty areas. Moreover, the overall poverty rate in poverty areas occupied mainly by whites is 26.7%, while the corresponding rate for tracts occupied by the poor blacks is 43.7%.

Similarly, while roughly a third (34.3%) of the nation's white poor live in central cities and one in seven (14.1%) live in central city poverty areas, the black poor experience a profoundly more concentrated poverty situation; three of every five (59.7%) impoverished black Americans live in a central city area, with two in five (40.0%) living in impoverished central city areas.[5]

Tract-level data from the 1990 census are not yet available for analysis, so little can be said about recent trends in these concentration indicators. However, Jargowsky and Bane (1990) have analyzed changes in the concentration of poverty between 1970 and 1980, finding that the number of ghettoized poor increased by 29.5% between 1970 and 1980, with almost 90% of this increase occurring among blacks and Hispanics (also see Massey and Eggers 1990). Using a 40% criterion (rather than the Bureau of the Census' 20% figure), Jargowsky and Bane also found that the increasing concentration of poverty was not at all uniform. While some metropolitan areas experienced increasingly concentrated poverty, other areas experienced little if any change and some even registered a decline. The authors conclude, "the phenomenon of large and growing ghetto poverty populations characterizes only a *minority* of SMSAs" (1990, p. 52).[6]

Nonetheless, the dysfunctional implications of the spatial concentration of poverty are severe and often serve to transcend individual motivation and efforts to escape the influence of degraded neighborhoods and the pathology of the streets. This structural impact is eloquently captured in Massey, Cross, and Eggers' (1991) summation of their empirical research on segregation and poverty in the nation's fifty largest SMSAs. Using both tract metro area and individual tract level data from the 1980 census, Massey, Cross, and Eggers (1991, 416–417) conclude that:

> . . . *personal behaviors that are widely associated with the underclass, and which outwardly appear to be idiosyncratic and wholly individual, are in fact linked to structural conditions in society that are beyond individual control or influence.* In particular, the degree of residential segregation and the rate of poverty that a group experiences in a metropolitan area interact to determine the con-

centration of poverty that its members experience in neighborhoods. *As poverty rises in a racially segregated environment, blacks are exposed to progressively higher levels of neighborhood poverty and increasing income deprivation, no matter what their individual social and economic characteristics.*

The *concentration of poverty* that arises from the conjunction of high poverty rates and high levels of segregation *leads, in turn, to a variety of deleterious individual outcomes.* Long-term residence in a poor neighborhood lowers the odds that a black man will find a job, and increases the probability that a black women will bear children out of wedlock and end up heading a family with children. (emphasis added)

HOW BIG IS THE UNDERCLASS?

With no firm consensus on the very definition of the underclass, there can obviously be no firm estimate of its size. We concluded at the end of the last chapter that the urban underclass, defined simply on the basis of demographic conditions, could not comprise more than about 3 or 3.5 million persons, or roughly a tenth of the total poverty population. But the demographic exclusions used to produce that number (e.g., children, the elderly, the working poor) would clearly include large numbers of urban poor living in underclass neighborhoods, who by our present definition would therefore have to be included. The earlier figure perhaps better represents the maximum size of the perpetrator subgroup, not the class as a whole.

There are several informative, even excellent treatments of the question, "How big is the underclass?" This notwithstanding, the lack of a common definition—or, barring consensus, dissimilar but precisely stated definitions that would allow reasonable comparisons across studies—has led to radically disparate estimates of the size of the underclass population (see Ricketts and Sawhill 1986; Ruggles and Marton 1986).

Auletta (1983, pp. 25–29) reviews a half-dozen studies of the topic and on that basis offers estimates ranging from 2 to 18 million persons. His preferred number, 9 million, is simply the midpoint of the range of estimates. A more recent estimate from the Urban Institute places the figure at approximately 250,000 persons, less than one-seventieth of Auletta's highest figure (Ricketts and Sawhill 1986; Wilkerson, 1987). Although only a small fraction of other estimates, the Urban Institute study also suggests that the size of the underclass more than doubled from 1970 to 1980. It has probably grown still further since. Also, as Sawhill has pointed out, the Urban Institute definition is highly restrictive, encompassing only the welfare dependent and the chronically unemployed. In testimony before Congress, she remarks, "The census tracts that meet the Urban Institute's underclass criteria, for example, include 2 million poor or working-class people who, though not themselves on welfare or chronically unemployed, can hardly escape the influence of their depressed surroundings" (quoted in Wilkerson, 1987). Including this latter group as part of the underclass would bring the Urban Institute estimate up into the range of estimates reviewed by Auletta.

Applying the definition formulated above—persons living in urban, central city neighborhoods or communities with high and increasing rates of poverty, especially chronic poverty, high and increasing levels of social isolation, hopelessness, and anomie, and high levels of characteristically antisocial or dysfunctional behavior patterns—is, sad to say, effectively impossible since there is no available data source that aggregates all the relevant variables into meaningful geographic units of analysis. Following the Urban Institute and others, one might arbitrarily select census tracts as the relevant geographical aggregation, arbitrarily select some poverty figure (say, 30% or 40% below the official poverty line) as the defining criterion, arbitrarily assume that all the other behavioral and attitudinal components are strongly associated with the degree of poverty, then sum populations across tracts that meet the poverty designation and announce the result as an estimate of the size of the urban underclass. This, unfortunately, binds the definition of the class to the characteristics of the available data. Our preference is to work with an appropriate, theoretically derived definition and simply admit that the existing data are not adequate at this time to come to any firm conclusions about the size of the underclass.

A CAVEAT ON GEOGRAPHY, REGION, AND CITY SIZE

Much of the literature on the underclass reflects the recent experience of large cities in the North—an unnecessary bias. Chicago, New York, Detroit, and Philadelphia are, of course, major national population centers sharing numerous developmental characteristics and historic patterns of industrialization and deindustrialization, migration, gentrification, and so forth; and these are, accordingly, the cities that figure most prominently in recent discussions of the underclass. But it would be wrong to infer from the emphasis on large Northern cities that cities in the South and West have been exempt from underclass developments, or that smaller cities have not experienced underclass problems.

To the contrary, large southern cities exhibit the full array of social pathology associated with the underclass: high rates of poverty, increasing proportions of female-headed households and out-of-wedlock pregnancies, violent crime and drug abuse, unemployment, welfare dependency, inadequate education. Indeed, the South suffers a higher rate of impoverishment than any other region (Duncan et al., 1984; U.S.

Bureau of the Census 1985, 1991c). Cities such as New Orleans and Atlanta rival or surpass Newark and Gary in their rates of poverty, and Houston matches Detroit homicide for homicide. Nor are places such as Birmingham, San Antonio, Miami, Mobile, Oakland, and other Sunbelt cities immune to underclass problems.

In fact, it is a plausible hypothesis that the underclass problem may be worse in the South than in other parts of the nation, for four reasons. First, the relative lack of an industrial base (rather than deindustrialization) may be indicative of a basic infrastructural incapacity to adapt to national and international market trends. Second, the South has a higher proportion of both minorities and poverty than other regions of the country. Third, southern states typically have a less developed welfare system that might otherwise "contain" underclass problems (Shapiro and Greenstein 1988). Finally, one must consider the region's unique history of race relations and the residual effects.

It is also not obvious why smaller cities would be immune to underclass developments. Many of the processes that have operated to create an underclass in the largest cities would also be found in smaller cities, although perhaps on a reduced scale. Many of the smaller cities have single-industry economic bases and might therefore be even more vulnerable to shifting economic developments. One of us (James D. Wright) recently had occasion to spend several days in Fort Wayne, Indiana, which, with a total metropolitan population of about 350,000, ranks as the 100th largest American city. During the visit, much concern was expressed about the city's escalating homicide rate, a spate of arsons involving abandoned and dilapidated buildings in the more run-down sections of town, several recent drive-by shootings involving rival gangs warring over drugs and territory, the expulsion of several high school students for carrying guns to school, the recent layoff of more than a hundred salaried (white-collar) workers at General Electric (the city's largest employer), and the worrisome effects of the deepening recession. The ten or twenty or fifty largest cities, it appears, have no monopoly on urban decay, concentrated poverty, or behavioral aberration; these, rather, have come to be commonplace in all American cities whatever their size.

CONCLUSIONS

The notion of an "underclass" is more a metaphor than a concept, and the term has been used in a bewildering variety of ways by numerous authors, critics, and researchers. To the extent that the term admits of precise definition, that definition must include economic, social-psychological, behavioral, and ecological aspects. For present purposes, as we have already said, we will use the term to refer to "persons living in urban, central city neighborhoods or communities with high and increasing rates of poverty, especially chronic poverty, high and increasing levels of social isolation, hopelessness, and anomie, and high levels of characteristically antisocial or dysfunctional behavior patterns," with the advance understanding that these neighborhoods or communities need not be (indeed are not) confined to the largest Northern cities.

Although our definition cannot be used to estimate the size of the underclass, it does point to the factors one must consider to understand how the class has developed and evolved over the past decade. And that, it so happens, is the topic to be taken up in the next two chapters.

NOTES

1. The relevance of "deviant" values to the definition of the underclass is an important source of disagreement among theorists and researchers. In one of the few empirically based studies of the question, Cook and Curtin (1987) found that the aspirations and values of the "underclass" did not differ substantially from those of the mainstream. There were, however, major behavioral discrepancies.

2. Cook and Curtin (1987) provide intriguing information on how "mainstream" Americans' perceptions of the "underclass" greatly magnify what appear to be rather minimal values differences. Such distortion may be understood as a logical cognitive defense, as the authors explain, but rather singular media portrayals of the ghetto poor as "different" from other Americans may also contribute to this perception (see Ellwood 1987, p. 49).

3. A central proposition in Wilson's analysis (and that of a number of others) is that the central cities have experienced increased *concentrations* of poverty, partly because of the out-migration of middle- and working-class families who can afford to "escape" the inner-city and also because recent economic trends have increased poverty among those remaining behind. Support for this proposition as it pertains to the fifty largest U.S. cities may be found in Danziger and Gottschalk (1987).

4. About 15% of the United States population as a whole lives in so-called census poverty areas. The poverty rate within the nonpoverty areas where 85% of the U.S. population lives is 10%.

5. The experience of impoverished Hispanics more closely resembles that of the black poor than the white poor in terms of its concentration. Several heavily Hispanic areas of south Texas are among the largest pockets of concentrated poverty in the country.

6. One of Jargowsky and Bane's (1990) most interesting findings is that in 1970, the ten metropolitan areas with the most ghettoized poor contained 36.2% of all poor people residing in census areas with poverty rates of 40% or higher. Ten years later, the figure had increased to 48.7%, with New York and Chicago alone accounting for more than a quarter (27.4%).

5

The Persistence of Poverty[1]

As the discussion in Chapter 4 makes clear, there is at best a loose agreement among researchers and commentators about who and what the underclass is and whether it is growing. On the other hand, nearly all analysts agree that *concentrated, chronic,* and *extreme* poverty lies somewhere close to the heart of a correct definition. Amidst the definitional confusion and ambiguity, that is, these related factors tend to stand out in common: the underclass is very and chronically poor over extended periods, and the poverty of the underclass has come more and more to be spatially concentrated in certain low-income urban areas.

Concerning the *concentration* of poverty, the relevant studies were reviewed at the close of the previous chapter and they are consistent with expectation; at least between 1970 and 1980, the poor were increasingly "ghettoized" in urban poverty areas. A definitive analysis of this process awaits the release of the 1990 census tract analyses, but the preliminary data that are available suggest a continuation of this trend. But what evidence, if any, can be marshalled to show that the *chronicity* of poverty has also increased?

Chronic poverty is poverty that persists across time or over generations and is to be distinguished from *episodic* poverty of the sort that results from short-term fluctuations in household composition or finances. That much poverty is in fact not chronic but episodic is one of the key findings from the research on poverty conducted in the 1970s (e.g., Duncan et al. 1984). While this no doubt remains true, there is nonetheless reason to believe that within the past fifteen or so years the rate of chronic poverty has been increasing and that this increase lies at the very core of the underclass problem.

Unfortunately, while the notion of chronic or persistent poverty ends and thus unites otherwise disparate claims about contemporary poverty and the underclass, the concept of chronicity itself is not without ambiguity. As we concluded earlier, the concept of the underclass is clearly intended to separate the experience of the long-term poor from the more commonplace, episodic forms of impoverishment that result from temporary economic dislocation, family dissolution, and the like; but no single standard or temporal benchmark of chronicity exists. How many years must a family be poor before that family can be considered chronically poor? (A related ambiguity that is not directly considered here is whether the notion of chronicity also implies an intergenerational component.)

Although various researchers have employed different conceptions and definitions of the chronicity of poverty, there is widespread agreement that during the past decade or so, chronicity has increased. Upon examination, however, this thesis of increasing chronicity often rests upon indirect, extremely limited, or often dated empirical evidence. More often than not, researchers infer increased chronicity from such developments as: (1) the allegedly more intractable nature of poverty over the past fifteen or so years, as evidenced by the tendency for the post-1973 incidence of poverty to remain high, especially among minorities; (2) the now well-documented trend toward an increasingly unequal distribution of income during the 1980s (see, e.g., Levy 1988; Mishel and Simon 1988; U.S. Bureau of the Census 1988a, table 12); or (3) the equally well-documented fact that a relatively large number of census tracts in almost all of the nation's large urban centers experienced an increasingly concentrated poverty population between 1970 and 1980 (see Danziger and Gottschalk 1987; Ricketts and Mincy 1988; Ricketts and Sawhill 1986).

Despite the consistency of these claims, there is little direct evidence on the chronicity of poverty or on the question whether chronic poverty has actually increased. Although Duncan (1984) and his associates' seminal work on the persistence of poverty clearly established the fact of chronicity in ways that Hunter (1904), Harrington (1962, 1984), Liebow (1967), Caudill on Appalachia (1963), and others previously could not, it is also true that this much-cited work dealt with the 1968–78 period.[2] As such, it does not bear directly on the widespread notion of increasing chronicity in the late 1970s and 1980s.

Towards the end of Chapter 1, we made mention of different types of data and metaphorically compared these to different visual media. Until this point in the discussion, however, we have restricted ourselves to looking at poverty either at a single point in time or in terms of highly aggregated trends over time. As yet, we have not focused on poverty from a dynamic perspective, one that allows us to follow specific individuals and families over time. By looking at poverty from this latter perspective we can speak to the issue of chronic or persistent poverty.

In this chapter, then, we test the hypothesis of increasing chronicity of poverty using data from the Panel Study of Income Dynamics (PSID).[3] Specifically, we operationalize several alternative quantitative definitions of intra-generational (i.e., within one generation) chronicity of poverty by creating a series of rolling multi-year windows to track PSID households' income experiences over the 1968–87 period.[4] Thus we assess the patterns of chronic poverty across time and ascertain whether the incidence of chronicity is or is not increasing. We also assess the nineteen-year record of chronic poverty among demographic subgroups based on the gender and race of household heads. All this perhaps sounds more complicated than it is; reduced to the essentials, our question is whether poor people these days spend more years in poverty on the average than poor people did in previous decades.

THE PANEL STUDY OF INCOME DYNAMICS (PSID)

As we have already mentioned, each year the Census Bureau provides a detailed count of how many Americans are poor (see *Current Population Reports,* Series P-60), with further information also given on demographic characteristics, educational attainment, work experiences, living arrangements, and other attributes. Unfortunately, these cross-sectional data do not tell us how poverty affects households and individuals over time. For instance, we have no direct way of knowing how many of the nation's 33.6 million poor in 1990 were also poor in 1989. The only way to know the answer to a question such as this is to follow the same people from one year to the next. Fortunately, the Panel Study of Income Dynamics (PSID) allows us to do exactly that.

The PSID began in 1968 with an initial national representative sample of almost 3,000 households and a subsample of about 1,900 low-income families. Since its inception, the PSID has purposely oversampled the poor in an effort to understand the determinants of family income and its changes over time. However, the combined sample is appropriately weighted to be representative of the U.S. population. Since 1968, heads of the same families have been reinterviewed, as have heads of families containing members of the original sample who have left to start households of their own or join other households. In 1987, the last year of PSID data we analyze, the twentieth wave of data collection had been completed. Due to family split-offs, the sample had grown to 7,061 households. In short, the PSID constitutes a unique ongoing national data set perfectly suited to the question at hand.

OPERATIONALIZING CHRONICITY

We initially undertake a crude comparative assessment of family composition differences between poor and nonpoor PSID households for each year by simply dividing all households into two groups according to

whether their total family income was higher or lower than the Bureau of
the Census' four-person poverty threshold. Results are presented in Table
5.1.[5]

These data suggest four things. First, for both poor and nonpoor families, mean household size has continued to decline throughout the 1969–
1987 period. Second, and perhaps contrary to expectation, throughout
this period the mean size of nonpoor families has *exceeded* the mean size
of impoverished households. For poor families, mean size has declined
from 3.12 to 2.19 persons, while non-poor families have gone from 4.18 to
2.95 persons. Third, the distributional profile of family size is substantially closer for both types of families than a comparison of the means
would indicate. Finally, as family units have become smaller, the size
differential has tended to shrink.

Using the information contained in Table 5.1 (and the potential bias
owing to differences in family size and the incidence of single-person
households among the poor and nonpoor), we break down both sets of
families by number of members. These data are reported in Table 5.2.

As we expected, the information in Table 5.2 indicates that while the
proportion of single-person households has grown substantially among
both groups throughout the period (from 30.2% to 45.8% and 8.0% to
15.4% among the poor and nonpoor respectively), among poor families
there is a far higher incidence of single-person households. Thus, the need
to explicitly account for family-size and compositional changes becomes
readily apparent. Although this is hardly surprising, these data do show
that the failure to account and adjust for household size would introduce
substantial bias in the calculation of chronicity.

As noted, this finding was anticipated since one of the most fascinating
aspects of the PSID has been the capacity to document the compositional
dynamism of American families (see Morgan 1974). As Rainwater observes in his Forward to Duncan et al.'s (1984, p. vi) *Years of Poverty, Years
of Plenty:*

> . . . one of the first things the analysts learned as they began to work with
> these data was that the commonsense category of "family"—by which we
> usually mean a nuclear family living together—is an extremely problematic
> concept when one takes a longitudinal perspective on families over time. A
> moment's thought reminds us that families are in fact constantly changing
> as time passes. . . .

The findings to which Rainwater speaks (based on analysis of the 1968–
1978 PSID data) are that "nearly one-half of the families in any given year
will be headed by someone other than the person who headed the 'same'
family eleven years ago" (Duncan et al. 1984, p. 4).

Table 5.1. Family Size Characteristics of PSID Families, 1969–1987

	Poor Families[a]				Nonpoor Families			
Year	Mean	S.D.	Range	N	Mean	S.D.	Range	N
1987	2.19	1.48	1–10	1746	2.95	1.46	1–11	5177
1986	2.21	1.48	1–11	1658	2.99	1.48	1–14	4910
1985	2.22	1.47	1–10	1573	3.01	1.50	1–14	4698
1984	2.30	1.51	1–9	1556	3.03	1.52	1–13	4337
1983	2.34	1.58	1–11	1488	3.05	1.55	1–13	4127
1982	2.29	1.55	1–11	1375	3.07	1.58	1–13	3969
1981	2.17	1.49	1–10	1285	3.14	1.62	1–13	3791
1980	2.23	1.58	1–11	1187	3.17	1.65	1–13	3633
1979	2.25	1.63	1–12	1039	3.18	1.67	1–12	3496
1978	2.32	1.68	1–11	946	3.26	1.75	1–12	3326
1977	2.39	1.76	1–12	928	3.31	1.81	1–13	3137
1976	2.32	1.68	1–12	835	3.38	1.89	1–14	2994
1975	2.43	1.84	1–12	764	3.42	1.94	1–16	2827
1974	2.41	1.85	1–12	729	3.56	2.01	1–15	2609
1973	2.51	1.97	1–13	624	3.67	2.06	1–16	2476
1972	2.63	2.05	1–10	565	3.81	2.17	1–16	2302
1971	2.83	2.25	1–12	533	3.88	2.21	1–15	2127
1970	2.99	2.30	1–13	478	3.97	2.23	1–17	1999
1969	3.12	2.32	1–14	463	4.18	2.31	1–17	1811

Note:
[a] According to official annual four-person poverty threshhold figure (U.S. Bureau of the Census (1989a, p. 156).

Table 5.2. Family Size of PSID Families, 1969–1987, Percent

Year	1	2	3	4	5	6+	N
Poor Families[a]							
1987	45.8	22.7	12.8	10.0	5.2	3.4	1746
1986	44.8	22.6	13.5	10.3	5.2	3.7	1658
1985	43.5	23.4	14.6	10.0	4.8	3.6	1573
1984	41.8	22.5	15.5	10.3	6.3	3.5	1556
1983	41.5	22.0	15.9	10.8	5.5	4.4	1488
1982	42.2	23.5	14.3	11.1	5.0	3.9	1375
1981	46.4	21.5	15.1	9.4	3.9	3.7	1285
1980	45.8	21.3	14.7	9.6	4.0	4.6	1187
1979	45.4	22.2	13.8	8.9	4.3	5.2	1039
1978	44.3	21.9	14.0	9.0	5.5	5.3	946
1977	42.2	22.1	15.5	9.2	4.1	6.9	928
1976	44.2	21.6	14.0	9.3	5.5	2.8	835
1975	43.2	21.3	14.9	7.6	5.2	7.8	764
1974	44.4	21.3	13.4	8.0	5.3	7.5	729
1973	42.1	22.1	13.1	7.7	6.1	8.9	624
1972	41.9	19.1	13.6	8.5	5.8	11.1	565
1971	38.3	20.3	13.3	8.3	7.5	12.4	533
1970	35.4	18.2	14.0	11.1	8.6	12.6	478
1969	30.2	20.3	16.0	11.4	9.3	12.7	463

Nonpoor Families

Year							
1987	15.4	28.5	20.5	20.5	9.4	4.7	5177
1986	15.4	28.5	20.7	20.5	9.9	5.0	4910
1985	15.9	27.2	20.8	21.1	9.7	5.4	4698
1984	15.0	27.8	21.0	20.7	9.7	5.8	4337
1983	15.5	26.8	20.9	21.0	9.8	5.9	4127
1982	15.8	26.2	21.2	20.5	9.9	6.5	3969
1981	14.4	25.8	21.9	20.2	10.5	8.0	3791
1980	14.8	25.2	21.4	19.7	10.7	8.1	3633
1979	14.7	25.1	21.8	19.3	10.7	8.3	3496
1978	14.3	24.5	21.2	19.4	10.9	9.7	3326
1977	13.5	25.0	20.9	19.2	10.6	10.7	3137
1976	13.0	26.0	20.0	18.0	11.1	12.0	2994
1975	12.8	24.9	20.9	17.6	10.7	13.0	2827
1974	11.2	24.3	20.6	17.6	11.3	14.9	2609
1973	10.7	22.6	20.9	17.8	11.6	16.2	2476
1972	9.8	22.6	19.0	17.1	12.9	18.7	2302
1971	9.9	21.8	17.7	18.1	12.4	20.0	2127
1970	9.5	20.6	17.0	18.8	13.0	21.4	1999
1969	8.0	18.6	17.1	17.9	14.2	24.5	1811

Note:
[a] Official annual four-person poverty threshhold figure (U.S. Bureau of the Census 1989a, p. 156).

This dynamism introduces a series of complexities that extend beyond the already difficult file structure inherent to a study as ambitious as the PSID. Although one must necessarily control for family size in looking at poverty trends, the entire notion of a family itself becomes an issue. In an effort to track the income history of family units over time, we must contend with the fact that family units gain and lose new members (including the head of the household) and suffer disorganization and reorganization due to birth, death, divorce, and remarriage. In addition, over a twenty-year span it is common to find children maturing and splitting off to form their own households.

In order to assess the poverty experiences of the PSID households, it is first necessary to establish the continuity of family units while simultaneously adjusting for fluctuating family size and structure.[6] The result of this effort to establish the poverty experiences of families is depicted in Figure 5.1, where we plot the annual incidence of poverty (adjusting for family size) of the PSID households versus the annual aggregate percentage poor reported by the Bureau of the Census. As evidenced in Figure 5.1, the percentage of poor within the PSID is consistently higher than the official incidence of poverty by a factor of two to four percentage points. This owes to the PSID's aforementioned purposive oversampling of low-income households. More important, these data indicate that the PSID and CPR measurements of poverty trends are extremely consistent over time.

ANALYZING PERSISTENT POVERTY

Having created the annual size-adjusted poverty dummy variable, we next sum the values for each family unit across all panel waves to discover the number of years particular households have experienced impoverishment during the 1969–1987 period. These data, namely, the percent of PSID households experiencing one or more years of poverty, are reported in Table 5.3.[7]

Each cell in Table 5.3 represents the percentage of the PSID sample that was poor in "X" or the number of interval years (defined by the columns) beginning with the two-year interval of 1969–1970 through the nineteen-year interval of 1969–1987. Thus, in the two-year interval spanning 1969–1970, 9.1% of PSID households were impoverished in just one of the two years, while 11.2% of the households were impoverished in both years. The remaining households (100.0% minus the sum of the cell entries across the columns, or 79.7%) did not experience poverty in either year.

As indicated in Table 5.3, 8.1% of the sample households were poor in

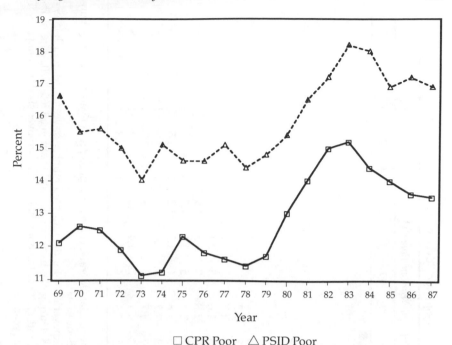

Figure 5.1. Annual incidence of poverty, CPR vs. PSID Series, percent, 1969–1987.

only one of the nineteen years (lower left cell), while 1.1% of the sample were poor in all years (bottom right cell). Alternatively, if we sum across the bottom row ("End Year" 1987, "Interval Years in Poverty" 1–19), we discover that 38.1% of the PSID households experienced at least one year of poverty and that 61.9% did not.

These initial findings are themselves worthy of note. We often tend to think of "the" poor as a relatively stable group in the population over time, which is to say, we tend to think of poverty as a chronic condition. During the era being examined, the *annual* rates of poverty range from 11% to 15% (more or less). And yet only one family in a hundred fell into this annual poverty population in each and every year. This also implies that nearly *all* poverty families spend some years out of poverty over the span of two decades, which is presumptive and persuasive evidence that the largest share of the poverty problem can indeed be solved (i. e., the poor—or most of them—are *not* poor forever). The poor that "ye have with you always," it seems, comprise something considerably less than a tenth of the total number of poor in any given year.

These initial results also demonstrate that the number of families that

Table 5.3. Persistence of Poverty, PSID Households Adjusted For Size-Specific Poverty Thresholds, by Percent[a]

Start Year 1969 End Year	Number of Interval Years in Poverty[b]																		
	1	2	3	4	5	6	7	8	9	10	11	12	13	14	15	16	17	18	19
1970	9.1	11.2																	
1971	8.7	5.4	8.6																
1972	8.0	5.5	4.1	6.7															
1973	7.7	4.8	4.1	3.2	5.5														
1974	8.5	3.9	3.7	3.1	3.2	4.4													
1975	8.5	4.3	3.0	3.1	2.8	2.5	3.9												
1976	8.5	4.1	3.3	2.6	2.7	2.0	2.6	3.1											
1977	9.2	3.9	2.9	2.9	2.2	2.1	2.3	2.1	2.8										
1978	9.1	4.6	2.4	2.7	2.3	2.0	2.2	1.7	1.7	2.7									
1979	8.3	4.6	3.2	2.2	2.4	2.0	2.1	1.5	1.7	1.7	2.3								
1980	8.2	4.5	3.2	2.6	2.1	1.7	2.4	1.0	1.8	1.6	1.5	2.1							
1981	8.2	4.5	3.2	2.6	2.3	1.4	2.1	1.9	1.0	1.8	1.3	1.5	1.9						
1982	7.6	4.9	3.1	2.6	2.7	1.4	1.7	1.4	1.7	1.3	1.5	1.1	1.7	1.6					
1983	7.9	4.9	2.9	2.4	2.6	1.7	1.5	1.2	1.5	1.8	1.1	1.3	1.2	1.7	1.5				
1984	7.8	5.0	3.0	2.4	2.4	1.6	1.8	1.1	1.2	1.7	1.6	1.0	1.1	1.4	1.4	1.5			
1985	8.1	5.0	2.8	2.8	2.3	1.4	1.6	1.6	.7	1.7	1.3	1.6	.8	1.2	1.2	1.3	1.4		
1986	8.1	4.8	2.8	2.7	2.9	1.1	1.7	1.2	1.2	1.1	1.7	1.4	1.2	.7	1.3	1.1	1.1	1.3	
1987	8.1	4.7	3.0	2.8	2.6	1.6	1.4	1.0	1.1	1.4	1.4	1.4	1.3	1.1	.8	1.2	.8	1.3	1.1

Notes:
[a] Household size-specific poverty thresholds are determined by the official federal income definitions promulgated by the U.S. Bureau of the Census and reported in annual *Current Population Reports*, Series P-60.
[b] Number of years in poverty refers to the percent of households impoverished for the indicated number of years within each interval. For example, the top left corner cell can be interpreted as follows: During the two-year interval spanning 1969-1970, 9.1% of PSID households were impoverished in one or another of the two years, and 11.2% of the households were impoverished in both years. The remaining households (79.7%) did not experience poverty in either year.

experience poverty over an extended time span is very much larger than the number who happen to be poor in any given year; the annual poverty rate, that is, proves highly misleading as an indicator of the true magnitude of our poverty problem. While the proportion of families officially designated as poor in any given year is somewhere between 11% and 15% (for the years in question), the proportion who experience at least one year of poverty over a two-decade span is nearly 40 percent—two or three times the annual poverty rate. If one could extend this analysis over the average lifetime of a family, the proportion experiencing at least a year of poverty would have to increase and might easily reach or exceed half. Is it truly possible that half the households in this affluent, postindustrial society are destined to spend at least one of their years beneath the poverty line? Remarkably, the answer appears to be yes.

While these data begin to provide information on chronicity, they do not yet directly test the hypothesis of increasing chronicity. It is to this issue that we now turn.

As noted, intragenerational (i.e., within a single generation) chronicity clearly depends on the particular definition of persistence employed (excepting, of course, qualitative criteria based on factors other than income, e.g., attitudes, behavior, lifestyle). Does being poor in two, three, or four out of five years effectively constitute persistent poverty? In analyzing the first ten years of PSID data, Duncan et al. (1984) employed what we consider to be a fairly stringent criterion: poor in eight or more of the ten years. Does a six-year criterion alter the picture substantially?

Clearly, there is no obvious or universally agreed on standard by which a poor family could be designated chronically poor, nor do we propose one. Our concern here is not with the absolute level of chronicity but rather with the trend in chronicity over time. Thus, we employ a number of different designations derived from a series of rolling or moving windows of two to five years duration in order to address the specific hypothesis of interest.

Procedurally, this entails computing a series of new variables ("windows") as per the following general formula:

Window $X_{i...j}$ = Sum (Poverty Dummy$_i$ + . . . + Poverty Dummy$_j$)

where the Window is of X year duration ranging from 2 to 5 that equals the sum of the value of the annual poverty dummies[8] beginning in year$_i$ through end year$_j$.[9] Inasmuch as the windows overlap like a series of moving averages, we conceptualize these variables as "rolling" or "moving."

The results of this procedure are reported in Table 5.4, columns 2, 5, 8, and 11. Readers should note that we arbitrarily define chronicity per each set of windows. Using a two-year window, we employ poverty in both years (i.e., 2/2 = 100% of the annual observations) as our criterion of persistence. With the three-year windows we use the standards of "poor in two of the three years" and "poor in three of three years" (i.e., 2/3 = 67% and 3/3 = 100% respectively). For four-year windows, we use the benchmarks of "poor in three of four years" and "poor in four of four years" (or, 3/4 = 75% and 4/4 = 100%) whereas the five-year windows employ the criterion of being poor in three, four, and five of five years (i.e., 3/5 = 60%, 4/5 = 80%, 5/5 = 100% of the annual observations). For ease of understanding and comparison, these data are plotted in Figure 5.2.

Inasmuch as the above measure of chronicity may be an artifact of the underlying base poverty rate, we also measure chronicity as a proportion of those who have experienced any poverty during the relevant window period. In essence, the latter allows us to analyze what proportion of poverty is chronic, independent of any underlying base trend in the overall poverty rate. This variable is also presented in Table 5.4, in columns 3, 6, 9, and 12. In addition, the trend in this proportional chronicity measure is displayed in Figure 5.3.[10]

Regardless of the size window we employ (or criterion of chronicity), the data unequivocally indicate that *chronicity has increased*. Specifically, each of the trend lines shows a decline in chronicity until approximately 1973. Thereafter, they begin to track upward as per the annual time series (see Figure 5.1). In the early 1980s, the upward trend is accentuated, thereafter leveling off in the post-1983 period, but at levels substantially higher than at any time prior to 1980.

In short, during the late 1970s and early 1980s, persistent or chronic poverty has indeed increased. This is true whether we measure chronicity in terms of the percent of all PSID households who are persistently poor (see Table 5.4, columns 2, 5, 8, and 11; and Figure 5.2), *and/or* prefer to think of the number of persistently poor households as a proportion of the households who have experienced any poverty during the window period (see Table 5.4, columns 3, 6, 9, and 12; and Figure 5.3).

The observed trend in chronic poverty is partly (although not exclusively) a function of the trend in the underlying base poverty rate. As the annual incidence of poverty tends to increase or decrease (see Figure 5.1) as per cyclical fluctuations in the economy, chronicity tends to follow suit. Consequently, to the extent that the base poverty rate continued to decline from 13.5% in 1987 to 13.0% and 12.8% in 1988 and 1989 respectively, we would expect the various measures of chronicity to exhibit some decline as well.[11]

However, the proportional data (as per Table 5.4, columns 3, 6, 9, and 12; and Figure 5.3) clearly document that the rate as well as the incidence of chronicity has increased during the period under study. While post-1983 data indicate some reduction in chronicity, they also suggest that at the end of the period under study, chronicity remains at higher levels than observed prior to the 1980s.[12]

Having empirically ascertained the increasing chronicity of poverty, we next examine the incidence and persistence of poverty across subgroups as defined by various demographic attributes of the household head.[13] Incidence data for the 1969–1987 period are presented in Table 5.5.

The top row of Table 5.5, labeled AGGREGATE, reproduces the information previously presented in the bottom row of Table 5.3. This is done to facilitate comparison with the poverty experiences of the subgroups. In addition, three columns of summary information have been added on the right-hand side of the table: the percent of the PSID sample group that has never experienced a single year of poverty throughout the nineteen years, the percent experiencing five or more years of impoverishment, and the percent poor in ten or more years.

Concentrating on the last three columns, we observe several dramatic differences across the demographic subgroups, all of them consistent with three decades of poverty data. Some of the more important differences are:

1. Three-quarters of white-headed households have not experienced a single year in poverty; the same can be said of less than a third of black households.

2. Nearly a third of black households (29.7%) have been poor in more than half of the nineteen years studied, while only 4.5% of white households have experienced ten or more years of impoverishment.

3. Attesting to the validity of the "feminization of poverty" thesis, female-headed households are more than five times as likely to have experienced five or more years of poverty and better than seven times as likely to have experienced ten or more years of poverty than male-headed households.

4. Only one in eight households (12.4%) headed by black females have not had a single year in poverty. The corresponding figures for households headed by white females, black males, and white males are 44.4%, 43.9%, and 79.6% respectively. Similarly, half of the black female-headed households were poor in ten or more years, while 21.9% of white female-headed households, 27.6% of black male-headed households, and only 1.8% of white male-headed households experienced this degree of impoverishment.

In sum, the data presented in Table 5.5 confirm previously well-documented trends in the location of poverty. Life chances are critically conditioned by race and gender.

Panel A—Two-Year Window

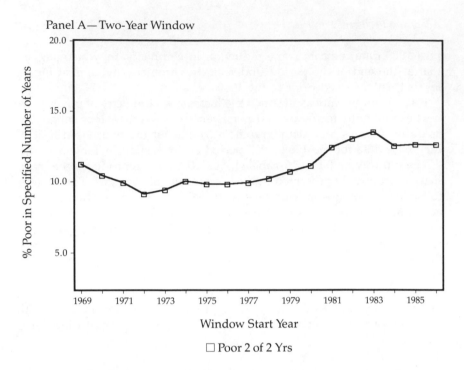

□ Poor 2 of 2 Yrs

Panel B—Three-Year Windows

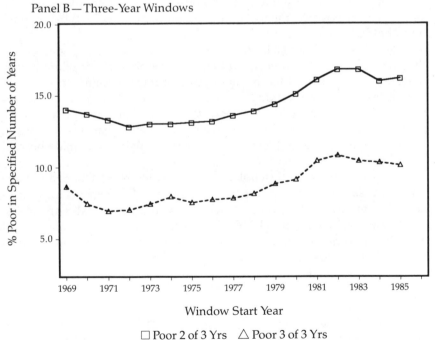

□ Poor 2 of 3 Yrs   △ Poor 3 of 3 Yrs

Figure 5.2. Two- to five-year windows, percent of PSID households poor in multiple years, 1969–1987.

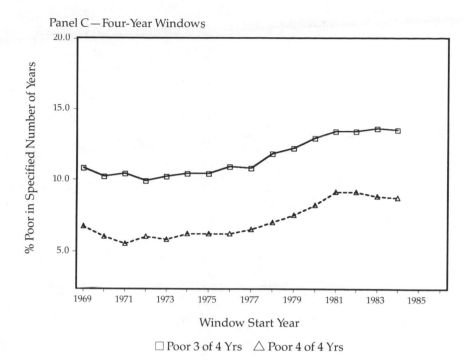

Panel C — Four-Year Windows

% Poor in Specified Number of Years

Window Start Year

□ Poor 3 of 4 Yrs   △ Poor 4 of 4 Yrs

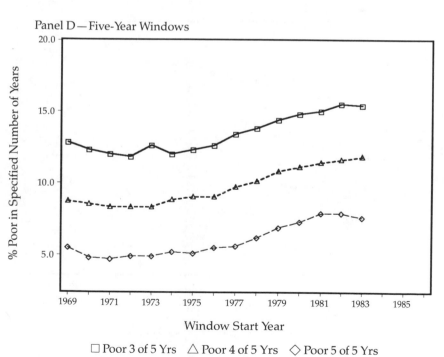

Panel D — Five-Year Windows

% Poor in Specified Number of Years

Window Start Year

□ Poor 3 of 5 Yrs   △ Poor 4 of 5 Yrs   ◇ Poor 5 of 5 Yrs

Panel A—Two-Year Window

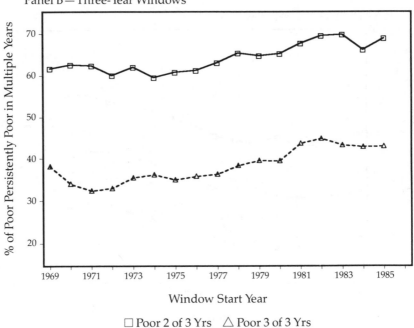

□ Poor 2 of 2 Yrs

Panel B—Three-Year Windows

□ Poor 2 of 3 Yrs   △ Poor 3 of 3 Yrs

Figure 5.3. Multiple year windows, PSID households persistently poor as a percent of PSID poor, 1969–1987.

Panel C — Four-Year Windows

Window Start Year

□ Poor 3 of 4 Yrs   △ Poor 4 of 4 Yrs

Panel D — Five-Year Windows

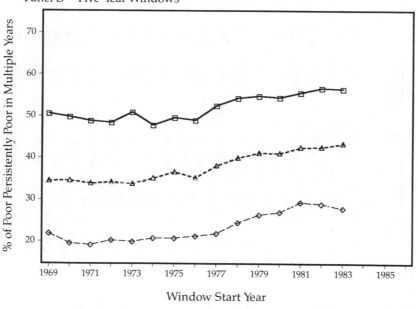

Window Start Year

□ Poor 3 of 5 Yrs   △ Poor 4 of 5 Yrs   ◇ Poor 5 of 5 Yrs

Table 5.4. The Chronicity of Poverty, Two- to Five-Year Windows, 1969–1987, by Percent of All PSID Households and Proportion Poor PSID Households[a]

Two-Year Windows			Three-Year Windows			Three-Year Windows			Four-Year Windows		
Years Covered	% Poor Both Years	As Proportion of Poor[b]	Years Covered	% Poor 2 of 3 Years	As Proportion of Poor[b]	Years Covered	% Poor 3 of 3 Years	As Proportion of Poor[b]	Years Covered	% Poor 3 of 4 Years	As Proportion of Poor[b]
1969–70	11.2	.553	1969–71	14.0	.616	1969–71	8.6	.380	1969–72	10.8	.484
1970–71	10.4	.533	1970–72	13.7	.625	1970–72	7.4	.338	1970–73	10.2	.435
1971–72	9.9	.507	1971–73	13.3	.623	1971–73	6.9	.322	1971–74	10.4	.450
1972–73	9.1	.486	1972–74	12.8	.600	1972–74	7.0	.328	1972–75	9.9	.427
1973–74	9.4	.505	1973–75	13.0	.620	1973–75	7.4	.353	1973–76	10.2	.448
1974–75	10.0	.527	1974–76	13.0	.595	1974–76	7.9	.360	1974–77	10.4	.438
1975–76	9.8	.526	1975–77	13.1	.608	1975–77	7.5	.348	1975–78	10.4	.451
1976–77	9.8	.503	1976–78	13.2	.612	1976–78	7.7	.356	1976–79	10.9	.459
1977–78	9.9	.528	1977–79	13.6	.630	1977–79	7.8	.361	1977–80	10.8	.457
1978–79	10.2	.545	1978–80	13.9	.653	1978–80	8.1	.382	1978–81	11.8	.496
1979–80	10.7	.555	1979–81	14.4	.647	1979–81	8.8	.394	1979–82	12.2	.498
1980–81	11.1	.546	1980–82	15.1	.652	1980–82	9.1	.393	1980–83	12.9	.503
1981–82	12.4	.594	1981–83	16.1	.676	1981–83	10.4	.435	1981–84	13.4	.517
1982–83	13.0	.596	1982–84	16.8	.694	1982–84	10.8	.447	1982–85	13.4	.523
1983–84	13.5	.607	1983–85	16.8	.697	1983–85	10.4	.431	1983–86	13.6	.523
1984–85	12.5	.581	1984–86	16.0	.661	1984–86	10.3	.427	1984–87	13.5	.518
1985–86	12.6	.586	1985–87	16.2	.688	1985–87	10.1	.428			
1986–87	12.6	.594									

Four-Year Windows			Five-Year Windows			Five-Year Windows			Five-Year Windows		
Years Covered	% Poor 4 Of 4 Years	As Proportion of Poor[b]	Years Covered	% Poor 3 of 5 Years	As Proportion of Poor[b]	Years Covered	% Poor 4 of 5 Years	As Proportion of Poor[b]	Years Covered	% Poor 5 of 5 Years	As Proportion of Poor[b]
1969–72	6.7	.276									
1970–73	6.0	.257	1969–73	12.8	.505	1969–73	8.7	.343	1969–73	5.5	.218
1971–74	5.5	.236	1970–74	12.3	.497	1970–74	8.5	.344	1970–74	4.8	.195
1972–75	6.0	.258	1971–75	12.0	.487	1971–75	8.3	.337	1971–75	4.7	.191
1973–76	5.8	.255	1972–76	11.8	.483	1972–76	8.3	.340	1972–76	4.9	.202
1974–77	6.2	.261	1973–77	12.6	.508	1973–77	8.3	.336	1973–77	4.9	.199
1975–78	6.2	.268	1974–78	12.0	.477	1974–78	8.8	.349	1974–78	5.2	.207
1976–79	6.2	.262	1975–79	12.3	.495	1975–79	9.0	.364	1975–79	5.1	.207
1977–80	6.5	.274	1976–80	12.6	.489	1976–80	9.0	.350	1976–80	5.5	.212
1978–81	7.0	.294	1977–81	13.4	.524	1977–81	9.7	.379	1977–81	5.6	.218
1979–82	7.5	.307	1978–82	13.8	.542	1978–82	10.1	.398	1978–82	6.2	.244
1980–83	8.2	.319	1979–83	14.4	.547	1979–83	10.8	.410	1979–83	6.9	.263
1981–84	9.1	.350	1980–84	14.8	.544	1980–84	11.1	.409	1980–84	7.3	.269
1982–85	9.1	.355	1981–85	15.0	.555	1981–85	11.4	.423	1981–85	7.9	.293
1983–86	8.8	.338	1982–86	15.5	.566	1982–86	11.6	.424	1982–86	7.9	.289
1984–87	8.7	.340	1983–87	15.4	.564	1983–87	11.8	.432	1983–87	7.6	.278

Notes:
[a] Household size-specific poverty threshholds are determined by the official federal income definitions promulgated by the Bureau of the Census and reported in annual *Current Population Reports*, Series P-60.
[b] Poor in indicated number of years (e.g., both, 2 of 3, 3 of 4, 3 of 5) as a proportion of number poor during window interval.

Table 5.5   Years in Poverty, Size-Adjusted PSID Households by Demographic Characteristics of Household Head, by Percent[a]

Start Year = 1969																						
	Number of Interval Years in Poverty[b]																					
End Year	1 1969	2 1970	3 1971	4 1972	5 1973	6 1974	7 1975	8 1976	9 1977	10 1978	11 1979	12 1980	13 1981	14 1982	15 1983	16 1984	17 1985	18 1986	19 1987	Never Poor	Poor ≥ 5 Years	Poor ≥ 10 Years
Aggregate	8.1	4.7	3.0	2.8	2.6	1.6	1.4	1.0	1.1	1.4	1.4	1.4	1.3	1.1	.8	1.2	.8	1.3	1.1	62.0	19.5	11.8
All whites	7.7	4.1	2.2	2.2	1.5	1.2	.6	.7	.4	.7	.5	.5	.3	.2	.4	.5	.3	.5	.6	74.9	8.9	4.5
White males	7.3	4.0	2.2	1.9	1.2	.8	.6	.3	.2	.1	.2	.4	.2	.1	.2	.1	0	.3	.2	79.6	4.9	1.8
White females	10.2	4.8	2.7	3.7	3.7	3.2	.5	3.2	1.6	4.8	2.1	1.1	1.1	1.1	1.6	3.2	2.1	1.6	3.2	44.4	34.1	21.9
All blacks	8.9	5.8	4.9	4.7	5.1	2.5	3.2	1.6	2.8	3.0	3.5	3.7	3.5	3.2	1.8	3.2	2.1	3.2	2.5	31.1	44.9	29.7
Black males	10.4	5.6	6.5	6.2	2.4	3.0	2.7	.9	2.1	3.3	3.0	1.5	2.1	1.5	.6	1.8	0	1.5	1.2	43.9	16.5	27.6
Black females	6.9	6.0	2.6	2.6	9.0	1.7	3.9	2.6	3.9	2.6	4.3	6.9	5.6	5.6	3.4	5.2	5.2	5.6	5.6	12.4	71.1	50.0
All males	8.2	4.5	3.1	2.7	1.4	1.4	1.1	.4	.6	.8	.9	.6	.6	.4	.3	.4	0	.6	.4	71.5	9.9	5.0
All females	8.1	5.3	2.8	3.0	6.7	2.5	2.5	3.0	3.0	3.5	3.2	4.4	3.7	3.7	2.5	4.2	3.7	3.9	3.7	26.4	56.2	36.5

Notes:
[a] Household size-specific poverty threshholds are determined by the official federal income definitions promulgated by the Bureau of the Census and reported in annual *Current Population Reports*, Series P-60.
[b] Percent of households impoverished for the indicated number of years. For example, the top row can be interpreted as follows: during the 1969–89 period, 8.1% of all PSID households were impoverished in one year, 4.7 were impoverished in two years, 3.0% were poor in three years, . . . 1.1% of the households were impoverished in all 19 years.

Table 5.6 and Figure 5.4 further illuminate the issue of chronicity by reporting results from five-year windows constructed across the same demographic subgroups examined in the previous table. Looking down the columns of Table 5.6, where we use the criterion of "poor in three of five years," we observe increasing chronicity as per the aggregate findings first reported in Table 5.4. Although the general trend in chronicity is approximately the same for all groups, across-column comparisons reveal rather different rates of chronicity occurring across population segments. Once again, the data indicate dramatic differences owing to both race and gender. This observation is clarified somewhat further in Figure 5.4, where the aggregate and subgroup trends in five-year windows have been normalized or expressed in standard deviation ("z-score") units.[14]

Figure 5.4 allows us to discern trend differences while holding constant highly variable base-poverty rates. Thus, we observe that during the post-1973 period, persistent poverty has exhibited an upward trend for almost all groups (see Panels A, B, and C). As indicated in Panel C, however, white female-headed households are somewhat of an anomaly. Throughout the mid- to late 1970s, these households experienced the steepest relative increase in persistent poverty. Following the 1981–1982 recession, however, this same group experienced the most pronounced (relative) progress against poverty.

In juxtaposition against the experience of white females, the trend for black female-headed households suggests a somewhat different story (see Panel B). The latter have continued to experience increasingly persistent poverty, once again confirming that our nation's most entrenched and persistent poverty has become increasingly concentrated among those living in black female-headed households.

SUMMARY

Much of the contemporary poverty literature claims that chronic poverty, by definition a less tractable form of poverty, has increased in recent years. As we noted at the outset of this chapter, however, much of this argument has rested on a weak empirical foundation. Therefore, in this chapter, we have sought to examine the thesis of increasing chronicity or persistent poverty in a direct empirical manner.

The increasing concentration of poverty in the urban core areas is a well-documented fact, and the evidence presented here shows unmistakably that more and more of this concentrated poverty is of the chronic and more obdurate variety. While the specific psychological and sociological mechanisms of causation have yet to be precisely deter-

Table 5.6. Chronic Poverty Among Population Subgroups, Five-Year Windows, 1969–1987, by Percent[a]

Five-year Windows				Percent Poor in 3 of 5 Years					
	All House-holds			Demographic Attribute of Household Head					
Years Covered		White	Black	Male	Female	White Male	White Female	Black Male	Black Female
1969–73	12.8	5.0	31.0	5.9	34.2	2.4	18.1	18.2	46.2
1970–74	12.3	4.7	30.4	5.4	33.2	2.4	16.8	17.2	46.0
1971–75	12.0	4.7	29.3	5.2	32.8	2.4	16.5	15.6	45.6
1972–76	11.8	4.9	27.8	5.0	32.8	2.3	17.9	14.2	44.6
1973–77	12.6	4.7	30.3	5.7	33.1	2.6	15.6	16.6	47.7
1974–78	12.0	4.9	27.9	4.9	33.6	2.5	16.9	12.9	47.7
1975–79	12.3	5.1	28.4	5.4	33.3	2.7	16.6	14.0	47.4
1976–80	12.6	5.4	28.5	5.2	34.9	2.6	19.0	13.7	49.0
1977–81	13.4	5.9	30.2	5.5	37.0	2.7	21.1	14.5	51.7
1978–82	13.8	6.0	30.7	6.0	37.3	2.8	20.4	15.2	52.6
1979–83	14.4	6.1	31.5	6.9	36.7	3.0	20.6	17.7	51.4
1980–84	14.8	6.1	32.7	7.4	36.8	3.2	19.8	19.0	52.2
1981–85	15.0	5.9	32.8	7.6	36.4	3.2	18.5	19.6	51.8
1982–86	15.5	6.1	33.5	7.8	37.4	3.3	18.8	20.0	52.9
1983–87	15.4	6.1	33.2	7.9	37.0	3.6	17.6	19.5	52.6
% Sample Attrition 1969–1987	8.2	6.6	17.2	<.1	27.8	<.1	30.5	<.1	27.2
1987 N	2038	1389	570	1605	432	1202	187	337	233

Note:
[a] Household size-specific poverty threshholds are determined by the official federal income definitions promulgated by the Bureau of the Census and reported in annual *Current Population Reports*, Series P-60.

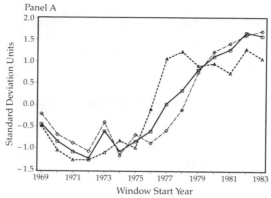

Panel A

□ All Households △ Female-Headed Households ◇ Male-Headed Households

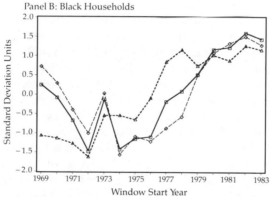

Panel B: Black Households

□ All Households △ Female-Headed Households ◇ Male-Headed Households

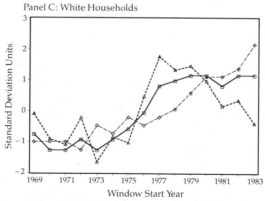

Panel C: White Households

□ All Households △ Female-Headed Households ◇ Male-Headed Households

Figure 5.4. Normalized 5-year window trends across demographic groups, PSID households poor in 3 or more of 5 year intervals, 1969–1987.

mined, in Chapter 6 we suggest how and why the increasing concentration and chronicity of poverty are related to rising rates of teenage
pregnancy, crime and violence, drug use, welfare dependency, and the
long list of similar developments that are now routinely linked with the
urban underclass. Whatever the exact causal connections, it is apparent
that the rise of persistent poverty and the growth of the underclass have
developed in tandem.

A FOOTNOTE ON HOMELESSNESS

Probably the most visible and certainly one of the most troubling
consequences of the 1980s-era increase in chronic poverty has been the
seemingly sudden rise of the urban homeless population. Homelessness
is not unique to the present day and age; to the contrary, we have
witnessed periodic episodes of widespread homelessness throughout our
history, beginning in colonial times (Wright 1989; Monkkonen 1984; Hopper and Hamburg 1984). Nor are we the only contemporary nation that
confronts a substantial homelessness problem; the problem appears widespread throughout the advanced industrial societies (Friedrichs 1988).
Still, homelessness seems especially anachronistic, even offensive, in contemporary American society, and the rise of homelessness has prompted
more than one observer to ask (more in exasperation than in genuine
uncertainty), What has gone wrong? We suggest that the increasing
chronicity and severity of poverty is high on the list of things that have
"gone wrong" and that have contributed to the homelessness crisis.

The past decade has produced a flood of research on who the homeless
are and how they got to be homeless. The evidence is clear, first of all, that
the incidence of homelessness grew throughout the 1980s (Burt 1992), in
close tandem with the increasing poverty rate and especially with the
increasing chronicity of poverty that has been documented above. Nearly
all observers also agree that homelessness is a consequence of extreme
poverty within a housing market that provides fewer and fewer options
to the poor (Rossi and Wright 1987). Indeed, the distingushing characteristics of the homeless are extreme poverty, high rates of personal
disability (alcohol and drug addiction, mental and physical illness), and
high levels of family and social estrangement (Wright 1989; Rossi 1990).

Concerning the first of these, it is clear that the homeless are drawn
overwhelmingly from the poverty population; indeed, they are among
the poorest of the poor, often surviving on less than 25% of a poverty-
level income (Rossi, Wright, Fisher, and Willis 1987). The advocacy community often argues that all of us are "only one paycheck" away from
homelessness and that "these days'" increasing numbers of formerly

middle-class people are found among the ranks. In fact, exceedingly few homeless people come from middle-class backgrounds. Most were born into poverty and have been poor all their lives; they are not only the poorest of the poor but also the most persistently poor.

Second, homeless people as a group exhibit extraordinarily high rates of personal and social disabilities. Approximately a third suffer from psychiatric impairments ranging from moderate to profound (Tessler and Dennis 1989; Wright 1988); about half abuse alcohol or other drugs (Wright, Knight, Weber, and Lam 1987); rates of chronic physical disorders among the homeless exceed those in the domiciled population by factors ranging from two to a hundred (Brickner et al. 1985; Wright and Weber 1987; Institute of Medicine 1988); indeed, more than a tenth are *physically* disabled and incapable of working. Many advocates and some researchers try to downplay the significance of these patterns; the argument is that excessive attention to mental illness, substance abuse, and the like "medicalizes" what is basically a social, not a medical, problem. But no one would deny that these disabilities are widespread among the homeless or that they present formidable barriers to successful reintegration of the homeless into society at large.

Finally, homeless people as a group tend to exhibit astonishingly high levels of estrangement from family and social networks. Relatively few have ever married or remain in contact with their families of origin; most of the people within their social networks are other homeless individuals. Robert Frost once wrote, "home is the place where, when you have to go there, they have to take you in" (quoted in Rossi 1990). It is not a bad definition; by the same logic, to be homeless is to be without such a place. Almost all of us know at least *someone* to whom we could turn in the face of catastrophe or in times of exceptional need. The homeless are those of whom this cannot be said.

Like poverty in general and extreme, chronic poverty in particular, homelessness impacts with particular severity on the young, racial minorities, and the socially unaffiliated. The average age of homeless persons in any number of credible studies is reported to be in the low to middle thirties; racial and ethnic minorities are heavily overrepresented. Most of the homeless were chronically unemployed for several years before their first spell of homelessness, this despite the fact that half of them have graduated from high school. For the most part, the homeless prove to be those most vulnerable to the chronicity trends discussed here and other untoward social and economic developments.

Right now, on any given night, there are perhaps three-quarters of a million homeless people to be found in the streets and overnight shelters of American cities (Burt 1992). Moreover, homelessness is known to be a transitory condition; the number of persons homeless at least once in the course of a year, that is, is much higher than the number homeless on any given night. Several studies have suggested that the annual homeless population is three to five times the one-night population, so in the span of a year as many as 3 or 4 million people may suffer an episode of homelessness—something on the order of a tenth of the American poverty population. A continuation of the chronicity trends analyzed in this chapter could easily double the size of the homeless population in the decade of the 1990s. One can only imagine the effect this would have on the quality of urban life. Homelessness is the inevitable and logical consequence of the many trends and developments that have been discussed in this and previous chapters. The rising tide of homelessness in the 1980s, in short, is an omen of just how bad things *could* become if present trends are allowed to continue unabated.

NOTES

1. We thank Mark Plunkett for his assistance on the analyses presented in this chapter. An earlier version of this material appeared in *Social Forces* 70(3), March 1992, pp. 787–812.

2. Contrary to many persons' expectations and the general thrust of "culture of poverty" arguments, Duncan et al. (1984, pp. 3, 41) found that slightly more than half of the individuals living in poverty in one year were impoverished in the following year, while only 2.6% of the sample was poor in eight or more (of ten) years. Alternatively, almost one-quarter (24.4%) of the population were in families who had experienced poverty in at least one of the ten years.

3. The data we use are from the PSID, Waves I–XX (1968–1987), cross-year merged family-individual file.

4. The PSID diverges from census practice inasmuch as the former does not draw any distinction between single-person and multiple-person families, while the latter treats single-person households as "unrelated individuals." Following PSID's lead we make no distinction (other than the obvious quantitative one) between single- and multiple-person households. Subsequently, we use the terms family and household interchangeably.

5. Incomplete family size and composition measures force us to exclude the first year (1968, Wave I) from these and subsequent calculations.

6. The procedural details of this are somewhat esoteric so we exclude them from the present discussion. Readers interested in them should consult Devine, Plunkett, and Wright (1992, Appendix A).

7. Except for the last cell in each row (i.e., all years) the number of years in poverty need not be continuous.

8. A dummy variable is a dichotomous measure coded "0" or "1" (e.g., no-yes, off-on, absent-present). In this case a family is coded "1" if poor in a given year and "0" if not poor.

9. Regardless of whether we use a set of two, three, four, or five year windows, each set ("X") of windows starts with 1969. For instance, using a two-year set of windows, we create a 1969–1970, 1970–1971, 1971–1972 . . . 1986–1987 window wherein each window takes a value of zero (not poor in any year), 1 (poor in one of the two years), or 2 (poor in both years). Similarly, a five-year set of windows produces a value of 0–5 (poor in none to all five years) for each window beginning in 1969–1973, 1970–1974 through 1983–1987.

10. In Figure 5.3, the proportional chronicity measure has been multiplied by a constant of 100. This has no effect other than allowing us to express the data in terms of percents rather than proportions.

11. Readers should also bear in mind that chronic poverty is not a pure linear function of the base poverty rate. Like the base poverty rate, though not necessarily isomorphic with it, chronic poverty depends on the economy and state welfare provisions as well as a host of other factors. To the extent that the experience of chronic poverty might impair an individual or family's capacity to escape poverty in the future, however, we might expect persistent poverty to exhibit some negative legacy. This, of course, remains an empirical question.

12. At the same time, it should be noted that while the documented trend in increasing chronicity holds for the period under study, it does not necessarily constitute a long-term trend.

13. Inasmuch as this yields a series of sub-groups defined by the racial and sexual characteristics of the household heads, it necessarily excludes from the analysis those households who experienced a cross-sex and/or cross-race change of head over the sample period.

14. The standard deviation is a widely used measure of the dispersion within a distribution of values. It is computed according to the following formula:

$$s = \sqrt{\frac{\sum (X_i - \overline{X})^2}{N}}$$

where each value ("X") is subtracted from the mean ("$\overline{X}$"), the resultant difference is squared, all differences are summed and then divided by the number of cases ("N"), and the square root is taken.

6

The Inner Logic of the Underclass

Considering the definition advanced in Chapter 4, one would be hard pressed to argue that the underclass is somehow a new development. To the contrary, some fraction of the American poverty population would have satisfied the elements of our definition at all times in the nation's history. And yet there is no mistaking the apparent urgency of today's situation. What makes the concentrated, chronic, urban poverty of the present era so troublesome and disturbing to so many?

We think the answer lies in the apparent *irrationality* of so much of the behavior that has come to be associated with the urban underclass. It seems irrational when young women bear many more children than they could ever possibly support or when HIV-positive women get pregnant and give birth to HIV-positive babies. It seems profoundly irrational when we read of teenage males who have shot one another to death over a pair of basketball shoes or when we see large groups of apparently able-bodied men hanging out drunk and stoned on the street corners while the newspapers are full of Help Wanted advertisements. More than one exasperated observer of the contemporary urban scene has been moved to ask, "What kind of moral universe do these people inhabit, anyway?"[1]

The apparent irrationality of much of the behavior that is associated with the underclass suggests in turn that an entire segment of the urban population has come to be indifferent to the sanctions, threats, rewards, laws, and customs that dictate the behaviors of the rest of society. Being immune to customary threats and sanctions, the behavior of the underclass—and with it the urban context in which it is embedded—seems wildly and perhaps irretrievably out of control. Since the behaviors that concern us appear to be essentially irrational, the fear is that nothing *reasonable* can be done to alter them, at which point repression, containment, and ultimately extinction by force loom as the only apparent alternatives. That there are some, even many, who relish this conclusion only adds to the urgency of the situation.

There is, sad to say, no lack of evidence to sustain such a conclusion. Every day, the media chronicle the escalating violence and degradation of life in the inner cities, often in graphic detail. Accounts of well-armed youth gangs shooting it out on the streets without regard for bystanders, assaults perpetrated against students and teachers in their schools, apparently random violence committed by bored youth "just having fun," street corner murders for a pair of Air Jordans or a sports team jacket—all this has become commonplace in the contemporary urban experience and suggests a fundamental erosion of the value of life itself. Disgust comes easily when one senses this apparent devaluation of life and turns just as easily to terror when isolation is no longer a viable means of protection. It is one thing when urban thugs kill each other but quite another when violence spreads into once-safe neighborhoods and threatens to overtake everyone. The middle-class dread evoked by such recent movies as *The Bonfire of the Vanities* and *Grand Canyon* lies fundamentally in the perception that any hope of containing the underclass has become an illusion. Pugnacious aggression against "them" is all that apparently remains.

More and more, the "them" of the preceding sentence are young black males, who, because of the double stigma of race and age, are now commonly perceived to be *the* major threat to the well-being of the inner cities. More often than not, sheer racism figures prominently in this equation, but we hasten to add that the fear of young black males is by no means restricted to whites. Neither is it entirely unjustified. It is a well-known and largely incontrovertible fact that males and females of all races and classes are more likely to be victimized by young black males than by any other demographic subgroup, and by a wide margin. It should go without saying that the large majority of young black males are not engaged in criminal behavior, but the fact that so much criminal behavior is committed by young black males means that all of them become stigmatized as potential or actual predators.[2]

The vast majority of African-Americans of all ages are responsible, productive, law-abiding members of society. (It is troubling that such an obvious point even needs to be made.) Still, the conditions of concentrated urban poverty and the behaviors associated with the underclass differentially affect the black poor (as both perpetrators and victims). In its substantial majority, the underclass is comprised of the bottom stratum of African-Americans living within the inner cities. That the poverty of the underclass is largely a black phenomenon unavoidably imposes a racial dimension on the entire discussion of urban woes. That most of the underclass is black, however, assuredly does not imply that most blacks are underclass, nor does it belittle the legacy of enslavement and continuing discrimination as the ultimate source of the many remaining disparities between black and white Americans' material well-being and life chances. It is a deeply racist error to equate black culture with the culture of the underclass or to forget that the immense majority of blacks in the inner city look upon "them" with as much disfavor as suburban middle-class whites do.

The behaviors of the underclass threaten more than the immediate physical well-being of the rest of the society (rich *and* poor, black *and* white). They also assault widely shared values and sensibilities. High rates of out-of-wedlock births, female headship and family disorganization, welfare dependency, drug abuse, low educational and occupational attainment, and other behavioral deficiencies associated with the underclass are seen, understandably, as a fundamental rejection of core national values that promote education, work, family, sobriety, self-sacrifice, and individual achievement as worthy, not to say sacred, goals.

Consequently, the behaviors and inferred values of the underclass are often seen to indicate fundamental psychological or characterological differences between "them" and "us." The rich, as F. Scott Fitzgerald remarked, "are not like you and me," and neither, or so it appears, are the poor. Ryan (1971), Edelman (1964), Gans (1972), Cook and Curtin (1987) and numerous others argue persuasively that middle-class people gain significant psychological and social benefit from believing that they are fundamentally different from the poor, and certainly from the "undeserving poor" (see Chapter 2). The ways in which the poor differ, in turn, are commonly attributed to a deviant and seemingly irrational subculture, a so-called "culture of poverty" that transmits aberrant values and behaviors from adults to children and thus reproduces itself in each generation.

"Culture of poverty" arguments provide seemingly solid grounds for expecting the intergenerational reproduction of poverty and the underclass. Values obviously have *something* to do with behavior, behavior in turn obviously has *something* to do with becoming and staying poor, and all parents, even poor parents, obviously impart their own values to their offspring. This apparently compelling logic, however, is contradicted by direct empirical evidence. In one of the few empirical tests of the proposition of intergenerational transmission, Long and Vaillant (1984, p. 341) conducted a long-term prospective study of 456 inner city men from highly and multiply disadvantaged families and found that:

> Men from chronically dependent and multiproblem families were on average indistinguishable by midlife from the children of more stable working-class families in terms of mean income, years of employment, criminality, and mental health. Although attained social class was somewhat lower for the disadvantaged, . . . the children from multiproblem welfare families did not inevitably perpetuate their initial disadvantages.

In large measure, the widespread appeal and legitimacy attached to Charles Murray's *Losing Ground* (1984) resulted from his ability to articulate this popular "culture of poverty" ideology, to dress it up in social scientific regalia, and to lay the blame for the deficient values of the poor and their associated behavioral manifestations—illegitimacy, family disorganization, crime, drug abuse, school separation, unemployment, welfare dependency, and all the rest—squarely at the door of well-meaning but misguided welfare programs of the Great Society (a theme also trumpeted with some insistence by Presidential spokesman Marlin Fitzwater in his explanation of the 1992 Rodney King riots in Los Angeles). Murray's analysis plays successfully on a deeply felt resentment against social welfare for those perceived to be undeserving; rather than fix problems, the Great Society (it is said) undermined the moral fiber of the poor and thus fostered the development of dependency and a deviant subculture. That nearly everything has gotten much *worse* in the past decade and a half, a period during which the welfare state has significantly *contracted*, seems to have escaped the attention of Murray and like-minded welfare critics.

Whatever the causes, the unmistakable worsening of urban conditions since 1980 has led many to look upon the urban underclass as a growing, possibly fatal, cancer. The seemingly endless, escalating, and inexplicable waves of illegitimate births, welfare dependence, wanton violence, drug abuse, and the rejection of education and hard work as routes to success have made the underclass repulsive and fearsome, a spreading malignancy that threatens the very fabric of society and perforce must be contained and eradicated.

The contempt with which the underclass is viewed is evident in some of the more commonly discussed solutions, which range from more police and more prisons to a stern and highhanded ("tough love") approach to welfare where fathers are required under threat of criminal prosecution to contribute to their offsprings' support, where mothers must be working or in school under threat of losing their welfare benefits, and where adolescents are expected (against all reason!) to "just say no" to drugs and sex and "yes" to studying hard and staying in school. Katz (1989, p. 125) has referred to these emphases as the "new authoritarianism," where policy stresses "the obligations of the poor instead of their entitlement to public benefits." What we apparently want, in short, is for the underclass to be the angels that the rest of us like to think we are (but frequently are not). Their continuing failure to adhere to behaviorally impossible standards then becomes the proof positive of what we suspected all along, that they lack the moral rectitude to go to school, get jobs, defer gratification, and sacrifice so they can care for their families. What choice remains but to beat or coerce their damnable lassitude out of them?

Of course, no one in their right mind would disagree that criminals should be imprisoned, that fathers should support their children, that people who can work should work in preference to receiving welfare, or that kids should aspire to and attain good educations and good jobs and then become responsible, independent, productive, self-fulfilled adults. Although we are not aware of any direct evidence on the point, we strongly suspect that even members of the underclass, or most of them at any rate, would agree wholeheartedly with each of these principles. In fact, despite the many barrels of intellectual ink that have been spilt on the "culture of poverty," there is a much larger discrepancy between underclass and mainstream patterns of *behavior* than there is between the *values* of the middle class and the poor. Most studies of the topic in fact stress the many strong *similarities* between the two groups in their basic aspirations and values (see e.g., Cook and Curtin 1987; Goodwin 1969).

Despite its considerable surface appeal, the concept of a "culture of poverty" proves misleading on at least this one critical point. The perspective suggests that poor people and affluent people value different things, whereas, fundamentally, all people value the same thing. Granted, there are many *specific* goals and aspirations to be pursued in life and everyone pursues a more or less unique mix of them. Some, that is, prefer more money, others prefer more leisure, and still others crave opportunities for self-actualization. But all of these specific goals and aspirations, each and every one, represents some variation on the same basic *value*, which is to be happy. "Happiness is what life is all about. Our goals, aspirations, dreams and fantasies revolve around happiness. Almost every decision we make is in terms of what we think will bring us the most happiness. Everything else that is important to us—love, faith, success, friendship, sex, recognition—is a means to the end of achieving happiness" (Freedman 1978, p. 3). Alexander Pope said the same when he referred to happiness as "our being's end and aim." Poor people wish to be happy as fervently as rich people do. Blacks wish it as deeply as whites. Happiness is the one universal goal that all pursue with equal vigor. What differs from person to person, group to group, subculture to subculture, is not so much life's premier value but the means at one's disposal to attain it. And since no one can possibly *wish* to be a miserable wretch, when we encounter miserable wretches we may be quite certain that they would strongly prefer their condition to be otherwise.

For the most part, the problems of the underclass are not simply attributable to a question of values or reducible to the existence of a deviant or irrational subculture. This is not to say that values do not matter or that an underclass subculture does not exist. It *is* to say that the truly meaningful distinction between the underclass and the rest of society lies in the *differential capacity to translate and actualize one's values into a socially desirable repertoire of behaviors*. Values themselves are relevant more as consequences than causes. Rather than being implicated in the causal etiology of the underclass, "deviant" values and the emergence of an underclass subculture are better seen as the consequences of structural conditions, contexts, and constraints that people face as they go about their daily lives. Values themselves depend mainly on how behavioral options and opportunities are structured, accessed, rewarded, and sanctioned. Given a structured set of options, individuals respond in similar ways, and those responses ultimately crystallize into recognizable and stable patterns of behavior. When many individuals respond behaviorally in like manner to a common set of options, we then refer to the crystallized patterns of behavior as a "culture" that is in turn transmitted, imitated, and reproduced.

In this view, culture is nothing more than a common response to a given structuring of life chances; and in that specific sense, every culture, subculture, or package of values may be said to contain its own inner logic, or as we might say, its own rationality. The underclass is thus no more or less "rational" than any other; if the elements of underclass subculture seem "irrational," it is only because they represent common behavioral responses to curiously grotesque conditions. And likewise, if we wish to alter those common behavioral responses (and we clearly do), the only hope lies in changing the conditions that breed the responses of which we disapprove. Just how this might be accomplished is taken up in our concluding chapter.

Our argument is thus that despite its seeming irrationality, there is an inner logic to the outlooks and behaviors of the underclass; the rest of this chapter is an effort to parse that inner logic, to show how the behavioral repertoire of the underclass is a *reasonable* response to the existential conditions of life in the impoverished inner city. Our aim is to demonstrate that the problems of the underclass concern *behavior*, not values, and that solutions will require a restructuring of life conditions in the inner city so that the behaviors we abhor are no longer necessary or rational. If we want teenage girls to stop having babies or teenage boys to stop packing weapons, we will need to create conditions in which these behaviors no longer *make sense*. Understanding that they *do* make sense under current conditions is the key to everything else.

The task before us, in so many words, is not to repair deficient or deviant values or to find harsh, new ways to punish their negative behavioral repercussions but to restructure the logic of underclass life. The need is to create conditions that (for example) enable parents to function as parents and within which it is *in the interests* of parents to function as parents, conditions where there is a tangible and efficacious linkage between aspirations and achievement, where the relationship between honest work and material well-being is restored. If we hope to inculcate values and behaviors among the underclass that accord with middle-class sensibilities, then it is incumbent upon society to provide the contexts, the conditions, the options in which more desirable behavioral choices make sense.

What, then, are those "curiously grotesque conditions" to which under-class culture is a rational, explicable response? As has been suggested earlier in this book and by many other analysts, *widespread joblessness* among the inner city poor lies at the very heart of the problem. Over time, large-scale unemployment and the lack of viable, legitimate economic opportunities result in far more than economic deprivation; they promote a chain of events that dissolve the foundations on which a positive and just sense of self and society are based.

> Ordinary life for most people is regulated by the rules of work and the rewards of work that pattern each day and week and season. Once cast out of that routine, people are cast out of the regulatory framework that it imposes. Work and the rewards of work underpin the stability of other social institutions as well. When men cannot earn enough to support fam-ilies, they may desert their wives and children, or fail to marry the woman with whom they mate. And if unemployment is longlasting entire com-munities may disintegrate as the able-bodied migrate elsewhere in search of work. In effect daily life becomes progressively deregulated as what Edel-man calls the "comforting banalities" of everyday existence are destroyed. The first signs of the resulting demoralization and uncertainty are usually rising indices of crime, family breakdown, vagrancy, and vandalism. (Piven and Cloward 1979, p.11)

This "deregulation" of life and the ensuing breakdown of mainstream societal mores is just another way of expressing the pathology of the underclass neighborhood, a pathology best understood as the inevitable consequence of a structure of opportunity that undermines or prevents individuals from fulfilling social obligations and roles (pointedly not as moral deficiency or psychological irrationality).

Joblessness among inner city nonwhite males now routinely exceeds 40 or 50% or even higher in some cities; most of those lucky enough to have a "job" find themselves laboring at or near the minimum wage. Consider some of the more or less obvious consequences of these facts.

Lack of access to meaningful, well-paying jobs upon graduation under-mines the rationale for staying in school; in consequence, dropout rates often exceed 50% in inner city public school systems. Widespread jobless-ness strongly enhances the appeal of crime or drug dealing as an econom-ic alternative; for many youth in the inner city, the drug trade and related criminal activities now represent nearly the only plausible route to eco-nomic success and material well-being. Ill-educated and jobless people make poor marriage partners, and so rates of illegitimacy soar. Lacking the usual and customary means by which teenagers become adults (finish school, find work, get married), teenage girls choose to "achieve" adult-hood by having babies, teenage boys "achieve" adulthood by fathering them, and jobless fathers, unable to support their offspring or their mates, split. Joblessness creates many bored and idle hours in the day, hours that are then free for drinking or using drugs or committing vandalism or violence. And there is nothing that promotes "welfare dependence" quite so strongly as the lack of any viable alternative to welfare.

In the most fundamental sense, and in every conceivable way, life in the context of widespread joblessness, underemployment, and extreme poverty is *life without a future*. With no legitimate prospects for the future, life then all too quickly becomes a quest for the immediate gratification of present impulses. Weighing the consequences of present behavior against their future implications in turn becomes a meaningless exercise. Arguments for staying in school, not getting pregnant, or not using drugs all require an orientation towards the future, a concern, in short, about tomorrow's consequences of today's behaviors. And this is precisely the sort of orientation that the structural conditions of the inner city have destroyed. In this sense, the behavioral pathologies of the inner city are not the cause of urban woes so much as they are indicative or symptomatic of a far more general unraveling of norms, values, and expectations that otherwise constrain behavior. What has arisen in the central city is a subculture where anything goes, a subculture that is essentially defined by estrangement from—indeed, hostility to—the norms and conventions of the larger society.

The alleged moral deficiency of today's underclass is often illustrated by contrasting the situation of lower-class blacks with the much more positive experience of other racial and ethnic minorities, most recently Asian-Americans, in their quest to realize the American dream. The basic observation is that even newly arrived Asian immigrants (for example, the Vietnamese and Koreans) experience fairly rapid upward mobility even when they lack formal education, English language skills, and other advantages. After all, Asian immigrants send their children to school, often with astonishingly positive results, display entrepreneurialism, and move up in the occupational structure. What explains the rather obvious difference between these minority groups and that portion of the African-American community that remains mired in the underclass? If Asian immigrants can do it, why can't lower-class blacks?

Again, differential *values* are commonly invoked as the explanation. Asian immigrants, it is said, value industry and thrift; they are willing and motivated to work, take low-paying, entry-level jobs, labor hard and long, be entrepreneurial, and consequently move up. Underclass blacks, by the same logic, must lack these motivations and drives and therefore remain in poverty.

Despite its evident appeal, this general line of explanation proves inadequate. In the first instance, the "basic observation" is as much stereotypical as it is empirical (see Steinberg 1981). It fails to recognize the considerable upward mobility achieved among many segments of the African-American community in the past two decades, and by the same token it fails to acknowledge the high rates of poverty, crime, and gang violence that have come to characterize many of the Asian immigrant communities (and other ethnic immigrant communities before them). Granted, comparative rates of upward mobility are higher among Asians than among blacks, but the experience is by no means universal.

We stress once again that the underclass is not *just* a black phenomenon and is surely not representative of mainstream black culture. The underclass represents the concentrated *conjunction* of class and race. When numerous racial restrictions on education, employment, housing, and the like were loosened in the mid-1960s, the African-American community experienced unprecedented achievement and upward mobility. However, as discussed in previous chapters, when upwardly mobile blacks achieved success and moved out, the inner city poverty that they left behind became more highly concentrated and entrenched. Over time, the conditions of these "abandoned" inner city communities deteriorated still further, evolving into what we now recognize as an underclass where traditional patterns of mobility no longer seem to hold.

Studies of the apparent success of recent Asian immigrant groups demonstrate that the strength of the family unit and the communal orientation that they bring to the problems of their assimilation are critical factors. To oversimplify somewhat, the relative success of recent Asian immigrants occurs within the context of a supportive family and social community. Individual success is enabled by collective effort. Intact families, parental involvement, and the pooling of risk and resources appear to be the key elements in their attainment (see, e.g., Light and Bonacich 1988; Caplan, Choy, and Whitmore 1992).

In turn, these familial and communal values that prove so important are part of a larger cultural constellation that recent (and many previous) immigrant groups brought with them at the time of their immigration, a constellation that evolved over centuries. During those same centuries, the familial and communal values of American blacks were being destroyed, first by enslavement and then by generations of oppression and discrimination.[3] Immigrants from Asia and Europe came to the United States because they chose to do so; immigrants from Africa came in chains. Those who would argue that slavery ended more than a century ago and therefore no longer matters fail to appreciate the grip of history on the present. Culturally, there is a direct link to be traced between the forced separation of enslaved husbands and wives and the selling off of their children, and the many aspects of "family disfunction" that characterize the present-day underclass community. For the most part, history and cultural legacy account for the differential success of

Asian immigrants and blacks, not inadequate outlooks, intrinsic laziness, or moral turpitude.

The comparison between recent Asian immigrants and underclass blacks contrasts two entirely different communities each having a decidedly different history. To the extent that the supportive, nurturant involvement of parents, families, and communities is the critical difference (as the available research tends to show), it is probably the same difference that distinguishes between successful middle-class blacks and their underclass counterparts. What we learn from the comparison is not that blacks as a group are lazy or morally deficient and that Asians as a group are thrifty and industrious, but that the critical element in the success of various "outgroups" throughout our history is to be found, fundamentally, in the strength of the family. It could hardly be otherwise: very few children can grow up to care for and value themselves, much less others, without first having had someone to do these things for them and thus to instill self-esteem and the corresponding capacity for self-improvement. Families do this better than any other institution.

In the remainder of this chapter, we explore some of the behavioral pathologies that have come to be associated with underclass life, with respect both to their empirical frequency and to the inner logic articulated above. Thus, we present and comment upon data concerning illegitimacy, welfare dependence, unemployment, leaving school, criminal activity and victimization, and drug abuse. While data on these topics are available from a variety of governmental and other sources, none of the statistical series that we employ recognizes the underclass *per se* as a separate analytic category. Consequently, like others who have travelled this same road (e.g., Murray 1984; Wilson 1987), we are forced to explore these behaviors with proxy indicators, typically by focusing on black-white differences. We therefore stress again that these comparisons are, at best, a crude "first approximation" and that the underclass and black populations are *not* one and the same. By our definition, the underclass consists of the most severely impoverished minority populations concentrated in the inner cities, those whose life conditions lie at the intersection of an impoverished class, a disadvantaged race, and a dysfunctional community setting. One may safely assume that if the underclass could be isolated as a separate category in these data, the contrasts would be even sharper.

OUT-OF-WEDLOCK BIRTHS

One of the dominant popular images associated with the underclass is that of the unwed mother who bears numerous children by several different fathers, all of whom are then supported by the largesse of AFDC. While these so-called "welfare queens" rarely have the five or six or more offspring associated with the stereotype (see below), it is nonetheless true that escalating nonmarital births represent a critical element in the emergence and perpetuation of the underclass.[4] A successful intervention to reduce the size of the underclass will require some attention to the rising number of nonmarital births and especially unmarried teenage pregnancies.[5]

Table 6.1 and the accompanying figures (Figures 6.1–6.4) document the recent trends in nonmarital births. In 1960, there were 142,000 births to unmarried black women and 83,000 births to unmarried white women. Since that time, the number of births to unmarried women has steadily escalated such that by 1988, births to unmarried black and white women numbered 427,000 and 540,000 respectively. In absolute numbers, the number of children born to unmarried black women increased threefold during the period while the number born to unmarried white women increased by a factor of six. (One interesting consequence of the differential trend is that since 1980, more *white* babies have been born out of wedlock than black babies.)

As the number of children born to unmarried women has increased, the number born to married women has declined, the latter trend being much more pronounced for black women than for white women. Thus the ratio of unmarried to married births has dramatically increased (see Figure 6.3). Among black women (ages 15–44) in 1960, 21.6% of all births were to unmarried women; in 1988, the percentage had climbed to 63.4%. Since 1976, more than half of all black children have been born to unmarried women, a trend that continues upward. (The percentage of unmarried births among white women has also increased but from a much lower initial base: from 2.3% in 1960 up to 17.7% in 1988.)

Births among unmarried *teenage* women have shown similar trends. In 1960, the birth rate for unmarried white teenage women was 6.6 births (per 1,000 unmarried white women ages 15–19), a figure that increased to 24.8 per 1,000 in 1988. Among unmarried black teenagers, the rate has increased from 76.5 in 1960 to 98.3 in 1988. Thus, in recent years, approximately 10% of the nation's unmarried black teenage women have given birth each year, a development that some have aptly labeled "children having children".

The economic disadvantages that accrue to children born of single women are generally considerable. There are certain to be *some* "Murphy Brown" babies contained in these data (children born to single but economically well-off professional women), but in general unmarried births are heavily concentrated in the lower reaches of the income distribution. The disadvantages are especially burdensome for children born to single

Table 6.1.   Trends in Nonmarital Births, 1960–1988

	Year							% Change 1960–88
	1960	1965	1970	1975	1980	1985	1988	
Births per 1000 nonmarried women								
Black women[a]								
Ages 15–44	98.3	97.4	95.5	84.2	82.9	78.8	88.9	−9.6
Ages 15–19	76.5	77.1	96.9	93.5	89.2	88.8	98.3	+28.5
White women								
Ages 15–44	9.2	11.6	13.9	12.4	17.6	21.8	26.6	+189.1
Ages 15–19	6.6	7.9	10.9	12.0	16.2	20.5	24.8	+275.8
Number of unmarried births (in thousands)								
Black women[a], Ages 15–44	142	168	215	250	326	366	427	+200.7
White women, Ages 15–44	83	124	175	186	320	433	540	+550.6
Unmarried births as a percent of all births within race/age category								
Black women[a], Ages 15–44	21.6	26.4	37.6	48.8	55.3	60.2	63.4	+193.5
White women, Ages 15–44	2.3	4.0	5.7	7.3	11.0	14.5	17.7	+669.6
Ratio of unmarried to married births within race/age category								
Black women[a], Ages 15–44	.276	.359	.602	.954	1.235	1.512	1.735	+528.6
White women, Ages 15–44	.024	.041	.060	.080	.125	.169	.215	+795.8

Note:
[a] Values for 1960 and 1965 pertain to nonwhite women.
Source: U.S. Department of Health and Human Services, National Center For Health Statistics, *Vital Statistics of the United States, 1988*, volume 1, 1990.

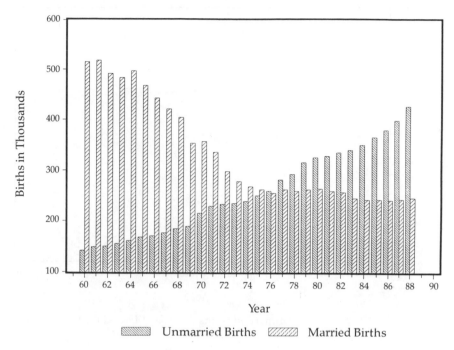

Figure 6.1. Births to black women ages 15–44, 1960–1988 (in thousands).

minority women inasmuch as these women tend to be younger, less educated, poorer, and living in more concentrated conditions of impoverishment. Their children are not only more likely to experience poverty, but to experience it for longer periods and with greater material deprivation than children born to unwed white mothers or into a two-parent family.

The absence of the father from the home environment has social as well as economic implications. All else equal, it is obvious that one parent (male or female) is less able than two to provide the authority, guidance, and structure necessary for a healthy childhood; one parent is also less able than two to earn a sufficient income. Many single people, of course, prove to be excellent parents, providers, and role models who raise children that grow up to be normal, healthy, fully functioning, contributing adults. This obvious point granted, it is still true that the normal difficulties of childrearing are heightened when only one parent is available.

In addition to the economic deprivation often associated with growing up in a single-parent household, there is recent empirical evidence that

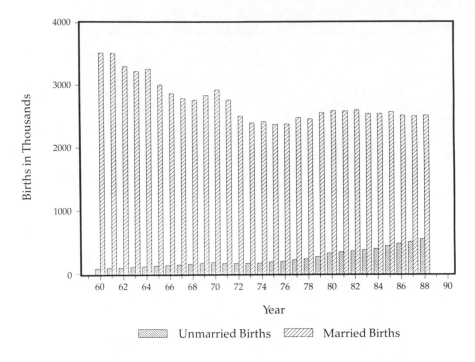

Figure 6.2. Births to white women ages 15–44, 1960–1988 (in thousands).

adolescent boys from single-parent households, especially female-headed households, are more likely to be involved in criminal activity than are teenagers from two-parent families (Sheley, Wright, and Smith 1992). Likewise, adolescent girls from single, female-headed households are somewhat more likely to become pregnant than are their peers from intact two-parent families. Using data from the *High School and Beyond* study (a representative national sample of 13,000 high school sophomore girls thereafter followed up in their sixteenth, seventeenth, and eighteenth years), Abrahamse, Morrison, and Waite (1988) found that rates of single parenthood ranged from a low of 1 in a 1000 for high-academic-ability, high-SES white respondents in intact families to a high of 1 in 4 among low-academic-ability, low-SES black respondents from female-headed families. Although a girl's chances of becoming a single teenaged mother depend on the complex interplay of individual, family, and social charac-teristics, the researchers were able to develop a "parenthood risk" scale. The most important factors were found to be: (1) parenting (as measured by the quality of parent-child relationship) and degree of supervision, (2) individual religious commitment, (3) attitudes toward having a child out of wedlock (as measured by a girl's rejection or acceptance of the idea and measures of peer influence and milieu), (4) a history of other problem

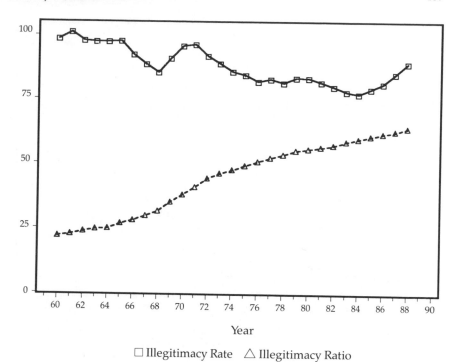

 Illegitimacy Rate   △ Illegitimacy Ratio

Figure 6.3.   Illegitimacy rates and ratio, black women ages 15–44, 1960–1988.
   Illegitimacy Rate: nonmarital births per 1000 nonmarried women ages 15–44.
   Illegitimacy Ratio: ratio of nonmarital births per 100 live births.

behavior, and (5) the perceived opportunity costs associated with having a child out of wedlock.

Not surprisingly, not all teenage women were equally responsive to all forms of restraint. The researchers note that:

> distinct forms of social restraint predominate for blacks, whites, and Hispanics. For blacks, close parental supervision has the strongest influence in lowering the rate of single childbearing; for whites a high-quality relationship with parents is the strongest influence; among Hispanics, religiosity appears to be strongest. . . . Where personal motivations exist for not getting involved with early unwed childbearing, young women manage not to. This effect appears far stronger among blacks than whites. *From a policy perspective, then, the individual teenager's own awareness and perception of what she would stand to lose can act as a powerful deterrent to becoming a single mother.* (Abrahamse, Morrison, and Waite 1988, p.vii, emphasis added)

Or, as a recent report from the Center for the Study of Social Policy (1992, p. 11) acknowledges, with only one parent:

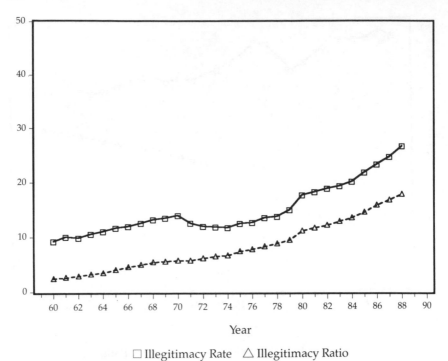

□ Illegitimacy Rate   △ Illegitimacy Ratio

Figure 6.4.   Illegitimacy rate and ratio, white women ages 15–44, 1960–1988.
        Illegitimacy Rate: nonmarital births per 1000 nonmarried women ages 15–44.
        Illegitimacy Ratio: ratio of nonmarital births per 100 live births.

it is difficult to secure the basic goods and services essential for raising a child, such as adequate food and clothing, child care, health care, good schools, and safe housing. As a consequence of their poverty, their children's opportunities are limited or sometimes even foreclosed: the chance to go to preschool, receive quality day care, hire a tutor or take music lessons, learn a sport, buy books, go to camp or college. Going without these basics and opportunities can rob children of their childhood. And too often poor children are at double jeopardy: They are the least healthy and the most likely to live in unhealthy neighborhoods and go without health care; they are at greatest risk of school failure and among the most likely to go to a failing school . . . .

In point of fact, the disadvantages associated with being born to a single parent begin well before birth. Single mothers are less likely to receive prenatal care and are more likely to bear low-birth-weight babies than their married counterparts (Center for the Study of Social Policy 1992). Consequently, these babies are at greater physical risk and suffer higher rates of infant mortality. Though many low-birth-weight babies grow up normally, these children do experience more health and developmental problems than other children. Among minority women, these disturbing statistical tendencies are even more pronounced.

When the single mother is also a teenager, especially a poor, black teenager, the disadvantages and problems associated with being in a single-parent household increase dramatically. Few teenagers have the requisite education, experience, or financial and emotional resources to care adequately for a child. When one adds the burden of poverty to these other deficits, it is quickly obvious that a child born to a poor, single teenage mother has severely diminished life chances. Judged in the light of cold, hard facts, the practice has virtually nothing to recommend it.

Given the many negativities associated with unwed parenthood, the trends reviewed in this section seem paradoxical, even irrational. If the difficulties associated with single parenting are so pronounced, if the consequent burdens imposed on children are so oppressive, then why in the world is the birth rate among unmarried women increasing so dramatically? How does it happen that each year, a tenth of unmarried black girls between ages fifteen and nineteen have a child? Why do these teenagers bear babies that they can rarely support?

Judged by a middle-class standard or in the light of statistical evidence, the fertility decisions of poor unmarried teenaged women do seem fundamentally irrational, even stupid or thoughtless. The imagery called to the middle class mind by the fertility trends we have reviewed is one of rampant and unprotected promiscuity in utter disregard of the consequences. However, poor, unmarried teenage girls do not assess their world from a middle-class perspective or in the light of national statistics. In the terms in which their own lives and life-chances must be assessed, early pregnancies and unwed parenthood may well represent positive, considered decisions.

The aspirations of a middle-class adolescent female might reasonably include education (at least through high school and in all likelihood beyond), a career, and subsequently marriage and a family. Given this aspirational frame of reference, a teenage pregnancy or an early childbirth would constitute a significant cost, an extreme and irreversible disruption in the life plan. Educational plans would need to be postponed or foregone; the necessity of supporting the child would force premature entry into the labor force, typically at a low-paying entry-level job; the presence of a child would presumably reduce the interests of potential marriage partners. For the average middle-class girl, in short, having a baby is a quick path to downward mobility. Understanding these realities and fully aware of the negative moral sanctions still associated with "illegitimacy," the middle-class girl makes a series of informed and sensible choices that reduce her odds of having a baby. If she is sexually active, she is more likely to use birth control and to use it effectively. If contraception is not used or used and fails, abortion remains as an option. If the pregnancy is brought to term, she is more likely to have married the father (Anderson 1989; Hacker 1987; Haynes 1987; O'Connell and Moore 1984).

For impoverished teenagers in the inner city underclass, the aspirational framework is different and in consequence their fertility decisions follow a very different logic. The "cold, hard facts" of their lives are that they are extremely poor and likely to remain so, that their high school is a cruel joke and that aspirations for education beyond high school are essentially pointless, that even a decent job (much less anything we would recognize as a "career") is probably more than one can realistically hope for, and that eventual marriage to a desirable mate is statistically improbable. With this sort of future staring one in the face, *what is there to defer*? Under these circumstances, just how does having a baby disrupt the life plan? The answer is that it does not.

To the contrary, in the circumstances just described, having a child confers numerous positive benefits. Bearing a child affirms the mother's womanhood, and not incidentally, siring a child affirms the father's manhood. As we suggested earlier, it is the one certain way to achieve the status that comes with being an adult. Having a child also provides purpose to life and the unconditional, unquestioned love and affection of another human being. Finally, is there any real purpose to be served in marrying the father when his prospects for an education and career are also dim?

Community and social context must also weigh heavily in these fertility decisions. The teachings of the black church and the sentiments of black culture are strongly pronatalist; in this context, there is much more ethical stigma associated with abortion than with unwed pregnancy. Finally, and inevitably given a national welfare system whose main provision is to assist impoverished parents of dependent children, the economics of early and unwed childbirth are vastly more favorable than they would be to middle-class teens. Indeed, given AFDC, food stamps, and a Medicaid card, there is every likelihood that one's standard of living would *improve* by bearing a child.

To critics such as Charles Murray, the solution to this problem is to cut AFDC and related benefits so that no woman can actually improve her material circumstances by having a child. Murray (1984, p. 227) argues that the elimination of welfare benefits to single mothers and their children will "drastically reduce births to single teenage girls . . . [and] increase the upward socioeconomic mobility of poor families." Murray apparently believes that the solution lies in making welfare *less* attractive; the alternative, which seems obvious to us but which is unmentioned by Murray, is to make options other than welfare *more* attractive. The solution is not to punish single teenage underclass girls for their sexual misconduct but to alter their aspirational frame of reference such that an early pregnancy would interfere with their *realistic, attainable* expectations for the future.

Despite a very common and longstanding presumption to the contrary, research has shown that AFDC and related welfare benefits are rarely an inducement to bearing children (McClanahan 1985; Wilson 1987). Indeed, given AFDC payment levels in most states and the pittances by which they are raised with each additional child, the very thought that lots of young women get pregnant specifically to make themselves eligible for AFDC or to increase their monthly payment is a bit strange. In any case, it has been shown that women who receive AFDC benefits are no more likely to bear additional children than poor women who do not receive AFDC. It *is* clear that AFDC often provides a young single mother with the option of setting up her own independent household, an inducement of sorts especially when it allows her to escape a difficult or abusive home situation. But this is scarcely equivalent to saying that the availability of welfare causes young girls to get pregnant, a proposition for which no credible evidence exists.

The principal effect of reducing or eliminating AFDC benefits would not be a reduction in fertility among young underclass women so much as a guarantee that the children of these women would be denied the resources necessary for adequate food, shelter, and health care. Cutting AFDC would mean *more* impoverished, ill-fed, unhealthy children, not fewer; in no way would such a measure improve the life chances of these young mothers or their children, reduce the number of unwed births, or promote marriage. If we wish to reduce early and unwed pregnancies among underclass women, we need to assure that there is a better future to which they can reasonably aspire, one whose attainment would be threatened by premature fertility. Seeking ways to punish these young women once they do get pregnant and bear children is mean-spirited and shortsighted.

What has been said about young underclass mothers applies as well to underclass fathers, although the dynamics are somewhat different. The young middle-class male has as much to lose by fathering a child as the young middle-class female has in bearing one. In contrast, underclass males are faced with the same realities as the females—extremely limited educational prospects and poor or nonexistent job prospects now and in the foreseeable future. These young men have little or no hope of being able to support their offspring in any case; thus they have no means of attaining the role of "father" except in the biological sense. Marriage confers no benefit to anyone, especially if it means the cessation of AFDC benefits. Thus, the social meaning of manhood is redefined to encompass the simple act of siring children regardless of one's capacity or intention to support them (see Anderson 1990). Reduced to a strictly biological function, males are accorded no integral role in family life and matrilineality becomes the family norm.[6] When the conditions that foster absent fathers become commonplace and spatially concentrated, then the male's role as nothing more than a source of viable sperm becomes a social fact, not aberrant but normative and expected.

Early and unwed childbearing *is* a serious problem and one obvious route by which the underclass perpetuates itself across time. But one cannot be hopeful that the solution will involve nothing more than asking teenagers to "just say no" to sex and then starving their children when they do not. If we want underclass males and females to adhere to our preferred adult roles and expectations—if we want fathers and mothers to marry and then raise, educate, and provide for their children—then as a society we must afford them a realistic opportunity to do so. If we give these young people good reasons for staying in school and deferring childbirth, reasonable job prospects, and the means to support themselves and their families—if, in short, we present them with a legitimate and attainable future—then surely their behaviors in the present will be more to our liking.

WELFARE

In the minds of many, the welfare system itself is responsible for the rise of the underclass. Welfare, we are told, encourages promiscuity and unwed pregnancy, promotes family dissolution, and fosters dependency. Who in their right mind would actually bother to work for a living when welfare is there to provide a free ride? The specter of able-bodied people getting handouts *they don't deserve* haunts every discussion of the welfare issue.

Ironically, most of the welfare dollars we spend are uncontroversial, and raise few if any hackles. Social Security and Medicare for the elderly are overwhelmingly the largest items in the social welfare budget, and yet the state of thinking about *these* welfare expenditures is such that it has proven impossible to reduce benefits even to very well-to-do elderly persons who have absolutely no need of them. No one would deny income and health care benefits to veterans of the U.S. armed forces either, whether they were truly needed or not. Only when government attempts to help the poor does welfare become stigmatized and execrable.

Indeed, it is not generally appreciated, but nonetheless true, that many more federal welfare dollars are spent on the middle class and the affluent than on the poor. Especially once "major tax benefits, like the home-mortgage interest deduction" are factored in, "the poor receive the smallest average benefit of any group—less than families with $30,000 to $50,000 incomes or those with $50,000 to $100,000 incomes. Most remarkable, the [average] benefit for the wealthiest group . . . was the highest of all" (Waldman 1992, p. 56). The *Newsweek* article also cites a recent study by the Census Bureau showing that "the portion of the benefit pie going to the poor has been shrinking in the past 25 years, while the slice going to the rest of the country has grown" (p. 57). As for those who find the very concept of welfare objectionable, the article offers sage advice: "Stop the griping. Most of us get our share of the government dole."

In general, when people object to "welfare" and "welfare dependence," the focus of their objections is either the general relief provisions of the states or Aid to Families With Dependent Children (AFDC). Concerning the former, it is worth noting that many states have very limited or even nonexistent state programs of general relief or assistance in place. At least one gubernatorial candidate has run for office with a promise to reform a state welfare system that *did not exist*.[7] States that do have programs of general assistance vary widely in their eligibility criteria, administrative procedures, and payment levels, making generalizations to the national scene nearly impossible. AFDC, in contrast, is a national program that is cofunded by the states, and so there are national data on AFDC participation that can be exploited in our present discussion. A brief examination of the relevant data (contained in Table 6.2 and Figures 6.5–6.7) shows that much of what people believe about "welfare" is wrong. Summarizing the critical points:

1. While total current-dollar AFDC spending increased almost fifteenfold between 1960 and 1988, the real-dollar increase (holding inflation constant) was less than threefold. In real (constant 1980) dollar terms, AFDC spending increased throughout the 1960s, peaked in 1976, and has since declined to a level commensurate with the expenditures of the early 1970s (see Figure 6.5, where total AFDC spending is indexed on the left axis). The idea that AFDC takes a bigger and bigger bite from the federal budget each year is wrong. In fact, expressed as a percentage of the total federal expenditure on welfare programs of all sorts, AFDC spending regularly *declined* throughout the 1980s and stands today at the *lowest* expenditure level in the entire history of the program. Doing away with AFDC altogether would save a mere 3% of the annual social welfare outlay.

2. Expressed in constant dollars, AFDC payments in recent years have become *less* generous, not more. The actual purchasing power of the average monthly AFDC payment increased considerably through 1970 and thereafter began a thirteen-year real-dollar decline from a high of $403 per month to about $260 per month since 1985 (see Figure 6.5, where

Table 6.2. Trends in Aid to Families with Dependent Children, 1960–1988

	Year							% Change 1960–88
	1960	1965	1970	1975	1980	1985	1988	
Total federal social welfare[a] (millions of constant 1980 $s)	69277	98277	163822	256104	303345	346894	364307	+425.9
Total AFDC spending (millions of current $s)	1056	1809	4853	9211	12475	15196	16827	+1493.5
Total AFDC spending (millions of constant 1980 $s)	2938	4724	10299	14102	12475	11640	11721	+283.6
AFDC as % federal social welfare (current $s)	4.2	4.8	6.3	5.5	4.1	3.4	3.2	–31.8
Avg. monthly AFDC family payment (current $s)	108	137	190	229	288	341	379	+250.9
Avg. monthly AFDC family payment (constant 1980 $s)	301	358	403	351	288	261	264	–12.3
Number of AFDC recipients (1000s)	3073	4396	9659	11401	11102	10921	10898	+254.6
Mean children per AFDC family	3.0	3.1	2.8	2.3	2.0	1.9	2.0	–33.3
AFDC Families as % all families	1.8	2.2	5.0	6.4	6.6	5.9	5.8	+222.2
AFDC Recipients as % all poor	7.7	13.2	38.0	44.1	37.9	33.0	35.5	+373.3

Note:
[a] Represents the sum of federal spending on social insurance, public aid, health and medical programs, veteran's programs, education, housing, and other expenditures classified as social welfare.
Source: U.S. Bureau of the Census, Statistical Abstract of the United States, various years, Washington, USGPO.

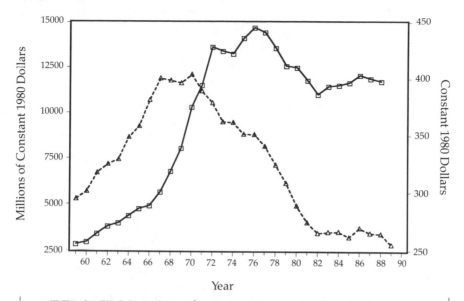

Year

☐ Total AFDC Spending   △ Average Monthly Family AFDC Payment

Figure 6.5. Aid to families with dependent children, expenditures and average monthly family payments, 1959–1988.

average monthly family AFDC payments are indexed on the right axis). Average monthly AFDC payments today are worth considerably *less* than they were when the program was first started in the 1960s.

3. In 1960, AFDC spending amounted to 4.2% of all federal social welfare dollars.[8] As we noted earlier, this percentage increased throughout the 1960s, peaked at 6.5% (in 1972), and has steadily declined since.

4. Table 6.2 and Figure 6.6 show that the mean size of AFDC families increased slightly through the middle 1960s but has declined significantly and regularly in the years since. In recent years, AFDC families have actually had *fewer* children than the American average family, contrary to a common misperception.

5. AFDC participation as a percentage of all American families increased dramatically through the 1960s, but has since plateaued at approximately 6%, declining slightly since the peak year of 1980. In like fashion, the total number of families receiving AFDC assistance climbed to more than 11 million by 1975 and has shown a small decline in the years since.

6. AFDC participation as a percentage of *poor* families has shown an equivalent trend. Through 1975, the proportion of the poor receiving AFDC assistance climbed sharply to a peak of nearly half; in the years

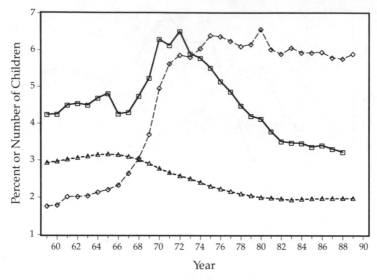

Figure 6.6. Characteristics of AFDC spending, family size, and incidence 1959–1988.

since, the proportion has declined and now hovers at approximately a third. (Figure 6.7 also chronicles the recent erosion of AFDC payments relative to the poverty threshold, median family income, and the annualized minimum wage. By whatever standard one chooses, AFDC payments have become relatively *less* generous, contrasting the dominant mythology.[9])

The data in Table 6.2 compel one to look upon the decade of the 1980s as a grand experiment testing the thesis that welfare per se is responsible for the emergence and growth of the underclass and for most of the other social woes that beset us. Between the beginning and end of the decade, AFDC spending as a percent of total welfare spending *declined*, the constant-dollar value of the average AFDC payment *declined*, the total number of recipients *declined*, and the proportion of poor families receiving AFDC assistance *declined*. By every measure, we had less "welfare" at the end of the decade than we had at the beginning. Following the logic of Charles Murray and his followers, one would therefore expect considerable improvement in the human condition to have followed from this retrenchment. The actual experience of the decade, of course, was precisely opposite to this expectation.

The oft-assumed effects of AFDC on the fertility of the poor are also contradicted by these data. The period of pronounced growth in the

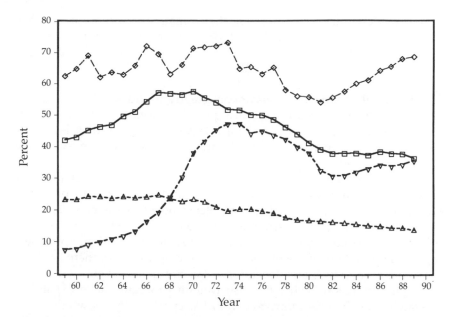

□ AFDC / Poverty Threshold (4-person)   ◇ AFDC / Annualized Minimum Wage

△ AFDC / Median Family Income   ▽ Poor Receiving AFDC

Figure 6.7.   Annual mean family AFDC payments as a percent, various income
levels and the percent of poor who receive AFDC, 1959–1988.

coverage and generosity of AFDC benefits *precedes* the escalation in out-
of-wedlock births. By the time unwed births began to show large increases, AFDC *retrenchment*, not expansion, was underway. Obviously,
there is more going on here than generous welfare benefits inducing poor,
young, unmarried, black women to have children. The empirical patterns
fail to support this simplistic conclusion.

Another invidious misconception about AFDC (and other forms of
welfare) concerns the pattern of usage over time. The dominant image,
perpetrated by critics such as Martin Anderson (1978) and Charles Murray (1984), is that AFDC recipients are typically long-term, perhaps inter-
generationally welfare-dependent African-American women, but the
empirical reality is very different. First, 60% of AFDC recipients are white.
Second, for the vast majority of recipients, AFDC provides temporary
supplemental income that allows mothers and children to weather an
episode of family dissolution owing to death, divorce, or separation of a
spouse, not a long-term source of regular income that substitutes for other
sources. Third, over half of all women who ever receive AFDC support
are off the welfare rolls within two years; only about 2% become

chronically dependent, meaning that they remain on welfare for a decade or more (Duncan et al. 1984; Levy 1988; Rein and Rainwater 1978).

None of this is meant to deny that *some* people become welfare dependent or that *some* people abuse the welfare system; clearly, the welfare system stands in need of meaningful reform. Federal studies of "welfare fraud" and abuse, however, have consistently found so little fraud that detecting the true abusers and getting them excised from the rolls costs more than fraud itself costs. The simple fact, clear in all studies, is that the large majority of welfare recipients are *not* abusive of the system or welfare dependent.

Further restrictions on welfare eligibility, further reductions in payment levels, or the outright abolition of AFDC and other welfare programs would only exacerbate our current problems, not solve them. Such, in any case, is the lesson we draw from the experience of the 1980s, when sizable rollbacks in welfare were accompanied by an intensification, not lessening, of the problems of the underclass. If in the present era there has been some increase in welfare dependence (an arguable proposition in any case), then it is surely not because welfare programs have expanded. Research over the past quarter century has consistently shown that welfare recipients prefer jobs that pay decent wages and provide health benefits instead of remaining on welfare. Welfare dependence results less from the provisions of welfare programs than from the large and growing shortage of decent work available to those of modest skills. The solution to welfare dependence, as we have already said, is not to make welfare *less* attractive but to make work *more* attractive; jobs with decent wages and benefits, training programs that provide access to those jobs, and the provision of appropriate child and health care to enable labor force participation are the genuine solutions.

UNEMPLOYMENT, SUBEMPLOYMENT, AND LABOR FORCE PARTICIPATION

The present section augments material covered in Chapters 2 and 3 concerning employment, unemployment, and subemployment (the latter meaning insufficient work or inadequate wages). Here, we briefly explore data on unemployment and labor force participation rates, subemployment, and employment at subpoverty wages and then consider some of the dynamics and implications of these issues for underclass communities.

Tables 6.3 and 6.4 show data on official unemployment and labor force participation rates by gender, race, and age. Not surprisingly, younger

persons (ages 16 to 34) routinely experience higher rates of unemployment and lower rates of labor force participation than their older counterparts. Also predictably, the differences are more pronounced among
blacks. For instance, official unemployment rates for *white* male and
female youths (ages 16 to 17 and 18 to 19) are in double digits throughout
the 1960–1988 period but never exceed 20%, even during the 1975 recession. Among comparable black youth, the rates never drop *below* 20%.
Although reduced in magnitude, this same basic pattern also holds for
blacks in the 20–24 and 25–34 age categories, prime years for labor force
participation and presumably the time in which marriage and family
formation would typically occur.

This same general pattern also holds for rates of labor force participation, although the disparities by race are somewhat smaller. The computed participation rates for 1988 show that among males in all age
categories, blacks have lower rates of labor force participation than
whites. Among women, the pattern is different: labor force participation
rates for black women as a whole and specifically in the age categories
25–34, 35–44, and over 65 *exceed* the participation rates of white women (a
useful result to keep in mind in confronting the stereotype of lazy black
women bearing welfare babies and living off the dole).

Official unemployment and labor force participation figures provide an
overly sanguine portrayal of labor market conditions: the unemployment
rate only reflects unemployment among those who are actively in the
labor force; the labor force participation rate only includes the officially
unemployed plus those who are currently working. Thus, unemployment
rates do not include persons who have dropped out of the labor force
altogether, the so-called "discouraged workers"[10], and participation rates
fail to capture both discouraged workers and those who have failed to
gain entry into the labor force.

Given these problems with the standard indicators, we have computed
a measure of "subemployment" from various additional materials gathered and published by the Bureau of Labor Statistics. This measure
consists of the sum of the number of persons who are (1) conventionally
unemployed, (2) discouraged workers, (3) involuntary part-time workers,
(4) employed workers on temporary unpaid leave, (5) 16–24 year olds not
in the labor force and not currently enrolled in school, and (6) persons
working full-time, year-round jobs but at incomes below the poverty
threshold. We thereafter divided this sum by the number of persons in the
civilian labor force and multiplied by 100 to arrive at a rate.

This subemployment index provides a somewhat more complete, thus
arguably better, indication of labor market conditions than conventional
indicators. Figure 6.8 plots the subemployment rate and the official unemployment rate for the years 1970–1987; as can be seen, both rates follow

Table 6.3. Male Unemployment and Labor Force Participation Rates, by Race and Age, 1960–1988

| | Unemployment Rate | | | | | | | Unemployment Ratio[a] |
| | Year | | | | | | | |
	1960	1965	1970	1975	1980	1985	1988	1988
Whites								
16+ years	4.8	3.6	4.0	7.2	6.1	6.1	4.7	1.38
16–17 years	14.6	14.7	15.7	19.7	18.5	19.2	16.1	4.74
18–19 years	13.5	11.4	12.0	17.2	14.6	14.7	12.4	3.65
20–24 years	8.3	5.9	7.8	13.2	11.1	9.7	7.4	2.18
25–34 years	4.1	2.6	3.1	6.3	6.0	5.7	4.6	1.35
35–44 years	3.3	2.3	2.3	4.5	3.6	4.3	3.4	—
45–54 years	3.6	2.3	2.3	4.4	3.3	4.1	3.2	.94
55–64 years	4.1	3.1	2.7	4.1	3.1	4.0	3.3	.97
65+ years	4.0	3.4	3.8	9.5	8.8	2.7	2.2	.65
Blacks & others								
16+ years	na	na	na	14.8	14.5	15.3	11.7	3.44
16–17 years	22.7	27.1	27.8	39.4	37.7	42.9	34.4	10.12
18–19 years	25.1	20.2	23.1	32.9	33.0	40.0	31.7	9.32
20–24 years	13.1	9.3	12.6	22.9	22.3	23.5	19.4	5.71
25–34 years	10.7	6.2	6.1	11.9	12.5	13.8	11.0	3.24
35–44 years	8.2	5.1	3.9	8.3	7.8	9.6	7.6	2.24
45–54 years	8.5	5.1	3.3	9.0	6.6	9.7	6.2	1.82
55–64 years	9.5	5.4	3.4	6.1	6.0	7.9	5.2	1.53
65+ years	6.3	5.2	3.8	9.5	8.8	8.9	5.6	1.65

Labor Force Participation Rate

	Year							Participation Ratio[b]
	1960	1965	1970	1975	1980	1985	1988	1988
Whites								
16+ years	83.4	80.8	80.0	78.7	78.2	77.0	76.9	1.24
16–17 years	46.0	44.6	48.9	51.8	53.6	48.5	49.3	1.94
18–19 years	69.0	65.8	67.4	72.8	74.1	66.9	71.0	1.34
20–24 years	87.8	85.3	83.3	85.5	87.2	86.4	86.6	1.10
25–34 years	97.7	97.4	96.7	95.8	95.9	95.7	95.2	1.00
35–44 years	97.9	97.7	97.3	96.4	96.2	95.7	95.4	—
45–54 years	96.1	95.9	94.9	92.9	92.1	92.0	91.8	1.04
55–64 years	87.2	85.2	83.3	76.4	73.1	68.8	67.9	1.41
65+ years	33.3	27.9	26.7	21.7	19.1	15.9	16.7	5.71
Blacks & others								
16+ years	83.0	79.6	76.5	71.5	70.8	70.8	71.0	1.34
16–17 years	45.6	39.3	34.8	30.1	31.9	29.8	32.7	2.92
18–19 years	71.2	66.7	61.8	57.5	56.3	60.0	56.0	1.70
20–24 years	90.4	89.8	83.5	78.4	78.9	79.0	79.3	1.20
25–34 years	96.2	95.7	93.7	91.4	90.4	88.8	89.3	1.07
35–44 years	95.5	94.2	92.2	90.0	89.7	89.8	88.2	1.08
45–54 years	92.3	92.0	88.2	84.6	83.9	83.0	83.5	1.14
55–64 years	82.5	78.8	79.2	68.7	63.5	58.9	59.4	1.61
65+ years	31.2	27.9	27.4	20.9	17.5	13.9	14.3	6.67

Notes:
[a] Ratio of race- and age-specific unemployment rate to rate for 35–44 year old white males (3.4%).
[b] Ratio of 35–44 year old white male participation rate (95.4%) to race- and age-specific rate.
Sources: U. S. Department of Labor 1988, 1989; Murray 1984, pp. 247–48.

Table 6.4. Female Unemployment and Labor Force Participation Rates, by Race and Age, 1960–1988

| | Unemployment Rate | | | | | | | Unemployment Ratio[a] |
| | Year | | | | | | | |
	1960	1965	1970	1975	1980	1985	1988	1988
Whites								
16+ years	5.3	5.0	5.4	8.6	6.5	6.4	4.7	1.38
16–17 years	14.5	15.0	15.3	19.2	17.3	17.2	14.4	4.24
18–19 years	11.5	13.4	11.9	16.1	13.1	13.1	10.8	3.18
20–24 years	7.2	6.3	6.9	11.2	8.5	8.5	6.7	1.97
25–34 years	5.7	4.9	5.3	8.4	6.3	6.2	4.5	1.32
35–44 years	4.2	4.1	4.3	6.5	4.9	4.9	3.7	1.09
45–54 years	4.0	3.0	3.4	5.8	4.3	4.5	3.1	.91
55–64 years	3.3	2.7	2.6	5.0	3.1	4.1	2.5	.74
65+ years	2.8	2.7	3.3	5.3	3.0	3.1	2.6	.76
Blacks & others								
16+ years	na	na	na	14.8	14.0	14.9	11.7	3.44
16–17 years	na	na	na	41.2	42.9	44.3	35.9	10.56
18–19 years	na	na	na	40.6	38.2	36.4	29.6	8.71
20–24 years	na	na	na	24.3	23.5	25.6	19.8	5.82
25–34 years	na	na	na	13.4	13.2	15.1	12.7	3.74
35–44 years	na	na	na	9.0	8.2	9.3	7.4	2.18
45–54 years	na	na	na	7.0	6.4	6.8	5.6	1.65
55–64 years	na	na	na	5.3	4.5	6.0	4.3	1.26
65+ years	na	na	na	na	na	5.2	5.4	1.59

Labor Force Participation Rate

	Year							Participation Ratio[b]
	1960	1965	1970	1975	1980	1985	1988	1988
Whites								
16+ years	36.5	38.1	42.6	45.9	51.2	54.1	56.4	1.69
16–17 years	30.0	28.4	36.6	42.7	47.2	45.2	47.7	2.00
18–19 years	51.9	50.6	55.0	60.4	65.1	64.8	66.3	1.44
20–24 years	45.7	49.2	57.7	65.5	70.6	73.8	74.9	1.27
25–34 years	34.1	36.3	43.2	53.8	64.8	70.9	73.0	1.31
35–44 years	41.5	44.4	49.9	54.9	65.0	71.4	74.9	1.27
45–54 years	48.6	49.9	53.7	54.3	59.6	64.2	69.2	1.38
55–64 years	36.2	40.3	42.6	40.6	40.9	41.5	43.6	2.19
65+ years	10.6	9.7	9.5	8.0	7.9	7.0	7.7	12.39
Blacks & others								
16+ years	na	na	na	48.8	53.1	56.5	58.0	1.64
16–17 years	na	na	na	25.0	24.6	27.5	28.1	3.40
18–19 years	na	na	na	43.8	45.0	47.9	48.2	1.98
20–24 years	na	na	na	55.9	60.2	62.5	63.2	1.51
25–34 years	na	na	na	62.8	70.5	72.4	73.7	1.29
35–44 years	na	na	na	62.0	68.1	74.8	78.1	1.22
45–54 years	na	na	na	56.6	61.4	65.7	68.3	1.40
55–64 years	na	na	na	43.1	44.8	45.3	43.4	2.20
65+ years	na	na	na	10.7	10.2	9.4	9.6	9.94

Notes:
[a] Ratio of race- and age-specific unemployment rate to rate for 35–44 year old white males (3.4%).
[b] Ratio of 35–44 year old white male participation rate (95.4%) to race- and age-specific rate.
Sources: U. S. Department of Labor 1988, 1989.

153

the same trajectory. At the same time, the subemployment rate is often more than twice the official unemployment rate. Subemployment exceeds unemployment by at least 7% in every year and never drops below 13.9% of the labor force (in 1979 and 1987), thus supporting the argument that labor market conditions are far worse than unemployment data indicate. We should also note that for the population of interest here, the under-class, this measure is still quite conservative since it is based on aggregate data for the entire labor force. Disaggregated figures based on race, age, poverty status and central city location would undoubtedly provide an even more distressing portrait of the labor market.

An incomplete but useful indication of the point comes from a recent report on workers with low earnings from the U.S. Bureau of the Census (1992). Some of these data are reproduced in Table 6.5, where we show the percentage of persons either not working at all during the year or work-ing but at subpoverty wages, broken down by race, sex, and age.

The data contained within Table 6.5 include teenagers and other depen-dents who may be comfortably provided for by their families or others; still, they are useful indicators of the discrepant and often debilitating labor market conditions experienced by African-Americans, especially males in their allegedly prime earning years. With few exceptions, the differences on this measure between white and black males range be-tween 10 and 24 percentage points, a remarkably consistent disparity illustrating the profound structural problems that black males of all ages confront when attempting to fulfill the traditional role of breadwinner.

Employment difficulties such as those indexed in the preceding tables and figures lie at the very core of the underclass problem. Granted, lack of jobs does not explain all of the problems of the inner city, nor can these job problems be adequately understood without also considering the low levels of educational attainment, high degrees of family disorganization, and many other attendant problems of underclass life. Nonetheless, chronic, concentrated unemployment and the lack of sufficient wages constitute a critical component in the general unraveling of the inner city and its pathological decline.

The chronic lack of adequate employment has both direct and indirect implications. Directly, deficient employment opportunities produce long-term, entrenched poverty (see Chapter 5), and with it the associated problems of inadequate housing, nutrition, education, and health care. Moreover, chronically poor communities suffer from an inadequate tax base and accordingly must confront an insufficient and degraded physi-cal and human infrastructure: schools and parks are not maintained; indigenous businesses and services cannot be sustained; housing deterio-rates as banks withhold loans; entrepreneurs, professionals, technicians,

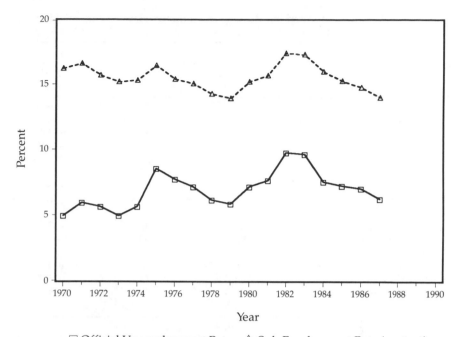

□ Official Unemployment Rate　△ Sub-Employment Rate (see text)

Figure 6.8.　Aggregate umemployment and sub-employment rates, 1970–1987.

and other skilled workers depart in search of work and better, more pleasant living conditions.

Indirectly and perhaps more insidiously, the lack of jobs undermines family formation and stability. It destroys the capacity for individuals to achieve independence and fulfill the obligations of parenthood. As we suggested earlier in this chapter, when the lack of adequate work becomes spatially concentrated and extended over long periods, it effectively deregulates social life. Without viable employment, men and women cannot provide for their children. Children suffer from the absence of positive role models and may grow up understanding quite well that the oft-professed connections between education, work, and material reward simply do not apply to people like them. Without a sense of (or belief in) these connections, connections that routinely inform and structure the lives and decisions of middle-class people, children may fail to develop any sense of an attainably better future or any feelings of accomplishment, obligation, and hope.

Within our inner cities, it has become distressingly common for children to grow up into early adulthood not having known a single individ-

Table 6.5. Persons Not Working during Year and/or Having Annual Earnings below the 4-Person Poverty Threshold, Percent, 1969, 1979, 1989

| | | *1969* | |
Sex & Age	Whites	Blacks	White-Black Difference
Males			
16 years and older	36.3	52.3	−16.0
16–17 years of age	99.2	98.8	+ 0.4
18–24 years of age	65.9	69.7	− 3.8
25–34 years of age	11.7	28.8	−17.1
35–54 years of age	10.6	33.2	−22.6
55–64 years of age	26.4	50.2	−23.8
65+ years	86.2	92.4	− 6.2
Females			
16 years and older	80.6	84.2	− 3.6
16–17 years of age	99.6	100.0	− .4
18–24 years of age	80.4	88.2	− 7.8
25–34 years of age	78.6	73.8	+ 4.8
35–54 years of age	73.0	78.7	− 5.7
55–64 years of age	76.3	88.0	−11.7
65+ years	96.5	98.4	− 1.9

| | | *1979* | |
Sex & Age	Whites	Blacks	White-Black Difference
Males			
16 years and older	39.1	56.6	−16.7
16–17 years of age	99.4	99.8	− .4
18–24 years of age	58.0	75.6	−17.6
25–34 years of age	17.0	36.5	−19.5
35–54 years of age	14.0	33.1	−19.1
55–64 years of age	33.5	55.3	−21.8
65+ years	90.7	94.0	− 3.3
Females			
16 years and older	74.7	75.5	− .8
16–17 years of age	99.8	99.4	+ .4
18–24 years of age	76.5	86.1	− 9.6
25–34 years of age	60.7	59.5	+ 1.2
35–54 years of age	65.2	64.2	− 1.0
55–64 years of age	76.1	78.5	− 2.4
65+ years	97.8	99.4	− 1.6

continued

(*Table 6.5.* continued)

Sex & Age	Whites	Blacks	White-Black Difference
	1989		
Males			
16 years and older	43.4	58.6	−15.2
16–17 years of age	99.2	100.0	− .8
18–24 years of age	71.2	81.2	−10.0
25–34 years of age	26.6	45.3	−18.7
35–54 years of age	18.7	36.6	−17.9
55–64 years of age	42.2	58.8	−16.6
65+ years	90.9	96.3	− 5.4
Females			
16 years and older	69.9	70.5	− .6
16–17 years of age	99.9	100.0	− .1
18–24 years of age	81.4	86.8	− 5.4
25–34 years of age	56.3	61.9	− 5.6
35–54 years of age	54.6	50.4	+ 4.2
55–64 years of age	74.0	80.7	− 6.7
65+ years	97.0	97.9	− .9

Source: U. S. Bureau of the Census 1992, Table 6.

ual for whom the celebrated work ethic and achievement relationships hold (Wilson 1987). The changing structure of the American economy has decimated traditional entry-level and blue-collar jobs that workers of modest skills have used throughout our history to support themselves and to sustain a viable family life. Those from the inner city fortunate enough to have gained an education and subsequently a career have chosen to escape the squalor and violence by leaving; thus, the communities and neighborhoods of the inner city are drained of their most talented potential leaders and their most positive role models. Those who remain behind find that work is often not available or, if available, intermittent and financially unrewarding.

Given this widespread, concentrated, long-term absence of legitimate opportunities, underclass youth easily discern that the materially successful are often those who play by a different set of rules. Why, then, are we surprised when so many inner city youth see no connection between hard work and material success, when they prove altogether indifferent to the roles, relationships, and connections that middle-class people simply assume as a way of life? Is it really any wonder that so many inner city youth prove unwilling to "defer gratification" and instead have babies, quit school, engage in crime, or fall into drug use? No one can be expected to defer gratification forever. The real mystery is not how or why so many inner city youth become hostile to social convention or pessimistic about their long-term life chances, but how it happens amidst such widespread human waste and misery that so many young people (and adults as well, for that matter) still try to make a go of it, still attempt to forge ahead into a better future, still hang on to the hope that they will somehow be able to improve their lives.

EDUCATIONAL ATTAINMENT

In an industrial society the need for education was far more limited than it is today. As recently as the 1960s, the booming U.S. economy provided tens of millions of well-paying manufacturing jobs that did not require much education but provided a sufficient livelihood to support a family. With deindustrialization and the closing or outmigration of vast sectors of American manufacturing, many of these jobs are now gone, especially in the older, once most heavily industrialized urban centers of the North and Midwest.

In contemporary society, job creation and economic growth have become highly dualistic: on the one hand, new technologies create highly skilled, well-compensated employment in information management, engineering, and related technical fields; on the other, the continuing growth in the "service sector" creates unskilled, minimum wage "Mc-jobs" in fast foods, domestic services, and the like. Access to the new technical occupations requires long years of advanced education; those lacking the means or motivation to acquire a requisite education find themselves confined to minimum wage service jobs. Without an adequate education, it is increasingly difficult to attain a job that pays a living wage, much less one that affords the opportunity for advancement, stimulation, and self-fulfillment. A good education, in short, provides the possibility of a better future; inadequate or nonexistent education consigns one to dead-end minimum wage jobs.

Figure 6.9 presents information on trends in school *enrollment* among 14 to 17 year olds (those of middle and high school age) by race. The good news, first, is that the trend is upward for both whites and blacks; that is, an increasing percentage of teenagers of both races are staying in school. Most of the increase in enrollment came in the 1960s, and by the late 1980s, about 95% of all 14–17 year old youth, black and white, were attending school. A second bit of good news is that by the early 1970s, the historic gap between white and black school *enrollments* had been closed, although the racial disparity in *graduation rates* still remains (Farley and Allen 1987).

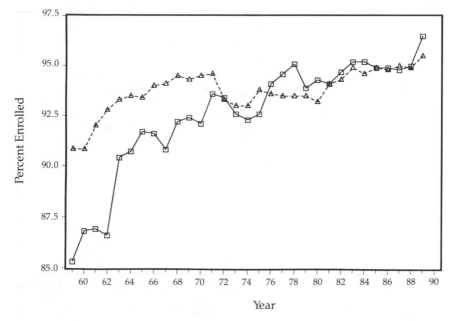

Figure 6.9. Teen enrollment in educational institutions by race, percentage, 1959–1989.

To a limited extent, the first of these patterns may be observed in Figure 6.10 as well, where school enrollment among 20–24 year olds is plotted (reflecting mainly enrollments in colleges and universities). Enrollment among both blacks and whites in this age category grew fairly rapidly during the 1960s. In addition, the racial gap in enrollment has been partially closed, although black enrollment stagnated at about 20% in the 1980s while white enrollment continued to edge upward (a reflection, we suspect, of the reductions in federal aid to college and university students during the 1980s and the lesser familial resources available to black students).

Related information on higher educational attainment for the period 1976–1989 is provided in Table 6.6. These data tend to support the picture gained from Figure 6.10. Overall, college enrollment has increased for both blacks and whites. However, the white trend is more stable. Among blacks, college enrollment actually began to decline in the late 1970s and the historic racial gap in college enrollment reemerged in the 1980s.

Table 6.6 shows that the percentage of blacks receiving bachelor's, master's, and doctoral degrees is *substantially* less than the corresponding

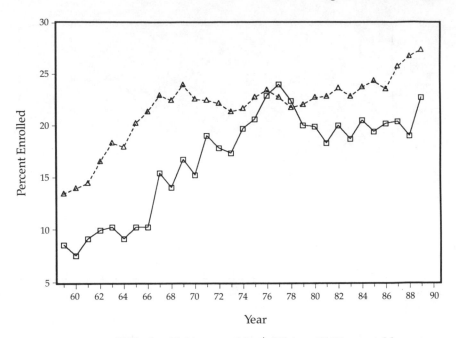

□ Blacks, 20-24 years old   △ Whites, 20-24 years old

Figure 6.10. Young adult enrollment in educational institutions by race, percentage, 1959–1989.

figures for whites, with the difference increasing at the higher educational levels. Even more troubling, the recent data show that the gains of the 1960s and 1970s are being eroded as black-white differences in enrollment and attainment beginning to reappear. Among whites in recent years, enrollment and attainment have been stable or increasing modestly, in terms both of absolute numbers and as a percentage of high school graduates. The pattern for blacks is different; whether expressed as an absolute number or as a percentage of black high school graduates, higher educational attainment among blacks has been in *decline* for at least the past decade. This is true for both BA degrees and postgraduate degrees.[11]

All our data on educational enrollments and attainments reflect the aggregate experience of black and white students; as in other cases we have considered, a disaggregation that identified poor, inner city underclass minority youth would inevitably yield a different and more troubling portrait. This point notwithstanding, the statistics on educational attainment that we do have are not particularly encouraging. They sug-

Table 6.6. Educational Attainment by Race, Number (in 1000s), and Percent, 1976–1989

| | College Enrollment of High School Grads[a] | | | | Bachelor's Degrees Conferred[b] | | | | Master's Degrees Conferred[c] | | | | Doctoral Degree Conferred[d,e] | | | |
| | White | | Black | | White | | Black | | White | | Black | | White | | Black | |
Year	Number	Percent	Number	Percent	Number	Percent	Number	Percent	Number	Percent	Number	Percent	Number	Percent	Number	Percent
1976	1291	48.9	134	41.9												
1977	1403	50.7	166	49.6	807.7	29.2	58.6	17.5	266.1	9.6	21.0	6.3	26.9	.97	1.3	.39
1978	1378	50.1	161	45.7												
1979	1376	49.6	147	45.4	802.5	28.9	60.2	18.9	249.4	9.0	19.4	6.0	26.1	.94	1.3	.40
1980	1339	49.9	151	41.8												
1981	1434	54.6	154	42.9	807.3	30.7	60.7	16.9	241.2	9.2	17.1	4.8	25.9	.99	1.3	.36
1982	1376	52.0	140	36.5												
1983	1372	55.0	151	38.5	826.1	33.1	57.5	14.7	223.6	9.0	13.9	3.5	23.9	.96	1.2	.31
1984	1455	57.9	176	40.2												
1985	1332	59.4	141	42.3	841.8	37.6	56.6	17.0	228.9	10.2	13.9	4.2	24.4	1.08	1.1	.33
1986	1292	56.0	141	36.5												
1987	1249	56.6	175	51.9	858.2	38.9	58.0	17.2	241.6	10.9	14.1	4.2	24.9	1.13	1.1	.33
1988	1328	60.7	172	45.0												
1989	1238	60.4	178	52.8												

Notes:
a Enrollment in college as of October of each year for individuals ages 16–24 who graduated from high school during the preceding twelve months.
b Degrees conferred at end of academic year as a percentage of high school graduates.
c Degrees conferred at end of academic year as a percentage of high school graduates.
d Includes PhD, EdD, and comparable degrees at the doctoral level. Excludes first professional degree.
e Degrees conferred at end of academic year as a percentage of high school graduates.
Sources: U.S. Department of Education 1991.

gest, first of all, that the considerable progress achieved during the 1960s and 1970s, years when longstanding racial disparities were beginning to narrow, has been at least partially lost during the 1980s; gaps in enrollment and attainment that had been closing are now widening again (see Orfield and Ashkinaze 1991). It seems rather unlikely that this pattern reflects a decline among blacks in their educational aspirations; more compelling explanations can probably be found in the federal government's cutbacks in education and scholarship funds in the 1980s and in the now-wavering commitment of many American colleges and universities to affirmative action.

What has been said to this point concerns only the *quantity* of education, not its quality; the quantitative measures that we have presented mask large racial differences in the quality of education being received. Even if high-school enrollment percentages are about the same for blacks and whites, there is every difference between a rat-infested, ill-equipped, poorly funded central city high school and its well-funded, well-appointed suburban counterpart. Data on enrollment and attainment in institutions of higher education do not distinguish between junior and community colleges, regional campuses, and lesser state institutions on the one hand vs. elite private and public colleges and universities on the other. One year of education at San Jose State or at the local community college is not the equivalent of a year's education at Harvard or Stanford or Berkeley. Once considerations of the *quality* of education are introduced, the black-white disparities rapidly grow larger.

The best of America's high schools, colleges, and universities are very good indeed, arguably the finest in the world. Alongside these world-class institutions of learning, however, we find a public school system that is in crisis and whose many failings threaten our collective capacity to be competitive in the emerging world economy of the twenty-first century. It is not enough to have schools that give the necessary tools for advancement and achievement to the middle class; the schools that educate the children of the poor must also provide the means of upward mobility. Instead, we are saddled with a bankrupt, ill-equipped, and poorly staffed system of institutions that attempt, however fitfully, to educate poor children of the inner city. All too often, the problems confronting students, teachers and administrators in these schools are so critical and overwhelming that the task of adequate education becomes secondary.

Realistically, inner city schools in poverty neighborhoods cannot escape the pathology that surrounds them. Thus, additional investments in these schools themselves, while necessary, will not prove to be sufficient; the inner city schools will continue to fail unless special efforts are made to ameliorate the attendant social conditions of the communities in question.

DRUG ABUSE AND THE DRUG/CRIME CONNECTION

Illicit drug use and drug dealing have come to figure prominently in the continuing degradation of life in the inner city. Although some commentators see escalating drug addiction and trade as major causal factors in the emergence of the underclass and blame drugs—particularly crack—for the increased violence of the contemporary inner city, drugs themselves are hardly the root cause. Rather, drugs are more symptomatic than determinant. Thus, government antidrug policies that ignore the social and demographic correlates of drug abuse while continuing to promote abstinence and enforcement without education and treatment are doomed.

A recent report from the White House, *National Drug Control Strategy* (January 1992), is factually correct in its particulars, but myopic and programmatically bankrupt in claiming that:

> Drug use is not caused by poverty (most poor people do *not* use drugs), racism (most minority individuals do *not* use drugs), or unemployment (most people who are unemployed do *not* use drugs). Nor is it caused by being a single parent or a teenage mother, or by low educational attainment. These are circumstances that can make life harder, indeed very hard, and they are important factors in locating and influencing drug use. But to explain the drug problem by pointing to social conditions is to "victimize" drug users and deprive them of personal autonomy—the freedom and will not to use drugs. It is to deny the dignity of those who live in similar circumstances and do not use drugs. *In short, the drug problem reflects bad decisions by individuals with free wills.* (p. 2, emphasis added, as quoted by Massing 1992, p. 46)

And likewise, most cigarette smokers die of something other than lung cancer, most abused children do not grow up to batter their own children, and most divorced women never end up in poverty. That the correlation among all these factors is less than perfect does not deny the reality of social conditions in fostering negative behavioral outcomes. To point to these predisposing social conditions is not to "deny the dignity" of those who have managed to escape their corrosive influence but to seek a reasonable, empirical understanding of why people make the choices they make.

The appeal of drugs in the inner city is easy to appreciate. For those without an attainable future to which they can aspire, those with little sense of hope or the opportunity for something better, drugs are a temporary expedient, a momentary high that affords escape and pleasure in an otherwise dismal life. Again we must ask, Why *should* people without a realistic future be expected to defer their momentary pleasures or forego some sense of escape from otherwise harsh and hopeless conditions? Drugs create an illusion of well-being. Is this fleeting illusion not preferable to the cold realities of inner city life? Is there really a "free will" choice to be made between momentary euphoria and endless misery?

None of this is meant to minimize or deny the physical, emotional, and social destructiveness of drugs, nor to suggest that individuals do not bear responsibility for their actions. Drugs have resulted in a great deal of property and violent crime and they have had a devastating impact on inner city neighborhoods now ravaged by rampant crack addiction.[12] However, to overlook the conditions that breed this destructive behavior and simply assert that drug addiction is a matter of "choice" dooms every intervention to failure.

Between 1972 and the present, the National Institute on Drug Abuse (NIDA) has conducted a series of National Household Surveys on Drug Abuse (NHSDA). As the name suggests, a key goal of these studies is to measure the prevalence and correlates of drug abuse among the US population. While much of the attention being given to drugs and the ensuing violence has focused on so-called hard drugs, specifically heroin, cocaine, and smokable cocaine or "crack," it is worth emphasizing at the outset of this discussion that the NHSDA surveys repeatedly document that alcohol and marijuana use is far more common among users of all ages.

Quite contrary to conventional understandings, the NHSDA surveys show that drug use peaked in the late 1970s and tended to decline throughout the 1980s. Table 6.7 shows the national trends for three age groups: 12–17 year olds, 18–25 year olds, and those 26 years of age and older. The data indicate that in the 1979 NHSDA, slightly more than a third (34.3%) of those aged 12–17 reported that they had ever used illicit drugs. By 1985, lifetime usage among 12–17 year olds had declined to a quarter. During the same period, the percentage of 12–17 year-olds reporting any illicit drug use during the past month declined from 17.6% to 9.2%.

Among those aged 18 to 25, the prevalence of drug use is considerably higher but has followed the same general trend. Between 1979 and 1988, lifetime usage of any illicit drug declined from 69.9% to 58.9% while use over the past month dropped from 37.1% to 17.8%. Among persons over 25, the data indicate a somewhat different pattern, inasmuch as lifetime use escalated between 1979 and 1988 while usage over the past month declined.

These data suggest that although drug use declined somewhat during the 1980s, experimentation with drugs still typically increases during the

Table 6.7. Estimated Trends in Use of Selected Drugs, Persons Ages 12 and Older, Percent, 1972–1988

	1972			1979			1988		
	Past Month	Past Year	Lifetime Use	Past Month	Past Year	Lifetime Use	Past Month	Past Year	Lifetime Use
12–17 year olds (N)	880			2165			3095		
Any illicit drug use	—	—	—	17.6	26.0	34.3	9.2	16.8	24.7
Marijuana/hashish	7.0	—	14.0	16.7	24.1	30.9	6.4	12.6	17.4
Inhalants	1.0	2.9	6.4	2.0	4.6	9.8	2.0	3.9	8.8
Hallucinogens	1.4	3.6	4.8	2.2	4.7	7.1	.8	2.8	3.5
Cocaine	.6	1.5	1.5	1.4	4.2	5.4	1.1	2.9	3.4
Heroin	—	—	.6	—	—	.5	—	.4	.6
Psychotherapeutics[a]	—	—	—	2.3	5.6	7.3	2.4	5.4	7.7
18–25 year olds (N)	772			2044			1505		
Any illicit drug use	—	—	—	37.1	49.4	69.9	17.8	32.0	58.9
Marijuana/hashish	27.8	—	47.9	35.4	46.9	68.2	15.5	27.9	56.4
Inhalants	—	—	—	1.2	3.8	16.5	1.7	4.1	12.5
Hallucinogens	—	—	—	4.4	9.9	25.1	1.9	5.6	13.8
Cocaine	—	—	9.1	9.3	19.6	27.5	4.5	12.1	19.7
Heroin	—	—	4.6	—	.8	3.5	—	.3	.3
Psychotherapeutics[a]	—	—	—	6.2	16.3	29.5	3.8	11.3	17.6
26 and older (N)	1613			3015			4214		
Any illicit drug use	—	—	—	6.5	10.0	23.0	4.9	10.2	33.7
Marijuana/hashish	2.5	—	7.4	6.0	9.0	19.6	3.9	6.9	30.7
Inhalants	—	—	—	.5	1.0	3.9	.2	.4	3.9
Hallucinogens	—	—	—	—	.5	4.5	—	.6	6.6
Cocaine	—	—	1.6	.9	2.0	4.3	.9	2.7	9.9
Heroin	—	—	—	—	—	1.0	—	.2	1.1
Psychotherapeutics[a]	—	—	—	1.1	2.3	9.2	1.2	4.7	11.3

Note:
[a] Includes nonmedical use of any prescription-type stimulant, sedative, tranquilizer, or analgesic.
Source: U.S. Department of Health and Human Services, National Institute on Drug Abuse 1990, Appendix Tables A-4–A-12.

late teens and early twenties—independently of race, income, educational status, and other factors. The NHSDA data further show that whites are significantly *more* likely than blacks or Hispanics to have used any illicit drug, though the incidence of cocaine use (including crack) is statistically comparable across race and ethnic categories (see U.S. Department of Health and Human Services, National Institute on Drug Abuse 1991). In addition, the 1988 study, which gave special attention to drug use among youths, reports no statistically significant difference (in the use of any substances noted in Table 6.7) by residence in large metropolitan, small metropolitan, and nonmetropolitan areas. Thus, contrary to myth, drug use is no more prevalent in large urban centers than in small cities, suburbs, and towns.

Also contrary to conventional wisdom, no meaningful differences in drug use among youths (ages 16–17) and young adults (ages 21–25) were found between school-enrolled and high school graduate populations on one hand versus school dropouts on the other. However, preliminary results from the 1990 NHSDA survey provide some evidence that the expected differences in marijuana and cocaine use between these groups may emerge later, after the age of 25.

Critically, adolescents' living arrangements are consistently found to yield statistically significant differences in drug use. Youth living with both natural parents have the lowest percentage of use of all illicit drugs; youth living with one natural parent, with a natural parent and a stepparent, or in some other arrangement show consistently higher rates of use (with some variation in the pattern depending on the specific drug).

Preliminary data from the most recent NHSDA surveys (1990 and 1991) suggest that these general trends persist for the population at large; illicit drug use, broadly defined, continues to abate. However, these most recent data also suggest an increase in the use of crack cocaine. The 1988 survey found that only a small percentage (1.1%) of youths aged 12–17 had used cocaine within the past month, though lifetime use was somewhat higher (3.4%). Among 18–25 year olds, the corresponding figures were substantially higher, 4.5% and 19.7% respectively (see Table 6.7). The most recent data indicate that there are some 850,000 persons who use crack at least weekly.

The NHSDA surveys provide the best available national statistics on drug use but they are highly aggregated and do not, in any case, allow us to examine any behavioral correlates, least of all within the underclass *per se*. However, a recent study of firearms use and acquisition among inner city youths in five large U.S. cities affords us the opportunity to examine drug involvement among 835 inmates (all male) in six juvenile correctional facilities and 1,653 students (both males and females) in ten inner city public high schools, groups popularly thought to engage in and experience violence, belong to street gangs, and engage in drug use and trafficking (see Sheley, Wright, and Smith 1992).

Data from this study are presented in Table 6.8. Like the NHSDA, this research also found that alcohol and marijuana use is far more common among both the inmate and student samples than is the use of harder drugs. Nearly 60% of male high school students had used alcohol at least a few times in the last year or so, and a quarter had used marijuana; any use of the harder drugs was reported by only 5–6%, finding roughly consistent with the national data reviewed above. The same patterns, albeit with much higher prevalence rates, characterize the incarcerated juveniles: 82% had used alcohol at least occasionally in the year or so before their current incarceration and 84% had used marijuana. While use of hard drugs was substantially less, it was nonetheless disturbingly high; 43% had used cocaine, 25% crack, and 21% heroin.

Combining results across types of drugs, 10% of the incarcerated youth and 40% of the student sample had not used drugs at all in the previous year or so. Complete abstinence from drugs, in other words, is characteristic of only a minority of the high school students and practically nonexistent among the inmates. Still, it is important not to exaggerate. Drugs are clearly present in the lives of both these samples (especially among the incarcerated youth), but perhaps less so than would be expected given common stereotypes. As already noted, the most commonly used drugs in both samples were alcohol and marijuana, not heroin or crack. And even here, 45% of the inmates and 81% of the students had *not* used alcohol more than a few times during the past year or two; 55% of the inmates and 93% of the students had *not* used marijuana more than a few times. Regular, heavy use of any of these substances was reported only by a minority of the respondents (the exception being alcohol use among the inmates).

As would be expected, the inmates were considerably more involved than students in the harder drugs, with heroin, cocaine, and crack having been used by 21%, 43%, and 25% respectively. In each case, about half of those who had used the drug did so only a few times; the other half were more regular, heavier users. Also, a third of the inmates (but only 4% of the students) had been in alcohol or drug treatment programs.

Using drugs is one thing; being directly involved in the drug business (as a dealer or as someone who works for a dealer) is quite another. Simply put, using drugs is a leisure time activity; dealing drugs is an economic pursuit undertaken for profit. For increasing numbers of inner city youth, it appears that the drug trade has become *nearly the only high-profit, well-paying economic activity available to them*. Both inmates and students were asked whether they agreed or disagreed with the statement that, "Dealing drugs is the best way for a guy like me to get ahead."

Table 6.8. Youth Inmate and Inner City Student Drug Involvement during the Past Year or Two, 1991

Item	Inmates		Students	
	Percent	*Number*	*Percent*	*Number*
Frequency of use				
Alcohol		741		586
never	18		42	
few times or less	27		39	
many times	26		14	
almost all the time	32		5	
Marijuana		744		585
never	16		75	
few times or less	39		18	
many times	26		4	
almost all the time	40		3	
Heroin		716		579
never	79		96	
few times or less	12		3	
many times	5		1	
almost all the time	4		1	
Regular cocaine		717		579
never	57		94	
few times or less	21		3	
many times	11		1	
almost all the time	11		2	
Crack cocaine		721		582
never	75		95	
few times or less	13		2	
many times	5		1	
almost all the time	7		2	
Ever in alcohol or drug treatment program?		751		592
never	64		96	
once	20		2	
few times	12		1	
many times	4		1	
Respondent's involvement in dealing		695		560
none	16		80	
user and buyer	12		2	
dealer	39		10	
worked for dealer	8		6	
user and dealer	25		2	
"Dealing drugs is best way to get ahead"		730		541
disagree	35		30	
strongly disagree	28		56	

Source: Sheley, Wright, and Smith 1992.

Nearly two-fifths of the inmates (37%) and even one in seven (14%) of the male high school students agreed with this sentiment. Attitudes notwithstanding, the large majority of inmates (72%) and a surprisingly large percentage of male high school students (18%) had either themselves dealt drugs or worked for someone who did. Among the inmates, drug dealing was as common as drug use.

Drug use patterns themselves tell us little about the relationships among drugs, crime, and guns; the data in Table 6.9 are more revealing in this regard. This table employs high-use, low-use, and nonusing groups of inmates by combining responses in the manner indicated at the bottom of the table, separately for each type of drug. These drug use variables are then cross-tabulated against selected items of interest. These cross-tabulations make it apparent, first of all, that substantial numbers of nonusers engaged in all the behaviors in question. For example, 44% of those inmates who never used heroin had committed robbery; 72% had fired a gun at someone. Similar findings apply to nonusers of cocaine and crack. Somewhat lower, but nonetheless substantial, percentages of alcohol and marijuana nonusers had also engaged in the criminal and gun activities in question. Nearly six in ten of the inmates who never even used alcohol, for example, said they had fired a gun at somebody at least once.

In a sense, these findings are scarcely worth mentioning; everyone in the inmate sample had committed enough serious crime to get themselves locked up in a juvenile corrections facility, so everyone in the sample was more or less destined to answer yes to at least one of these questions regardless of their pattern of drug use. On the other hand, in an era when drugs and youth crime have become inextricably linked in the popular consciousness, when the "drug problem," "juvenile crime problem," and the "underclass problem" are seen to be essentially synonymous, it is certainly worth noting that a great deal of juvenile crime and violence are perpetrated by youth who in fact never touch drugs.

That important point made, it is also clear that there is a definite relationship between patterns of drug use on the one hand and criminal and gun activity on the other; drug users were generally more likely than nonusers to have done nearly everything asked about. Those who had used heroin were more likely than those who had not to be involved in crime and in gun ownership and use, and to believe that it is okay to shoot someone to get something one wants. Those who had used cocaine were more likely to have been involved in robbery, burglary, and property crimes committed for drug money but not more likely to commit homicide. They exhibited greater involvement in all types of gun ownership save carrying a gun generally and possessing a military-style gun. They were more likely to feel that shooting someone for material gain was

Table 6.9. Youth Inmates' Drug Use, Crime, and Gun Activity

	Drug																			
	Heroin				Cocaine				Crack				Alcohol				Marijuana			
	% Use Level			(N)	% Use Level			(N)	% Use Level			(N)	% Use Level			(N)	% Use Level			(N)
Item	Hi[a]	Lo[b]	No[c]		Hi[a]	Lo[b]	No[c]		Hi[a]	Lo[b]	No[c]		Hi[a]	Lo[b]	No[c]		Hi[a]	Lo[b]	No[c]	
Burglary	61	84	59	(697)	82	75	53	(701)	82	80	59	(704)	74	57	35	(723)	73	60	32	(726)
Robbery	60	58	44	(697)	57	52	42	(700)	59	52	45	(702)	55	43	29	(722)	55	40	31	(724)
Homicide	47	47	35	(661)	43	33	37*	(666)	51	28	37	(662)	42	29	40*	(675)	41	32	44	(678)
Property crime for drug money	60	64	31	(700)	67	48	22	(700)	70	62	29	(704)	49	27	14	(726)	47	29	14	(728)
Carried a gun	90	91	80	(700)	86	85	81*	(706)	86	88	81*	(710)	89	80	65	(730)	89	78	65	(731)
Owned military gun	51	49	46	(700)	48	44	45*	(700)	50	40	46*	(702)	50	42	36	(724)	51	42	33	(725)
Owned shotgun	71	72	53	(698)	71	65	52	(699)	69	67	56	(700)	67	55	34	(720)	68	52	38	(721)
Owned sawed-off shotgun	71	78	58	(702)	69	65	58	(700)	58	57	62*	(702)	70	55	44	(724)	69	56	44	(725)
Owned revolver	78	82	70	(698)	80	72	70	(698)	78	70	72*	(701)	81	66	51	(722)	79	67	52	(724)

	Hi	Lo	No	(N)	Hi	Lo	No	(N)	Hi	Lo	No	(N)	Hi	Lo	No	(N)	Hi	Lo	No	(N)
Owned automatic handgun	67	77	62	(702)	71	69	62	(702)	68	74	63*	(707)	70	62	51	(727)	72	63	45	(729)
Fired gun during crime	81	88	71	(711)	82	76	71*	(711)	77	78	73*	(716)	80	72	54	(735)	81	69	55	(738)
Fired gun at some-one	83	88	72	(694)	80	77	73*	(695)	76	76	74*	(698)	81	72	59	(716)	81	70	66	(721)
Easy to get gun	73	73	70*	(677)	72	69	71*	(681)	62	63	72	(684)	73	70	58	(705)	74	67	59	(707)
OK to shoot some-one who has something you want	73	76	60	(686)	74	59	62	(690)	67	67	62*	(693)	68	57	53	(710)	68	63	45	(710)

Notes:
a Hi = high: used many times or almost all the time during past year or two.
b Lo = low: used a few times or less.
c No = no use.
* Not statistically significant at p = .05; difference is statistically significant.
Source: Sheley, Wright, and Smith 1992.

171

acceptable, but they were not more likely to have fired guns during a crime or at someone.

Users of crack were more likely than nonusers to have committed all types of crime in question but, with the exception of shotgun possession, were no more likely to be involved in gun activity or to have fired a gun during a crime or at someone. They viewed shooting someone to get something one wants as no more acceptable than did nonusers. Finally, while heroin and cocaine users and nonusers viewed ease of acquisition of a gun in the same fashion, crack users were more likely than nonusers to perceive acquisition as easy.

The relation of drug use to involvement in crime and gun activities was even more pronounced for alcohol and marijuana than for the harder drugs. Only involvement in homicide was unrelated to level of alcohol use. For all other activities and perceptions, users of alcohol and marijuana exceeded nonusers in their level of participation.

Involvement in crime and gun activity, perception of ease of gun acquisition, and assessment of the acceptability of shooting someone for material gain were progressively more likely with increased involvement in all drugs except heroin. This pattern is most pronounced for alcohol and marijuana use. For most items, lower-level heroin users score somewhat higher than higher-level users.

In sum, drug use is clearly associated with crime and gun activity among criminally active youth (see also Huizinga et al. forthcoming). This is the case for all five types of drug use examined individually, for heroin, cocaine, and crack use combined in index form, and for all five drugs viewed in combination. Whether this is in fact a causal relationship is more difficult to say; most studies that report an association between delinquency or crime and drug use are careful to explain "that the relationship may be spurious rather than causal" (Fagan 1990, p. 184). An argument could be made that involvement in drugs leads one to become involved in other crimes or leads one to possess, carry, and use firearms. At best, however, the use of drugs cannot be a necessary precondition since nonusers were also heavily involved in all the activities in question.

Perhaps the most likely possibility is that drugs, guns, and criminal activity are all manifestations of the emerging inner city underclass youth subculture, and that participation in this subculture itself is the critical variable, not participation in any particular manifestation of it. The suggestion, in other words, is not that some inner city youth get involved in drugs, which then leads them causally to guns or crime, but that these youth get involved with peer structures and values (or in other words, affiliate with peer groups) where hanging out, getting high, carrying guns, and committing crime have become part and parcel of the daily routine of existence. In the same vein, Fagan has pointed out that "the association [between drug use and crime among youth] seems to be facilitated by the strength of involvement in peer social networks where drug use and delinquency are normative" (1990, p. 184). No one element is causally prior to any other; all, rather, result directly or indirectly from the anger, estrangement, and profound cultural isolation that have come to characterize so many of our inner city youth.

This interpretation is bolstered by the finding that alcohol use and marijuana use are as strongly related to criminal activity as is the use of harder drugs. It is not likely that these findings reflect some direct behavioral link (whereby youth get drunk or high on pot and as a result are driven to commit crimes). The suspicion, rather, is that these variables reflect the degree to which a juvenile is a participant in the street culture of the inner city. Getting high is very much a part of that street culture; the choice of specific drugs largely seems a matter of convenience and avail-ability. Thus alcohol and marijuana, being generally more available, are more commonly used than the harder drugs. What the data suggest, in other words, is that youth who spend the most time "high" (be it on alcohol, crack, or whatever) are also the most criminally active—not because of the direct effects of the drugs but because routine drug use is an element in a street subculture that also entails high rates of criminal activity, gun carrying, and gun use.

CRIME AND VICTIMIZATION

Within recent years, homicide has become the leading cause of death among black males aged 16–30. Each day, newspapers in large cities carry grim reports of shootouts and drive-by killings. In many inner city neigh-borhoods, the probability of a young black male meeting a violent death now exceeds the probability of his going to college. With statistics such as these, it is any wonder that many inner city youths find it difficult to conceive of any future, much less one that includes an education, career, marriage, and family?

Turning to a somewhat broader consideration of the issues of criminal activity and victimization, it is readily apparent that African-Americans have higher rates of violent crime. It is equally apparent that the vast majority of crimes are intraracial; thus black Americans experience higher rates of criminal victimization as well.

Table 6.10 presents race-specific data on homicide victimization rates along with arrest rates for the crimes of homicide, robbery, and burglary for 1959 through 1988. Since males are responsible for the vast majority of these crimes, the data are given for males only. Figure 6.11 graphically depicts the trends in black and white male homicide rates; while Figure 6.12 portrays the homicide, robbery, and burglary arrest data.

The homicide victimization data contained in the first two columns of Table 6.10 (see also Figure 6.11) indicate a modest increase for both black and white males, with relatively major increases occurring in the 1960s.[13] In general, however, the homicide rate among blacks appears somewhat more variable: that rate escalated fairly dramatically during the 1960s and has oscillated within the range of 50–70 per 100,000 since. The homicide rate for black males is consistently five to ten times higher than the rate for white males.[14]

Arrests for homicide, robbery, and burglary show similar disparities. As per Table 6.10 (columns 3–8) and Figure 6.12, it is apparent that for both blacks and whites a secular increase in arrest rates has occurred, more so for the crimes of robbery and burglary than homicide. While the increase among whites has been fairly steady and absolutely small relative to the increase in the rate for blacks, it has approximately doubled over the 1959–1987 period. For black males, the escalation in arrests was most dramatic during the 1960s and has more or less stabilized or ex-

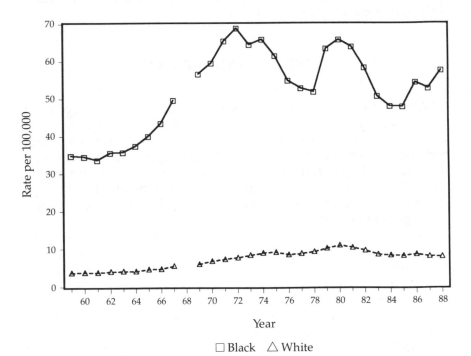

□ Black   △ White

Figure 6.11.   Male homicide rates by race, 1959–1988.

hibited a slight downward trajectory since. Further comparison of the black and white arrest data indicates that black arrest rates for burglary run two to five times higher than the arrest rates for white males throughout the period. This difference, in turn, is dwarfed by the differential arrest rates for homicide and robbery.

Victimization data suggest that these continuing disparities in arrest rates are not attributable to racially discriminatory police practices, but accurately reflect the profile of perpetrators provided by victims in various national surveys conducted by the federal government. In short, arrest data match up extremely well with victimization reports so far as race of perpetrators is concerned (see Smith, Devine, and Sheley 1992).

Given that blacks are more likely to commit these and other street crimes, they are heavily overrepresented in the correctional population (Table 6.11). In 1988, 3.7 million persons, or approximately 2% of the adult population, were either incarcerated or on probation or parole. While the majority of these persons were white, slightly more than a third (35.7%) were black.[15] In 1988, 6.6% of adult African-Americans were under correctional supervision; the corresponding figure for whites was 1.5%.

Data on the correctional population broken down simultaneously by sex *and* race are not published in annual Bureau of Justice Statistics' publications. We do know, however, that 86.7% of the correctional population is male. If this figure is the same for both whites and blacks, then there are roughly 1.1 million black males in the correctional population (.867 × 1,325,273 = 1,149,012). In 1988 there were approximately 9.5 million African-American males age 18 or higher; thus, or so it would appear, nearly 12% of adult male African-Americans are under correctional supervision. In the same year, incidentally, only 303,000 black males (or 3.2% of African-American males age 18 and or older) were enrolled in colleges and universities, which suggests that black males are 3.5 times more likely to end up in prison or on probation or parole than to go to college (see U.S. Bureau of the Census 1990, table 252).

Data from the Federal Bureau of Investigation's annual Uniform Crime Reports (UCR), annual National Crime Surveys (NCS) undertaken by the U.S. Department of Justice, and other sources indicate that African-Americans consistently experience higher rates of violent and household crime than whites. Also, violent crimes committed against blacks tend to be more serious and are more likely to involve weapons (see Whitaker 1990). Table 6.12 documents these differences in forms and rates of criminal victimization for the years 1979–1986. Simple assault is the only crime of violence where the white rate exceeds the black rate. For rape, robbery, homicide, and aggravated assault, African-Americans experience higher rates of victimization.

While the victimization rate for crimes of theft is lower in the aggregate

Table 6.10. Homicide Victimization and Arrest Rates per 100,000 Males for Homicide, Robbery, and Burglary, by Race, 1959–1988

| | Homicide Rate | | Arrest Rates per 100,000 Males | | | | | |
| | | | Homicide | | Robbery | | Burglary | |
Year	Black[a]	White	Black[a]	White	Black[a]	White	Black[a]	White
1959	34.7	3.5	27.3	2.0	143.2	13.7	343.7	86.7
1960	34.5	3.6	32.5	2.4	183.0	16.9	433.5	101.7
1961	33.6	3.6	26.9	2.2	176.7	17.7	458.4	112.6
1962	35.5	3.8	25.7	1.9	172.8	14.7	403.1	94.2
1963	35.7	3.9	23.5	2.2	138.7	14.5	367.8	104.2
1964	37.4	3.9	23.9	2.2	141.5	14.5	408.3	109.2
1965	40.0	4.4	27.3	2.4	165.9	15.0	439.2	107.1
1966	43.4	4.5	29.1	2.6	167.7	14.6	419.8	111.3
1967	49.5	5.3	32.9	2.7	211.5	16.4	491.8	124.0
1968	na	na	38.1	3.0	246.6	18.1	539.4	131.2
1969	56.5	5.8	43.7	3.2	291.6	18.1	562.6	131.5
1970	59.4	6.6	44.8	3.6	304.7	19.8	576.2	139.8
1971	65.4	7.1	50.4	3.7	339.6	20.7	601.2	150.3
1972	68.8	7.5	49.1	3.9	350.4	21.4	563.9	148.3

Year							
1973	64.4	8.1	45.5	4.1	323.6	23.5	548.7	160.6
1974	65.8	8.7	50.2	4.5	393.0	29.1	684.9	197.5
1975	61.4	8.9	42.5	4.5	333.9	29.6	616.9	200.3
1976	54.8	8.2	34.4	3.8	268.2	23.4	550.3	172.8
1977	52.8	8.5	38.2	4.6	304.5	29.2	571.0	182.8
1978	51.8	9.0	38.3	4.9	343.1	29.8	581.7	184.0
1979	63.3	9.9	36.2	5.1	309.1	30.3	553.6	182.7
1980	65.7	10.7	36.6	5.3	328.4	32.1	568.7	186.8
1981	63.8	10.2	39.5	5.5	349.5	31.4	584.4	182.7
1982	58.2	9.4	41.3	5.6	376.0	32.9	618.8	182.3
1983	50.6	8.4	37.2	5.2	348.9	28.4	543.3	163.4
1984	47.9	8.1	28.4	4.8	308.5	26.6	440.1	153.2
1985	47.7	8.0	30.9	4.6	302.4	26.1	450.3	154.4
1986	54.2	8.4	31.9	4.8	319.1	27.3	459.7	154.2
1987	52.6	7.8	35.5	4.5	316.2	25.7	476.9	147.0
1988	57.5	7.7	—	—	—	—	—	—

Notes:

a Nonwhite prior to 1978.

Sources: Homicide rates are from the U.S. Department of Health and Human Services, National Center For Health Statistics, *Vital Statistics of the United States*, annual editions, volume 2, part A; Arrest data computed from the U.S. Department of Justice, Federal Bureau of Investigation, *Uniform Crime Reports*, annual editions.

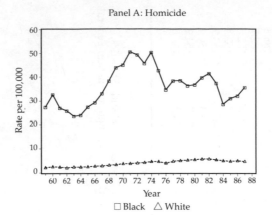

Panel A: Homicide

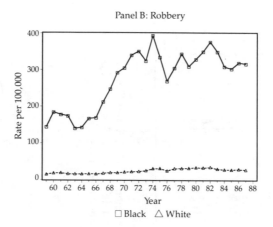

Panel B: Robbery

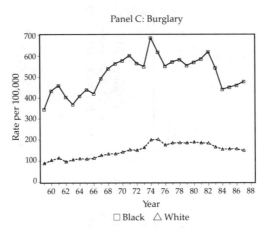

Panel C: Burglary

Figure 6.12. Male arrest rates for selected crimes by race, 1959–1987.

178

Table 6.11. Adult Correctional Population of the United States, 1988

| | Total | Sex | | | | Race | | | |
| | | Male | | Female | | Black | | White | |
		Number	Percent	Number	Percent	Number	Percent	Number	Percent
Total	3,713,163	3,222,150	86.7	491,013	13.3	1,325,273	35.7	2,348,075	63.2
Jail	341,893	311,594	91.1	30,299	8.9	143,658	42.0	194,361	56.8
Probation	2,356,483	1,955,881	83.0	400,602	17.0	706,945	30.0	1,625,973	69.0
Prison	606,810	575,256	94.8	31,554	5.2	289,448	47.7	309,473	51.0
Parole	407,977	379,419	93.0	28,558	7.0	185,222	45.4	218,268	53.5

Percent of Adult Population Groups

	Total[a]	Males	Females	Blacks	Whites
Percent of group under correctional care or in custody	2.04	2.6	.5	6.6	1.5
Jail	.19	—	—	—	—
Probation	1.30	—	—	—	—
Prison	.33	—	—	—	—
Parole	.22	—	—	—	—

Note:
[a] Total adult resident population.
Source: U.S. Department of Justice, Bureau of Justice Statistics 1991, Table 1.2.

for whites, these data also indicate that this difference owes entirely to
the category of larceny without contact, or those situations in which there
was no direct contact between the victim and offender. For larceny with
contact, that is, where there is direct involvement of victim and
perpetrator—albeit without violence or the threat thereof—blacks had
more than double the victimization rate of whites (i.e., 5.6 vs. 2.6 per
1000).

Figure 6.13 presents this same basic information graphically, using the

Table 6.12. Average Annual Victimization Rates and Number of Victimizations, by Race of Victim and Type of Crime, 1979–1986

	Race of Victim	
	White	Black
Victimization rates[a]		
Crimes of violence	34.5	44.3
Rape	.8	1.5
Robbery	5.4	13.0
Aggravated assault	9.3	13.8
Simple assault	18.9	16.0
Crimes of theft	80.5	77.1
Personal larceny with contact	2.6	5.6
Personal larceny without contact	77.9	71.4
Household crimes	201.0	260.7
Burglary	72.4	108.4
Household larceny	113.7	127.9
Motor vehicle theft	14.9	24.5
Number of victimizations		
Crimes of violence	5,638,350	937,960
Rape	135,420	31,460
Robbery	890,570	276,010
Aggravated assault	1,526,060	292,790
Simple assault	3,086,300	337,700
Crimes of theft	13,172,080	1,630,430
Personal larceny with contact	427,970	118,680
Personal larceny without contact	12,744,110	1,511,740
Household crimes	15,063,000	2,448,720
Burglary	5,426,690	1,017,850
Household larceny	8,518,440	1,200,880
Motor vehicle theft	1,117,880	229,980
Number of persons	163,599,680	21,159,700
Number of households	74,945,970	9,392,490

Note:
[a] The victimization rate is the annual average of the number of victimizations for 1979–86 per 1,000 persons or households in that racial group. Detail may not add to total because of rounding.
Source: Whitaker 1990, Table 1.

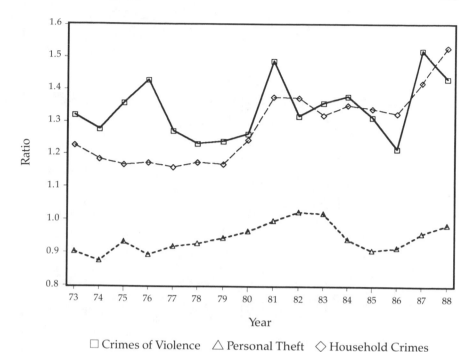

Ratio

☐ Crimes of Violence △ Personal Theft ◇ Household Crimes

Figure 6.13. Black to white ratios of criminal victimization, 1973–1988.

ratio of black to white victimization rates as the essential indicator. As indicated, black rates of violent victimization and household crimes consistently exceed white rates, while whites typically experience a somewhat greater rate of theft.

In Table 6.13, race-specific criminal victimization rates are further broken down by victim's family income for the years 1965–1966, 1979, and 1990. Although the income categories change over time and some specific crimes are not comparable across years, these data demonstrate generally that poor people are more likely than the affluent to be victims of violent crime regardless of race, and that blacks are more likely victims than whites, regardless of income.

With respect to property (vs. violent) crimes, the pattern is not as clear, but if we set aside larceny without contact, victimization remains higher among the less affluent and among blacks. Thus, whatever the specific type of crime in question, blacks and poor people typically experience higher rates of criminal victimization.

Finally, it is well known that residential location plays an important role in patterns of victimization; crime, that is, tends to be largely an urban

Table 6.13. Criminal Victimization Rates per 100,000 Persons by Race and Income, 1965–1966, 1979, 1990

	Family Income in Current Dollars			
	≤$2,999	$3,000–$5,999	$6,000–$9,999	≥ $10,000
	Family Income in Constant 1980 Dollars			
	≤$7,829	$7,830–$15,659	$1,660–$26,099ª	≥ $26,100
Panel A: 1965–1966				
Type of Victimization				
Forcible Rapeᵇ				
White	58	46	10	17
Black & others	111	60	121	—
Robbery				
White	116	91	42	34
Black & others	278	240	121	—
Aggravated assault				
White	146	289	147	220
Black & others	389	420	121	—
Burglary				
White	1310	958	764	763
Black & others	1336	1261	2056	—
Larceny ($130ᶜˑᵈ)				
White	378	700	565	916
Black & others	501	300	363	—

	Family Income in Current Dollars					
	≤ $2,999	$3,000–$7,499	$7,500–$9,999	$10,000–$14,999	$15,000–$24,999	≥ $25,000
	Family Income in Constant 1980 Dollars					
Panel B: 1979	≤ $3,419	$3,420–$8,549	$8,550–$11,399	$11,400–$17,099	$17,100–$28,499	≥ $28,500
Type of victimization						
Rape and attempted rape[b]						
White	314	168	118	127	72	65
Black & others	467	99	342	120	30	0
Robbery						
White	758	807	744	586	401	439
Black & others	1632	1455	905	1474	455	894
Aggravated assault						
White	2183	1173	1477	971	910	678
Black & others	1819	1320	2038	1364	766	738
Burglary						
White	—	—	—	—	—	—
Black & others	—	—	—	—	—	—
Personal larceny with contact[c]						
White	474	385	257	220	182	230
Black & others	786	511	456	730	469	204

Table 6.13 continued

		Family Income in Current Dollars					
	≤ $7,499	$7,500–$9,999	$10,000–$14,999	$15,000–$24,999	$25,000–$29,999	$30,000–$29,999	≥ $50,000
			Family Income in Constant 1980 Dollars				
Panel C: 1990	≤ $4,729	$4,730–$6,307	$6,308–$9,460	$9,461–$15,767	$15,768–$18,921	$18,922–$31,535	≥ $31,535
Type of Victimization							
Rape[e]							
White	130	30	140	70	30	50	40
Black	130	—	—	50	—	—	270
Robbery							
White	790	810	680	500	280	280	280
Black	1950	1100	1410	1040	910	950	940
Aggravated assault							
White	1350	1010	1120	740	640	580	390
Black	1560	1100	1990	1030	700	550	1010
Theft[f]							
White	6610	5010	5170	5710	5440	5760	6890
Black	4970	3970	6900	5650	7170	7120	6720
Personal larceny with contact[c]							
White	430	360	260	320	290	170	320
Black	900	390	270	330	320	620	350

Notes:
[a] Blacks & others data for all families with incomes ≥ $15,660.
[b] Includes attempted rape according to Murray (1984, p. 260).
[c] See differences with larceny in other years.
[d] $130 or more in constant 1980 dollars.
[e] Does not include attempted or statutory rape.
[f] Category is not comparable to earlier burglary category.
Sources: Panel A: Ennis 1967, p. 31. Panel B: Murray 1984, p. 260. Panel C: U.S. Department of Justice, Bureau of Justice Statistics 1992, Table 16.

problem. Blacks and low-income persons suffer from higher rates of crime regardless of city size, but these racial and income disparities are most pronounced in central city areas with the highest crime rates.

SUMMARY

All societies promote acceptable behavior among their members with a series of rewards and sanctions whose moral force and behavioral consequences depend on a social contract. This contract (between society and its members) imposes obligations and responsibilities on all parties while simultaneously granting rights and rewards. Granting rights and rewards to some and systematically denying them to others undermines or perhaps dissolves that tacit contract.

The urban underclass has become a surplus population in every sense of the word: economic, political, and social. The underclass has effectively been excluded from the compact that otherwise binds society together. If we are to insist that the underclass hold up its end of the social contract, then we, society as a whole, must do the same. How much longer can we afford to exclude an entire class of the urban population?

To reiterate the essential theme: Without some realistic sense of a better future, there is little or no reason to conform to the mores and expectations of mainstream society, little or no reason to aspire to its benefits when the reality of one's existence precludes their attainment. Within the inner city we are witnessing the unraveling of the social fabric and the dissolution of the social contract; the evidence reviewed in this chapter has recorded some of the details of the process.

Entrenched, concentrated, and chronic poverty fuels social pathologies that now thrive in the inner city. Despair has replaced hope, predation has replaced aspiration, and society at large suffers the inevitable consequences. As we have attempted to argue here, what is often seen as pathological is frequently a rational, realistic response to distorted social conditions. If the essential reality is as we have described it—an entire class of people with no stake in their own future—then it is that reality which must be changed. Just how this might be accomplished is a topic we consider in the final chapter.

NOTES

1. These are the "words of one ethicist" quoted by Levine and Dubler 1990, p. 322.

2. An illuminating and sensitive discussion of this phenomenon and its associated perceptual and interactional consequences is contained in Anderson (1990).

3. Among historians and others, the relationship between black family instability and slavery is widely disputed. Gutman (1976), for instance, argues that the family structure of slaves and free people of color paralleled that of whites with the overwhelming majority of African-Americans living in nuclear families. Thus, black family disorganization is deemed a more recent phenomenon. The alternative view is aptly captured in Moynihan (1965).

4. Nonmarital births represent one of the two main mechanisms that result in single-parent, female-headed households, the other being family dissolution owing to divorce, separation, death, or abandonment. Inasmuch as we have previously documented rates of poverty within female-headed households (Chapter 3), we confine the present discussion to out-of-wedlock births.

5. Moralistic policies that advocate "just say no" while withholding contraception and contraceptive education are decidedly absurd inasmuch as they simply deny the reality of teenage sexuality. At the same time, making contraception available on demand without any attendant changes in the structural conditions that promote illegitimacy will only have a marginal impact on the problem.

6. The literature on family disorganization within the black community is quite extensive and controversial. See Hacker (1987, 1992) and Wilson (1987) for useful overviews and summaries.

7. The reference here is to the late and unlamented candidacy of David Duke for governor of Louisiana, who promised to "do something" (just what was not clear) about the state's "welfare mess." Louisiana has no state welfare system in place; its annual outlay for "welfare" consists principally in the state's matching contribution to federal outlays for Louisiana's AFDC recipients. (Duke also made vague references to reforming the food stamp program, apparently unaware that this is a federal program in its entirety, with no contributions from the states and with no state jurisdiction over eligibility criteria or benefit levels.)

8. The data in these tables and figures only reflect the *federal* welfare expenditure; the *total* expenditure is higher inasmuch as states and localities also spend on AFDC, general assistance, and the like. See Chapter 7 for more details.

9. Though complete data are not available beyond 1988, preliminary data indicate that the decline in the purchasing power of AFDC has continued since 1988.

10. The current official governmental operationalization of unemployment refers to those persons who had no employment but were available for work, and (1) had engaged in any specific jobseeking activity within the past 4 weeks, such as registering at a public or private employment office, meeting with prospective employers, checking with friends or relatives, placing or answering advertisements, writing letters of application, or being on a union or professional register; (2) were waiting to be called back to a job from which they had been laid off; or (3) were waiting to report to a new wage or salary job within thirty days (see U.S. Bureau of the Census 1991c, p. 198).

11. Due to data availability, specifically, pre-1976 data on black educational attainment, the college and postgraduate degree percentages in Table 6.6 are computed as a percent of high school graduates in the same year rather than for

the college and postgraduate cohorts themselves. While less than optimal, this should not distort the basic trends we discuss.

12. The inexpensiveness and potency of crack cocaine have made it the clear drug of choice among the inner city poverty population. In New Orleans, one of the poorest of major United States cities, crack first made its appearance in 1986. Once introduced, it spread epidemically and quickly ravaged already deeply impoverished and tenuous neighborhoods, bringing with it violence on an unprecedented scale. In New York, Washington, Chicago, Detroit, Atlanta, Philadelphia and virtually every other large United States city, this same basic scenario has been replayed.

13. As indicated in note "a" of Table 6.10, the pre-1978 data (in column 1) pertain to all non-white males rather than blacks only as do the data since 1978. The latter data indicate that the homicide statistics for blacks only consistently run higher than the nonwhite data, indicating that the early part of the time series actually underestimates the black male homicide rate by 3–8 per 100,000.

14. In 1988, there were 10.2 million black males fifteen years of age and older. With a homicide rate of 57.5 per 100,000, this translates into approximately 5865 deaths. If black males had the same homicide rate as white males (7.7 per 100,000), the resulting death toll would be only 785 deaths.

15. In 1988, African-Americans comprised 12.3% of the U.S. population (U.S. Bureau of the Census 1990, table 11).

7

An Agenda for the Future

INTRODUCTION

American society at the brink of the twenty-first century presents us with a troubling contradiction. On the one hand, we are a remarkably affluent society whose economic achievements and standard of living are the envy of the rest of the world. And yet we find ourselves saddled with a higher poverty rate, a higher crime rate, a higher infant mortality rate, more homelessness, more drug abuse, more violence, more hunger, than any other advanced Western democracy. Despite pious incantation, we are not "one nation, under God." Rather, we have become two nations: the first a nation of affluence, where material well-being is taken largely for granted, and the second a nation of poverty, where desperation, deprivation, and violence are the rule. Surely, this is not the example we want to set for the world or the legacy we wish to bequeath to our children.

Although no known present-day society has managed to eliminate poverty altogether, many have found the means and the political will to reduce the level of poverty well below the American standard. If other advanced industrial societies can do this, then so, surely, can we. Thus steps that might be taken to reverse the developments about which we have written comprise the topic of this concluding chapter. Our interest is in what can and should be done to make the American Dream equally available to all citizens, to create a society that is as free of poverty as it can be, one that truly offers "liberty and justice for all." At the same time, we do not intend this to be an exercise in utopian fantasy, but rather a blueprint for practical action towards attainable goals. Thus, desirability must be balanced against feasibility, merit against cost, good will against the practical economic, social, and political realities of present-day American life.

The essence of realism in thinking about poverty, and especially about the underclass poverty that has been the focal theme of this book, is the grudging but firm acknowledgment that all will not be saved. God, it is said, has a place in heaven for all His children, but on earth, or at least in our particular corner of it, one finds a large number of impoverished

189

inner city residents who have passed the point of no return and for whom an independent, productive adult existence is, by now, probably out of the question. This is not to say, as others indeed have said, that we must be prepared to write off an entire generation and start over with the next. It is to affirm, rather, that there has arisen in the central city underclass a discernibly large stratum of (predominantly) young people whose futures already amount to a choice between permanent dependency and early death.

We think it obvious beyond all question that this stratum of lost and hopeless souls does not number 33 million people or even anything close to that figure. That is to say, the largest share of the American poverty problem can indeed be solved. To solve it requires, we think, fundamental new directions (or, in more than a few cases, resurrection of old but now-abandoned directions) in income and welfare policy, in employment and education policy, in health care and substance abuse policy, and in a host of other policy arenas, many of which are discussed later in this chapter. But even if we were to do *everything* that needs to be done, everything that *could* be done, we would still find ourselves burdened with a residual group of permanently impoverished, estranged, and hostile persons who resist our every effort, persons who, through "their own folly and vice," will forever remain outside the mainstream.

In Chapter 6 we discussed the inner logic of the underclass, and attempted to show that from the viewpoint of impoverished inner city residents, much of the behavior that society at large finds aberrant and abhorrent indeed has an explicable rationale. That is to say, within the practical day-to-day reality of inner city life, behavioral decisions that people make can be understood as realistic adaptations to existing economic, social, and cultural conditions. If one wishes to alter those behavioral decisions—and we clearly do—then the obvious key is to alter the conditions to which they are a response. As we have suggested, the essential reality in this connection is an entire class of people who no longer have any realistic future to which they might aspire. Thus the solution to the problem of the underclass is to change this essential reality. Just how this might be accomplished is the topic we consider in this chapter.

It proves useful to begin the discussion with a recitation of first principles, certain basic propositions that we assume to be self-evident and that form the basis for what follows. It is not that we consider these to be inarguable principles; rather, we choose simply not to argue them. We think they are the sorts of things that most sensible people would agree with; whether this is true or not, these few basic points comprise the valuative framework for our discussion.

First, *it is better to work for a living than to be given handouts.* Productive labor (including, to be sure, the rearing of children) is the main responsibility of every functioning adult member of society; it is the means by which each person contributes to the collective good. Moreover, work is an essential component of self-esteem, a principal means of achieving a sense of personal worth. There is no value in being a parasite and no reason for society to support parasites. Those who are poor through indolence and sloth, who remain in degraded and impoverished conditions even in the face of every opportunity to improve themselves, have no legitimate claim to our compassion or our money.

At the same time, *society has an obligation to provide all people with the opportunity and means to make their maximum positive contribution to the collective good.* If all who can work are expected to work, then there must be ample work to go around. And the wages to be earned from work must be sufficient to provide an acceptable standard of living; otherwise the insistence on work has no practical or moral force. It is the responsibility of society at large to provide the opportunities by which each person can fit himself or herself for their productive adult roles.

Although work is always preferable to handouts, *there are many persons in this and all other societies who, through no fault of their own, cannot work and who must therefore be maintained at a comfortable level through appropriate social programs.* The aged and infirm, the physically disabled, the mentally ill, the maimed, and the deformed represent permanently dependent groups in society for whom the insistence on productive labor is pointless. In such cases, it is preferable that the requisite care and support be provided by the families involved, but families often lack the resources or will to do so. Government programs can and should compensate for the inability of families to support their dependent members, whether children or adults.

A degree of inequality in the distribution of the social good is a necessary feature of modern society. Some, that is, will have more and earn more than others; perfect equality is neither desirable nor attainable. *Extreme material deprivation, however, is not essential or desirable in any way,* and neither is extreme wealth. It is sometimes argued that poverty fulfills certain critical "functions" in a complex society. The prospect of poverty represents the stick that keeps the rest of the society hard at work; the existence of poverty maintains an essential definitional boundary that demarcates the middle class. These arguments are without merit. Even if the clever apologist can conjure up something positive about the existence of poverty, the social dysfunction created by our current poverty situation dwarfs any modest positive function. More equality in the distribution of well-being and less material deprivation are unalloyed goods.

All societies and all subgroups within societies develop their own unique customs and values that we identify as cultures or subcultures;

this is as true of the poor as it is of any other group. But *the extreme relativist position—that all cultures and subcultures have equal legitimacy and are therefore to be supported and defended—is counter-productive, and nonsensical.* That some cultures sacrifice virgins to appease their gods or to launch their canoes does not make it an acceptable or valuable practice. That there are groups within society who think it is okay to spend one's day hanging out drunk or stoned on the street corner does not mean that it is. One can defend the right of people to be "different" or to reject "middle-class" values and at the same time condemn attitudes, outlooks, and behaviors that detract from the collective societal good. At the same time, ethnocentrism, racism, and xenophobia have no legitimate place in modern society. There is every difference between cultural elements that detract from the collective well-being and elements that annoy us or that we simply don't like. Loud music can be an annoyance; thuggery degrades the aggregate quality of life.

Affluence is preferable to poverty; it is better to have money than to be without it. The cleric's vows of poverty may be spiritually uplifting but only if the sheer essentials of food, clothing, and shelter can be assumed. In the absence of these essentials, nothing about poverty is ennobling. Likewise, *health is preferable to illness and satiation is preferable to want.* Self-denial is often a virtue and piggery a vice, but the aching gut that results from too little to eat is damaging to the flesh and spirit.

All else equal, *it is better that children be raised and cared for by their parents than in foster care or institutional settings.* Conversely, it is the responsibility and obligation of parents to care for their children and thus not to bear children that they cannot comfortably support. Policies that foster family dissolution or excessive childbearing are perverse. *Intact families are better than broken families;* that is, it is better for children to be raised by two parents than by one, if for no other reason than that the presence of two parents doubles the potential resources available to raise the child.

Many people come into this world with deficits over which they have no control; these might be the deficits of genetic inheritance, or inadequate maternal nutrition, or the deficits of race, class, or culture. No persons should suffer or be punished for that over which they have no control; to the contrary, *every effort should be made to compensate for any initial deficits and to enable a independent, productive adult existence in spite of them.* Among the many deficits that need concern us, being born into poverty is perhaps the most consequential, and we shall discuss at length later just what society might do to compensate for this terrible accident of birth.

Wisdom is preferable to ignorance; the proper goal of the educational system is to create informed and intelligent citizens and fit them for a productive social role. While everyone has an undeniable right to his or her own heritage, everyone has an equal right to be instructed in matters necessary for successful, independent existence. Talent, unquestionably, is unevenly distributed in any population, but even the least talented deserve the opportunity to develop what talents they do have, just as society as a whole has an obligation to provide them with something worthwhile to do.

Finally, American society is not so exceptional or unique that we cannot profit from the lessons of other societies. Measures that successfully reduce poverty in Germany or Canada are likely to be successful here. If the Dutch have found a way to eliminate their drug problem, there is no *a priori* reason why we cannot do the same. If Japanese students consistently do better in math and science than American students, it is probably not the result of innate genetic differences between them and us; it is because they are doing things educationally that we are not. Emulating the positive experiences of other industrial democracies, and avoiding their mistakes, is not "un-American"; rather, the failure to do so is stupid.

POVERTY, POLICY, AND ECONOMICS

What do existing antipoverty programs cost us? What does poverty itself cost us? What is a realistic, workable budget for a 1990s version of a War on Poverty? These are obviously not idle questions; in an era of massive federal deficits, we would be hard pressed to afford policy initiatives that might add tens or hundreds of billions to the annual federal expenditure, especially if there were no compensating benefit.

There is no easy way to calculate the overall cost of poverty to the nation as a whole. Some of these costs—for example, the annual expenditure on Aid to Families with Dependent Children (AFDC)—are direct, expressible in dollars, and easy enough to look up. Other costs—for example, the costs of treating poverty-related diseases—are also direct and theoretically expressible in dollars, but these costs are buried in the general health care expenditure and virtually impossible to isolate as a separate item. Still other costs are indirect and not readily expressible in monetary terms: for example, the aesthetic and symbolic costs we must all bear as a result of the continuing physical deterioration of central city poverty neighborhoods.

The total annual federal budget these days conveniently rounds off to one and a half trillion dollars. About half that sum is spent on social and human services. Spending on specific antipoverty programs amounts to something less than $200 billion annually, less than 15% of the total federal budget and less than 30% of the social and human services budget. The largest single federal outlay is for indigent health care, principally Medicaid, which in recent years has been on the order of $50 billion annually (to which one would need to add contributions by the states). A second major outlay is for Aid to Families with Dependent Children (AFDC), the costs of which have averaged about $25–30 billion per year. (AFDC costs are also shared with the states.) The Food Stamp program adds $20 or $25 billion to the total; various HUD housing subsidies and Section Eight certificates add another $20 billion. State expenditures on general welfare (relief, general assistance) total less than $10 billion annually. Combined annual federal and state expenditures on all the above programs therefore total somewhere in the neighborhood of $180–$200 billion. Other antipoverty programs (e.g., WIC, Head Start) represent small pittances by comparison. So the annual direct expenditure on antipoverty programs is on the order of $200 billion, give or take 20 billion.

Two hundred billion dollars a year is a large sum but is not by any means the total cost we pay for the poverty in our midst. For example, it is obvious that poverty dramatically worsens the American crime problem; most crime is committed by young men who lack legitimate alternative means to support themselves. Direct federal, state, and local expenditures for criminal justice—for police, courts, and prisons—amount to about $65 billion yearly. To this one would have also to add the dollar value of property lost through crime (conservatively on the order of $10 billion annually), the costs of treating persons injured by criminal violence, the sums paid by businesses and individuals to protect themselves from crime, and so on. When all is said and done, it is easy to imagine that crime costs the nation at least another $100 billion or so a year; that half of this is a direct result of poverty is probably a reasonable assumption.

Poverty is also directly implicated in the nation's drug and alcohol problems. Drug and alcohol abuse is estimated to cost the nation another $100 billion or so per year in lost productivity alone; other costs (e.g., for treatment, antidrug education and programs, drug interdiction efforts) are not directly known but are presumably high. Just what fraction of these costs can be ascribed to poverty is also unknown, but here too, half seems a reasonable assumption.

Some but certainly not all of the poverty-related health care costs are subsumed in the annual expenditure on Medicaid. First of all, many poor people are not covered by Medicaid. In many states, for example, *only* persons receiving AFDC are eligible for Medicaid, a restriction that leaves many of the poor uncovered (especially single males). Indeed, there are about 37 million Americans who lack health insurance of any sort, whether private or public, and the largest share of them are poor or near-poor. Lacking health care insurance, the uninsured rarely receive medical attention until their condition has degenerated to emergency status, at which point they seek care in hospital emergency rooms (where by law and custom care cannot be denied to persons unable to pay). Just how much this arrangement costs us is anybody's guess, but emergency room care is the most expensive form of health care available. Many recent public health trends are directly related to the poverty situation, among them AIDS, the increasing incidence of tuberculosis, and the venereal disease epidemic. What have these trends added to the annual health bill? How much productivity is lost annually when poor people miss days of work because they cannot afford to see a doctor or purchase medication? What does it cost us to provide neonatal intensive care when poor mothers give birth to high-risk infants because appropriate prenatal attention was not forthcoming?

Every state has an office of child and youth services (they go by many different names) and a foster care system; most of the children who go through this system are children of the poor. Often, the payments made by the states to foster parents handsomely exceed the equivalent AFDC payments. The costs of the foster care system, case investigators, social workers, administrators, and so on are dispersed across fifty state budgets and so cannot be easily estimated, but they are certain to be considerable.

Poverty youth are strongly overrepresented among high school dropouts and contribute disproportionally to the problem of teen pregnancy. Teenage pregnancies tend to be high risk and therefore to pose additional burdens to the health care system; the children of teenage mothers often end up in foster care. In many central city public school districts, it has become common for half or more of the students to leave school before completing their degrees. Teenage mothers and high school dropouts often become a permanent part of the underskilled, undereducated labor force that contributes to America's lack of competitiveness in the world economy and whose annual costs in lost potential productivity must run well into the tens of billions of dollars. It is worth asking, how many possible computer operators, scientists, nurses, police officers, teachers, or day care workers do we lose annually when discouraged and hostile youth leave school prematurely? And what does it cost us as a nation to do without the inventions, products, and services they might have otherwise provided? The same question might be asked of the twenty or thirty infants out of every thousand who are born to the poor but fail to survive their first year of life. (The rate of infant mortality among the poor is about three times the rate for children of the middle class.) How many potential Thurgood Marshalls or Colin Powells or Ralph Bunches or Martin Luther Kings do we bury each year?

It is not possible to add everything up and get to a bottom-line statement about what poverty costs us, but the order of magnitude is clearly somewhere in the hundreds of billions annually. As a rule of thumb, one would be on apparently defensible grounds in assuming that the total cost is on the order of a half trillion dollars a year, which in turn is something like a tenth of the gross national product. Costs of this magnitude provide nearly overwhelming economic justification for efforts to reduce the rate of poverty, whatever additional justifications might be offered on other grounds. After all, if a billion dollar increase in anti-poverty spending would produce a 2 billion dollar reduction in criminal justice or health care costs, then it would be rational to spend that billion and foolish not to. By any reckoning, poverty costs us a great deal of money and so we can afford to spend a great deal of money to be rid of it.

NATIONAL INCOME AND WELFARE POLICY

How much money, then, would it take to be rid of poverty altogether? And how might one go about getting that money into the hands of the poor? The first of these is a question about what is called the income deficit—the difference between the aggregate income of persons below the poverty line and the income they would need to be above it; the second is a question about a workable, equitable, distributional mechanism.

There are, as we have said, about 33 million persons below poverty in the United States. Some of them are very far below the poverty line and would therefore need a large increase in income; others are only slightly below the line. In general, the average (median) income of persons in poverty is about half the corresponding poverty line (adjusted for household size). In 1990, the poverty income deficit amounted to about $60 billion, or approximately $1,700 per poor person. This, interestingly enough, is about what the federal government spends annually on Medicaid and AFDC combined, which is to say that it is not an oppressively large or unattainable sum.[1]

Properly distributed, then, $60 billion per year would raise every person and household in the United States above the current poverty line, and that would effectively mean the end of poverty as we presently define it. At the least, it would mean the end of extreme material deprivation. This would *not* assure a comfortable middle-class existence to every household; to the contrary, life right at the poverty line is only marginally more comfortable than life below it. But a $60 billion annual expenditure would guarantee to all a minimal standard of living below which no one would be allowed to fall. In terms of national income policy, this amounts to a *guaranteed annual income* (GAI).

The customary reaction to GAI proposals is that they would destroy the motivation to work and thereby wreak havoc with the national labor supply. If all persons receive a guaranteed income whether they work or not, then why bother to work in the first place? But it is a simple matter to develop GAI policies such that people are *always* better off by working than not working, through the expedient of what is called *negative income taxation* (NIT).

Let us illustrate how NIT works with a simple example. First, any given NIT scheme is defined by two parameters: a guarantee level (the income below which no one is allowed to fall) and the effective tax rate on earned income. For purposes of this example, we will use the 1990 poverty line for a single individual, $6,800, as the guarantee level and 50% as the tax rate. Now, imagine a single person who has had no earned income in a given year (that is, who did not work at all). This person would receive a transfer payment in the amount of $6,800 over the course of the year (presumably, in the form of monthly checks for $567 per month). Next, imagine a single person whose earned income for the year was $5,000. Since the tax rate on earned income in this example is 50%, then the person's income would equal the guarantee ($6,800) plus 50% of the earned income ($2,500) or $9,300, and the annual transfer payment would be the difference between that sum and the earned income, or $4,300. Thus, the person who earns $5,000 per year ends up with $9,300 in spendable income and is therefore much better off than the person with no earnings who must, perforce, survive on the guarantee alone.

Two additional features of NIT schemes can now be pointed out. First, they are called *negative* income tax schemes because up to a certain point, the annual income tax owed is *negative*, not positive. In the above example, the person with the earned income of $5,000 was owed an additional $4,300 at the end of the year. Secondly, that "certain point" is the *break-even* level at which point persons fall over into the positive income tax brackets. If the tax rate on earned income is 50%, then the break-even point would be twice the guarantee level, so that (in the above example), a single person with earnings of $13,600 would receive no transfer (and also pay no tax) and a person with earnings of more than $13,600 would pay the usual tax on all earnings above the break-even point.

In theory, NIT is an attractive alternative to conventional approaches to welfare because NIT provides work incentives by allowing earners to retain a fractional portion of their earnings without sacrificing any portion of the guarantee level. This can be contrasted with existing welfare programs, which tend to reduce the transfer payment dollar for dollar against every dollar of earned income. (Thus, an AFDC recipient typically has her AFDC check reduced by one dollar for each dollar she earns through work.) In essence, existing welfare programs tax earnings at the rate of 100%, so that the person is no better off by working than not working. The appeal of NIT schemes of the sort sketched here is that people are *always* better off if they work than if they are idle; at the same time, all persons are guaranteed a minimal standard of living whether they work or not.

A second strong appeal of NIT schemes is their administrative simplicity. A negative income tax program can be implemented within the existing structure of the Internal Revenue Service. Basically, at the end of Year One of such a program, everyone calculates his or her income tax statement (just as everyone now does). Based on the tax statements, the guarantee levels, and the tax rates, the IRS would determine whether the filer was in the negative or positive brackets. Those in the positive brackets would be assessed the taxes owed (just as they currently are); for those in the negative brackets, the necessary transfer would be calculated and persons would be sent a monthly check each month of the following tax year that represented their guarantee for the previous year. Thus the transfer payments would always reflect the person's income situation of the previous year, whereas the determination of eligibility would be based on earned income in the current year. This, needless to say, represents a vast simplification of the existing welfare bureaucracy that administers AFDC, SSI, SSDI, Unemployment Compensation, the Food Stamp program and a wild congerie of other federal, state, and local income transfer programs, all of which could be readily subsumed under an NIT program administered through the IRS tax system, at considerable savings in the administrative overhead.

Yet another appeal of NIT schemes is their equity. In essence, the NIT scheme sketched above represents a single national income and welfare policy whose eligibility requirements and payment levels are the same in every state—this in sharp contrast to the existing system of separate programs, separate eligibility standards, and different payment levels in each state. NIT thus represents the nationally standardized welfare policy that welfare rights proponents have advocated for several decades. It would also address the perverse problems introduced by large state-to-state differences in the generosity of welfare benefits, differences that cause (for example) poor people in Illinois to attempt to receive welfare in Wisconsin, where benefits are much more generous (*Newsweek*, 1992, p. 6).

There are many similarities between NIT schemes and our current tax and welfare system; an NIT approach is *not* a radical departure from existing arrangements in certain important respects. At present, persons with incomes below a certain level owe no tax and are not even required to file; under an NIT scheme, persons with incomes below the break-even point would also owe no tax (instead, they would receive a transfer payment). At present, eligible persons with sufficiently low incomes receive monthly cash transfer payments from the government (in the form of AFDC or other welfare checks); under an NIT scheme, the same would be true. At present, the earned incomes of welfare recipients are effectively taxed at the rate of 100%; under an NIT scheme, they would be taxed at something less than 100% (and in our suggested scheme, at 50%). At present, certain forms and amounts of income are exempt from taxation; under an NIT scheme, *all* earned income up to the break-even point is exempt from taxation. The principal difference between current arrangements and an NIT approach is that the latter is administratively much simpler and more equitable, and does *not*, at least in theory, remove the incentive to work. GAI and NIT thus represent a simple, expedient, workable alternative to the existing welfare system that would effectively eliminate poverty and guarantee a minimum standard of living to all.

Still, many find it hard to shake the fear that if we guarantee all persons a certain income whether they work or not, many among the poor will content themselves with the guarantee and choose not to work (despite the economic advantage that accrues under NIT to those who do work). A number of large-scale field experiments were undertaken in the late 1960s and early 1970s to assess this very possibility, and as a matter of fact, the results of these experiments did *not* show generally significant reductions in labor force effort among poor persons whose incomes were guaranteed through an NIT scheme.

One of the most comprehensive reviews of the methods and findings of the many NIT experiments is by Rossi and Lyall (1976). These experiments were undertaken in a number of urban areas in New Jersey and Pennsylvania (the experiment discussed by Rossi and Lyall), in Denver and Seattle, in Gary, Indiana, in Manitoba, and elsewhere. All of them tested variations on the NIT approach to income maintenance through diverse combinations of guarantee levels and tax rates. The basic design of all the experiments was quite similar. Samples of the poor were enrolled in the study and randomly assigned to either treatment or control groups. Persons and households in the treatment groups were given a guaranteed annual income through some NIT scheme (defined by the specific guarantee level and tax rate for any particular treatment condition); persons in the control groups were interviewed regularly (usually quarterly) but had no income guarantee. All the experiments ran for periods ranging from three to five years. A large number of outcome variables were monitored, such as family stability, attitudes, labor force participation, and earnings.

It is difficult to summarize the results of these several large, complex social experiments in a few sentences. The labor supply response of men to NIT was somewhat different than that of women, and there were also some important differences by ethnicity. Concerning male heads of households (that is, married men), "the measurable effect of experimental treatments . . . was generally very small and almost never statistically significant" (Rossi and Lyall 1976, p. 113), this in definite contrast to the image of the "NIT 'goldbricker' . . . who dropped out of the labor force to live on his guarantee." That is, the labor force behavior of poor male heads of households whose incomes were being guaranteed through NIT was identical to that of the control group. The pattern for wives was somewhat more complicated: white women showed a relatively substantial percentage *reduction* in labor force activity in the treatment condition; black and Hispanic women showed either no change or some increase. Still, the overall reduction in labor supply in the least favorable case, white married women, was on the order of 9% (i.e., these women worked 9% fewer hours if their incomes were being maintained than if not). All scholars who are familiar with the NIT experiments understand full well that they are by no means definitive, but they provide the best data we have on how poor persons respond to an income guarantee. And there is little or no solid evidence in these data to suggest substantial reductions in aggregate work effort.

It is also inappropriate to consider the "work disincentives" that might be posed by a GAI/NIT scheme of the sort we have discussed (or other related problems) in isolation from the rather massive disincentives of the current system. Consider the situation of a poor, black, uneducated, untrained, single central city woman with two children. For most women of this description (and for poor people generally), "work" implies a low-skill job with no benefits at the minimum wage. Assuming full-time, year-round employment, this woman can expect to earn about $8,500 (2000 hours at $4.25 an hour = $8,500). The poverty line (in 1990) for this three-person household (one adult and two dependent children) is $10,530; thus, this woman cannot escape poverty simply by working, even full time year round. In fact, under these circumstances, this woman would still be eligible for food stamps. If she is working forty hours a week, there will also be day care costs that further reduce her effective income (especially if her children are young and not in school), and since minimum wage jobs rarely provide health insurance coverage, she will either have to pay for a private health insurance plan (a very unlikely strategy because of the expense), or pay for health care for herself and her children on a fee-for-service basis (also unlikely, for the same reason), or do without medical care (the most probable of the three).

Consider in contrast this same woman's situation if she is not working but survives instead on AFDC. In the more generous states, AFDC eligibility means that she will receive (1) a monthly cash payment of several hundred dollars (the national average monthly AFDC cash payment is about $350, or roughly half the monthly minimum wage), (2) a Section 8 housing certificate that subsidizes the monthly rent, (3) a monthly allotment of food stamps to subsidize the costs of groceries, and (4) a Medicaid card that will provide health care for her and her children at no cost. Further, since she is not working and can care for the children herself, she incurs no day care expenses. One need not be an antiwelfare conservative to understand that this woman is much better off on welfare than at work.

This is not to say that our AFDC recipient is "well off" or that she and her children live comfortably on these AFDC benefits. Adding up the transfer payment and the cash value of the housing subsidy and food stamp allotment would still leave this woman well below the poverty line. She will prefer welfare to work—in a word, will become welfare dependent—*not* because the welfare alternative is so attractive but because work with no benefits at the minimum wage is so *un*attractive. And that is perhaps the leading absurdity of our current welfare and income situation, one that a national NIT program would resolve.

The relevant question, then, is not whether an GAI/NIT approach would give us the best of all possible worlds, but whether such an approach would represent an affordable improvement in human well-being. AFDC and other welfare programs exist in the first place because we believe—at least for certain classes of people such as children, the elderly, and the disabled—that there is a minimum standard of living below which people should not be allowed to fall. The guaranteed annual income approach that we recommend simply extends this noble idea to the entire American population. And we further believe, on the basis of solid evidence, that an NIT mechanism of the sort we have discussed could accomplish this end and still reward people for working.

Yet another advantage of an NIT approach is that it would essentially define a certain minimum standard of living as a right of citizenship guaranteed to all (just like the right to vote or to speak freely) and thereby remove the stigma associated with being "on welfare." It would also replace our current cumbersome and degrading welfare process—an endless and demeaning process of eligibility determination and recertification, long lines and hostile caseworkers at the welfare office, the need to go to one office for the food stamp certification, another office for AFDC, and still another for Medicaid—with a simple process geared to the annual income tax statement and administered through the IRS. Finally, GAI/NIT is an attestion that what poor people lack is money, that they can be trusted with cash—this in contrast to our strong present preference to give them programs or non-cash transfers (such as food stamps or housing vouchers or free school lunch programs) instead of cash. An NIT approach to welfare dignifies the poor by guaranteeing them a certain level of money income and letting them assume the responsibility for how it is spent.

There is little doubt that the NIT scheme we have proposed would add somewhat to the annual poverty outlay, especially since many existing programs would still be necessary (especially Medicaid). Still, the total dollar value of means-tested cash transfers in 1990 (mainly AFDC and other public assistance payments, Supplemental Security Income [SSI], and means-tested veterans' payments) was about $31 billion; means-tested noncash benefits (principally food stamps and rent subsidies) added another $30 billion. These two components alone virtually equal the $60 billion in cash transfers necessary to guarantee all people an income above the poverty line. Several additional billions would doubtlessly be saved through the much greater efficiency with which the NIT scheme could be implemented. Thus, a guaranteed standard of living above the poverty line, assured through a negative income tax method that rewarded people for working, could be had for not much more than what we currently spend in cash and noncash benefits to the poor (*not* including the present costs of Medicaid, which would, we feel, remain necessary even under a GAI policy).

The $60 billion annual cost projection for our GAI/NIT scheme, of course, takes the number of the poor as a given, that is, it assumes that we cannot achieve any significant reduction in the number of persons who would fall below the break-even point and thus be eligible for NIT transfer payments. If the number of eligibles were somehow reduced— which is to say, if we could increase the cash earnings of the poor so that more and more of them fell above the break-even point and in the positive tax brackets—then the annual cost of GAI/NIT would obviously fall dramatically.

One obvious method to reduce the numbers of persons who would receive NIT transfer payments under our proposed scheme (or to reduce the average amount of the transfer) would be to raise the minimum wage to a point where full-time, year-round work at the minimum wage would place earners above the break-even point. In our proposed scheme, break-even comes at $13,600 (for a single-person household), and so the corresponding minimum wage would equal $6.80 per hour, an increase of $2.55 per hour over the existing minimum wage. This, in essence, shifts a share of the cost of the guaranteed annual income off the government and onto employers. It also guarantees that full-time work even at the minimum wage would always leave earners better off than the NIT transfer would leave them, thus removing the work disincentive effects of a minimum wage that does not raise earners above the poverty line.

With a minimum wage that exceeds the NIT cutoff and that thus provides an ample incentive to work, and with a GAI/NIT policy in place to guarantee the minimum standard of living to those who cannot work, the next step would be to provide ample work for all who can work. And this brings us to the matter of employment policy, the second major component of an effective antipoverty program.

NATIONAL EMPLOYMENT POLICY

We and many others have identified the high rate of joblessness among central city youth as an essential (even decisive) component of the emergence and development of the American underclass. The exceptional rate of joblessness in the central cities and elsewhere raises an obvious but troubling question, namely, *how can there be so much joblessness when there is so much work to be done?*

Anyone familiar with the American urban scene will have noticed the immense quantity of useful work that needs doing but goes undone. Consider: every major city is plagued to a greater or lesser extent by abandoned and dilapidated houses on the one hand, and by widespread homelessness on the other. All that seemingly separates these houses from the people who need housing is capital to acquire them and labor to make them fit for human habitation. The decay of the nation's physical infrastructure has been widely noted, indeed, has become a matter of urgent national priority and federal initiatives. It is more than mildly ironic that beneath many of our deteriorating bridges sleep men who, with some minimal training, could help repair them. A concerted effort to rebuild the national infrastructure could by itself eliminate joblessness in the central cities. And this is work that needs to be done *now.*

The reconstruction of urban America is by no means the only example of work that needs doing. Every city of which we are aware suffers to some extent from the blight of unmowed lands and uncollected litter; every urban school system has classrooms that would be more attractive and more conducive to learning with a fresh coat of paint; every city street department could profit from more street repair crews. There are serious national shortages of nurses, teachers and teachers' aides, day care workers, and workers in many other "helping professions." Obviously, many of the poor would need considerable training in order to fill these shortages, but this is an asset, not a liability, in that the training need creates work for trainers and thus further stimulates economic growth. (Training the children of the poor for a useful adult role would also give the nation's urban high schools something to do, a point to which we return in a later section.)

Consider, as one example, the day-care problem. There are about 33 million poor people in the United States; of those, 40% are children and a third are the mothers of the children. Many of the mothers, as we have already suggested, find work uneconomic in part because of the day care cost. Training a large cadre of day care workers to provide child care for the dependent children of the poor would thus enable labor force participation among many poor mothers and create day-care employment opportunities at the same time.

How many day care jobs could be created by providing all poor women with day care that would in turn allow them to work? And what would it cost? As a rule of thumb, it can be assumed that about half the children of the poor are under school age; assume further that one trained day care worker can care adequately for five children. These assumptions give us an estimate of about 7 million poor children who need day care and of about 1.4 million new jobs that would be created in providing that care. If these new jobs were compensated at the break-even wage in our proposed GAI/NIT scheme ($13,600 per year), then the entire system would add up to an investment of about $19 billion annually, or roughly the same as the current annual food stamp expenditure.

Consider next what this annual expenditure of $19 billion would buy. First, it would purchase about 1.4 million new nonpoverty jobs for which the currently poor could be trained. Secondly, it would enable the labor force participation of perhaps 12 million poor women for whom the lack of affordable day care is now a substantial barrier. Third, it would create many thousands of training jobs to prepare people for their day care roles. Finally, it would be possible with sufficient training to offer a Head Start type of programming along with custodial day care and thus to give the children of the poor an important advantage as they prepare to begin their schooling.

Much the same could obviously be said about the nation's deteriorating housing stock. Every city in the U.S. finds itself saddled with abandoned and dilapidated housing units on the one hand and with people who need housing on the other. Millions of jobs could be created in a national program to rehabilitate marginal buildings; an ancillary benefit would be a sharp improvement in the housing conditions of the poor.

The point is an obvious one: Given the immense mass of socially useful work that needs to be done and the large numbers of able-bodied people who need useful work to do, allowing widespread joblessness to continue among the able-bodied poor is madness. Economic growth *and* social justice would be equally well served by identifying the work that needs to be done, by training the jobless poor to do it, and by paying a decent (nonpoverty) wage to get it done. In this connection, it is useful to recall one of our first principles. If, as a society, we are to insist that the able bodied work, then there is a corresponding obligation to assure that socially meaningful and amply compensated jobs are available; otherwise, the insistence on work is meaningless, even punitive.

We, of course, are not the first to stumble upon job creation and job training as necessary components of antipoverty policy. To the contrary, the concept has been resurrected on numerous occasions and in numerous guises: the Works Project Administration and the Civilian Conservation Corps of the Depression, the Manpower Development and Training Act (MDTA) programs of the early 1960s, the Job Corps of the War on Poverty, the Comprehensive Employment and Training Act (CETA) programs of the 1970s and early 1980s, and the Job Training Partnership Act (JTPA) programs of today. Indeed, the federal government has been investing in job-related training efforts at least since the Smith-Hughes Act of 1917 (Levitan 1985, p. 117). What has this long history of job training programs taught us? And why, given this history, does the problem of joblessness continue to plague us?

The answer to the second of these questions is reasonably straightforward. Among the more successful of the nation's jobs programs was the CETA program of the 1970s. CETA was a federal-state-local partnership designed to develop employment and training services that were maximally responsive to the local labor market situation. "During the 1970s job creation in the public sector was a major component" of the program (Levitan 1985, p. 116). That is, CETA-participant cities identified public-sector work that needed doing (this ranged from casework in social service agencies to maintenance work in city parks); the CETA program provided funds to train jobless people to do the work, to provide stipends during the training, and to pay the wages necessary to get the work accomplished. In the ideal case, the skills obtained by CETA participants were ones that would later transfer into the local labor market. Evaluation studies of CETA programs found that participants experienced less subsequent unemployment and had higher earnings than nonparticipants; in the peak year of 1978, 750,000 people were employed through CETA programs around the nation.

So what happened? "As part of the Omnibus Budget Reconciliation Act of 1981, however, the [CETA] program was eliminated. No other major job creation program has since been enacted to take its place" (Levitan 1985, p. 117). Indeed, as a result of the Omnibus Budget Reconciliation Act, the overall federal investment in employment and training programs was more than halved, from an outlay in excess of $14 billion in 1980 to less than $7 billion in 1982, with further reductions since. As we have already remarked, the years since 1981 have witnessed an increasing rate of poverty and the rapid deterioration of the urban social and economic situation. Can this just be a spurious correlation?

The successor program to CETA is the JTPA, which relies mainly on tax credits to the private sector for job creation. In and of itself, this is not a bad thing; federal investments that stimulate the creation of private-sector employment should be continued, even expanded. Unfortunately, most of the jobs created via JTPA incentives have been minimum wage jobs that are scarcely better than welfare; indeed, *half* the new jobs created in the 1980s paid an annualized wage less than the poverty line for a family of four. A second problem is that private sector efforts invariably strive to keep the training costs as low as possible, which results in ill-trained workers who are not sufficiently skilled to work at anything other than minimum wage jobs.

A renewed national investment in job training and job creation efforts along the lines of CETA seems to us an eminently sensible recommendation. Structural changes in the international economy and progressive technological upgrading have eliminated vast numbers of jobs from whose earnings workers previously supported families and modest but respectable standards of living; this process has accelerated during the past decade as the federal government has cut back on job training programs. The net result is now equally vast numbers of poorly educated and ill-trained persons with nothing useful to do, persons for whom the available work is scarcely better than welfare (and markedly inferior to the income that can be earned through drug trafficking or crime). Would a policy of full employment at nonpoverty wages, with the public sector as a major employer, wreck the economy or destroy America's competitiveness in the world market, as many evidently fear? Perhaps the better question is, If we cannot find a way to provide gainful and socially useful work for the able-bodied jobless and to compensate them at a nonpoverty wage, then is there any hope at all?

Large numbers of impoverished youth now spend their time hanging out on the street corners getting drunk or stoned, this mainly because they have nothing better to do with their time. Many might prefer to be in school except that the inner city schools are in disarray and do not adequately prepare a young person for a productive economic role in any case. Others might prefer to be in some sort of job training program except that these programs no longer exist. Still others would prefer gainful employment but find that no jobs are available or that the going wage rate is so low that hanging out and getting drunk becomes the preferred alternative. Those who find themselves distressed by this "underclass" behavior and its sequelae—crime, drug use, violence, predation—would do well to ask themselves about the realistic alternatives these young people face.

We have already said that a decade of indifference to the decaying social and economic infrastructure of the inner city has bred an entire class of young people who have no stake in their own future. If we cannot find a way to provide them a realistic and attainable future, then we will continue to live with the consequences. If providing a realistic and attainable future results in some degree of economic dislocation, then so be it. It seems a tolerable trade-off for an urban environment where people are not in constant fear for their lives.

Although the welfare, income and employment schemes suggested above may seem "radical" (and certainly expensive), they are for the most part similar to welfare-state policies that are well established throughout the advanced industrial democracies—nations whose poverty rates are but a fraction of ours. To illustrate, using a constant definition of poverty (40% of the national median income), the poverty rates among families with children in an assortment of advanced industrial nations are as follows (Smeeding and Rainwater 1991):

Sweden:	2.9%	Britain:	8.6%
France:	5.3%	Netherlands:	3.9%
West Germany:	3.1%	United States:	17.5%

There are, to be sure, many differences among these several nations; one of the most important is that the United States is the only nation of the seven that "has failed to give a significant proportion of its poor a measure of income security," which is to say, does not have a guaranteed annual income policy, an income "floor" below which hardly any household is allowed to fall. To varying degrees, the other six also have full employment policies with substantial employment through the public sector. And while the nations listed above are not without their economic and social problems, the citizens of each enjoy a standard of living that compares quite favorably with that of middle-class people in the United States. One will definitely find homeless people in Germany or Canada or the Netherlands, but the homeless problem in these societies pales in comparison to the problem of homelessness here. And by American standards, all six would also be considered virtually crime free. All are burdened with residual pockets of poverty, but the poverty population in each is a matter of a few percent of the total, not a sixth of the national population as in the US case. Can we afford to emulate policies in this nation that have proved successful in reducing (indeed, nearly eliminating) poverty elsewhere in the industrialized West? Or should we ask instead whether we can afford not to?

NATIONAL EDUCATIONAL POLICY

A major cause of joblessness among the inner city young is a system of public education that is in disarray, one that routinely fails to prepare its students for productive adult roles. Dropout rates in urban public high school systems now approach (and in some cases even exceed) 50%; many who stick with it and earn a high school diploma against long odds find that the diploma gives them no advantage in the job market and that their years of high school education have not prepared them for any meaningful workplace role. If public high schools did what they are supposed to do, the need for job training programs of the sort recommended earlier would certainly lessen.

There are, it seems to us, two related aspects of the schooling problem. The first is in keeping young people in school until they earn a diploma; the second is in creating programs and curricula that make it worth one's while to have that diploma. Presumably, solving the second of these problems would go a long way towards solving the first.

Reforming the system of inner city public education confronts the twin barriers of entrenched interest and the dead weight of tradition. Much that is done in the public schools is done for no other reason than that it has always been done. In the meantime it has become commonplace to find high school *graduates* who cannot read past the third-grade level and who are unable to perform the simple arithmetic needed to balance a checkbook. As the mental faculties necessary to do these things are possessed by nearly everyone, one wonders how twelve years of schooling could possibly produce so many students who are apparently unable even to read and write.

There are, it seems to us, three essential missions that must now be pursued in public education (both elementary and secondary). The first and overwhelmingly the most important concerns instruction in essential basic skills—traditional skills such as numeracy, literacy, and the like to be sure, but also increasingly important skills of hygiene, safety, comportment, speech, and others. Many of the nation's inner city schools obviously fail even in this most rudimentary and essential mission. It could have once been assumed, perhaps, that much of the behavioral and intellectual repertoire necessary to function in society would be taught in the home, but this is apparently no longer the case, and since public policy can intervene in the schools more effectively than it can intervene within families, there is little choice but to insist that schools assume these responsibilities.

Schools that do not adequately prepare students for their adult lives are failures in every sense, and in this connection a few essential but easily overlooked priorities can be recommended to the attention of every inner city public school in the nation. Arithmetic is *much* more important than algebra. Arithmetic is an essential skill in negotiating life; algebra is useful mainly to prepare one for the study of geometry, which in turns prepares one for trigonometry, which is essential in learning calculus. It is *much* more important that students be able to read and complete a job application than to have read *Beowulf* or Shakespeare or any other particular piece of text. It is *much* more important to be able to speak, read, and write English than to speak, read, or write in some other language. Ability to communicate with the citizens of other nations is highly desirable; ability to communicate with one's fellow citizens is essential. It is *much* more important to know how the AIDS virus is transmitted than to be able to point to one's kidneys. It is even more important to understand the value of punctuality in the workplace than to understand where or what Canada is. As an absolute first priority, then, the emphasis in the schools should be on these practical, applied skills that have direct utility for successful functioning in later life.

A second mission of the public schools—undeniably important but considerably less important than the first (and even the third, or so we would argue [see below])—is instruction in what might be called the "civil religion," those aspects of geography, history, society, polity, and culture that bind us as a nation. A good deal of the curriculum in any school is devoted to these important but decidedly secondary matters. And surely, this is curriculum that needs to be taught, but not a word of it needs to be mentioned until the basic survival skills have been mastered. Apparently, most of it now gets taught (certainly not learned!) whether the essential skills are present or not, and that, we suggest, is a case of misplaced priorities.

Finally, secondary education needs to prepare students for whatever comes next in their lives. For some, "what comes next" is higher education, and for others, it is the labor force if they are lucky and idleness and drifting if they are not. Schools have long recognized this fundamental distinction by tracking students into college preparatory curricula on the one hand, and into something else on the other. At one time, that "something else" was specific vocational training: typing, bookkeeping, home economics, auto mechanics, welding, or whatever. But with some few exceptions, the urban public high schools have largely abandoned the vocational training function for students not destined to continue in college. And so, students graduate from these "other" tracks, the non-college-prep tracks, having never mastered a single useful skill that would assist them in the transition from school to work. It seems to us that next to the basic skills, some sort of marketable skill, craft, or trade is the minimum "payoff" any student should expect to receive from his or her high school education.

The recommendation is thus to emphasize "life preparation" for the non-college-bound as strongly as "college preparation" is now emphasized for students destined to continue their education beyond high school. This is *not* to argue that the traditional high school curriculum—

civics, social studies, English, math, science—should be abandoned for students not going on to college. In an ideal world, every citizen would have a detailed appreciation of the common history of the nation, its geography, polity, society, and its relationship to other nations, and all would have some feel for science, literature, the arts, and so on. But these high-minded goals seem more than a little anachronistic when high school graduates are commonly found to be illiterate, innumerate, and entirely bereft of work skills.

An urban high school that took "life preparation" seriously would work closely with local business and industry to identify job skills that were in demand, then develop the appropriate programming and curricula that would impart those needed skills to the young (much as is currently done in some junior and community college programs). Job placement for those in the "life preparation" track would be taken as seriously as college placement for those in the college-prep track. The high school diploma for those in the "life placement" track would amount, in essence, to an attestation that the student had mastered certain basic skills and a certification that the student could ably perform some specific, defined, work role. In this fashion, the high schools would provide every student, college bound or not, the opportunity to maximize his or her contribution to the collective good.

A closer and more discernible link between schooling and work for the non-college-bound, such as that suggested above, would presumably lessen the high-school dropout problem, which has become a leading social problem in the inner city. Drug use, crime, teenage pregnancies and so forth are all much more common among high school dropouts than among any other group of youth. The concentration of dysfunctional behavior among dropouts is sufficiently strong, however, that even further "stay in school" measures can be recommended.

One obvious measure—so obvious that one wonders why it has never been seriously considered before—is simply to require students to stay in school until they complete a high school degree. At present, there are mandatory school attendance laws in every state, all geared to the attainment of some specific *age* (at which leaving school becomes legal). Our proposal is to require school attendance until a specific level of *accomplishment* has been attained instead. Presumably, if one were required to stay in school until the completion of a degree, marginally talented students would have a much greater incentive to take their school work seriously. Students beyond a certain age (say, 21) who had still not earned a degree could petition to be relieved of the requirement by showing that they had secured gainful employment. Several states have also begun to experiment with a requirement that young people either be in school or have earned their high school diploma in order to obtain a driver's license;

some states now even require school attendance of the children of welfare recipients in order to remain eligible for payments. Under the GAI/NIT scheme proposed above, one could also tie participation (that is, eligibility for the guarantee) to the completion of the high school diploma.

A system of carrots and sticks along the lines suggested above should be sufficient to keep nearly everyone in school until he or she had achieved a basic level of skill and a diploma. At the point of graduation, three options would then be open: continuing one's education beyond high school (including additional vocational or liberal arts education in junior and community colleges), entering the normal labor force (or the military), or, for those unable to secure normal employment, enrolling in a CETA-style program as suggested earlier. What we have in mind is something along the lines of a National Youth Corps that would provide additional training, job skills, experience, and maturity through socially useful public-sector employment offered to all recently graduated youth who were unable to find work in the private sector. The list of socially useful public-sector work that might be offered in a National Youth Corps is limited only by one's imagination: day care and recreation workers, teacher's assistants, nurse's aide, maintenance workers, nursing home and hospital attendants, and public works construction laborers, to name a few.

The point of the overall system sketched above is, first, through educational reform in the high schools, to make it possible for all young people to prepare themselves for useful, productive adult roles and then, through various stay-in-school requirements, to insist that they do so; and second, through aggressive job placement efforts and through the National Youth Corps, to enable youth to assume productive, adult roles shortly after the completion of their schooling. The obvious payoff in this system is that once it is in place, *no reasonable excuse for joblessness remains.* Those who would then *choose* joblessness in the face of every opportunity to be a contributing member of society are parasites to whom we have no further obligation, not even the minimum income guarantee proposed earlier in this chapter.

Three more aspects of national educational policy also need to be mentioned here, if only briefly. *First,* to compensate the children of the poor for the entering deficits that the poverty of their parents inflicts upon them, a substantial expansion of the Head Start program needs to be considered. The obvious "location" of this expansion would be within the national day care system proposed earlier. *Second,* greater attention must be given to identifying academically talented children of poverty and assuring that they are provided with the opportunity and means to continue their education through and beyond high school. *Finally,* additional investments must be made now in adult education, adult literacy,

212 An Agenda for the Future

and adult training and retraining programs so that the present generation as well as the next is given ample opportunity to maximize its positive contribution to the collective good.

NATIONAL FAMILY POLICY

The decay of the traditional family and the disorganization of the poverty (or minority) family have become all-purpose scapegoats for the ills of modern society. That a great deal of "family decay" is a consequence, not a cause, of larger woes is regularly overlooked. Moreover, however much one might wish it to be otherwise, there is very little that social policy can do to dictate what goes in within families. The proper role of "national family policy" is mostly to remove perverse incentives that otherwise encourage dysfunctional outcomes.

Many of the perverse incentives associated with current policies would be removed by other policy initiatives that we have already discussed. One obvious example is the existing incentive that encourages young inner city women to drop out of school, get pregnant, and go on AFDC. Given our present-day educational and employment situations, AFDC and the associated benefits (housing subsidies, Medicaid, food stamps) represent, for all practical purposes, the only route to independence and upward mobility available to many poor young women. After all, there is no guarantee that a poor young woman will successfully complete high school, no guarantee that a decent job will be available to her even if she does, and no guarantee that if she is fortunate enough to get a job, the income to be earned from it will raise her above the poverty line. If she has a child, on the other hand, she is pretty well guaranteed to receive AFDC and the associated benefits. Welfare, in short, has become a principal means by which young poor women can leave their parental households and set up families of their own; in turn, having a child is the necessary entry pass into the system of welfare benefits. We have already explained why existing AFDC benefits are often preferable to low-skilled, unbenefited work at the minimum wage; our proposed emphases in education and employment policy would make schooling and work by far the more attractive alternative and thereby remove a major incentive for poor teens to become pregnant in the first place.

Likewise, under the current system, AFDC recipients are penalized heavily if there is a second potential breadwinner in the home; many fathers of poor children do their children and their spouses a favor by splitting, most of all when the welfare payment is taxed dollar for dollar against any earned household income. A negative income tax system that would allow families to retain a proportional share of their guaranteed income in spite of their earnings would encourage (rather than discourage) fathers to remain in the household. Policies that penalize households for their earnings foster single-parent households and welfare dependency; policies that reward households for their earnings encourage family stability and economic self-sufficiency. As we have already stressed, people become welfare dependent *not* because welfare is so attractive but because the alternative is frequently so unattractive. Increasing the attraction of the alternative would go a long way towards removing many of the "dysfunctional" aspects of the poverty family.

Much of the present-day concern about the "breakdown of the family" reflects the precipitous increase in unwed teenage mothers among the inner city poor. In point of fact, as we have already explained, unwed motherhood has become a means of upward mobility for poor, young women. A second factor is, of course, the dearth of marriageable young black males. A recent study suggested that 42% of black males ages 18–35 in Washington DC were either in jail (15%), awaiting trial or being sought on active arrest warrants (6%), or on probation or parole (21%). Among the slim majority that remains, many will be unemployed, or involved in illegal activities, or drug addicted, or in some other way ill suited to assume the responsibilities of spouse and parent. Many young black women will therefore, on the average, face three choices: not to have children at all (strongly at odds with the matrilineal organization of the inner city black community), to marry an otherwise undesirable mate and have children with him, or to become an "unwed mother." The evident and pragmatic solution to the problem is therefore to increase the pool of desirable mates, which implies providing meaningful educational and employment opportunities to an entire class of young black men to whom these basic things are now systemically denied. Joblessness, not AFDC, lies at the very heart and core of the "family disorganization" problem.

NATIONAL HEALTH POLICY

There are about 37 million Americans without health insurance of any sort, most of them poor or near-poor. In many states, eligibility for government-subsidized indigent health insurance (Medicaid) is tied to participation in AFDC, an arrangement which, as we have already suggested, creates a great deal of "welfare dependency." Those who are ineligible for Medicaid for one or another reason will have health insurance only if it is provided as a fringe benefit of their employment. The uninsured are therefore persons who are ineligible for Medicaid, who have no job or whose job does not provide health insurance benefits, and whose incomes are insufficient to purchase a private health insurance plan—in short, the poor and near-poor.

The emerging crisis in indigent health care is amply indexed by the situation of the nation's poor children. A fifth of our children live in families below the poverty line; children suffer the highest aggregate poverty rate of any age group in the U.S. population. This is especially true of children in female-headed households, nearly a quarter of all children. One indicator of the deteriorating condition of children is the declining proportion who are covered by medical insurance.

> The percentage of children without private or public health insurance grew sharply (40 percent) between 1977 and 1987. In 1987, 17.8% of children age seventeen or younger were uninsured (11.2 million uninsured children), compared to 12.7 percent of all children (8.1 million uninsured children) a decade earlier." (Cunningham and Monheit 1990, p. 80)

Even more precipitous was the decline in public insurance coverage among children in households with working single parents: in 1977, a third of these children were covered by public insurance (mostly Medicaid), and in 1987, barely 13%.

Most private health insurance for children is that made available to their parents as a fringe benefit of their jobs. These days, most intact husband-wife households have both adults in the labor force, thus doubling the chances that at least one parent will receive health insurance that covers the children. As the proportion of children living in single-parent households increases, the odds on having health insurance coverage therefore decline—minimally by a factor of two. And of course, most single-parent households are headed by women, whose employment remains concentrated in the lower-paying, traditionally "female" occupations where fringe benefits are less generous when they are offered at all. Thus, the reduced availability of employment-related private coverage explains the declining proportion of children insured through this mechanism.

The declining proportion of children covered through public insurance reflects "the significant retrenchment in Medicaid eligibility that affected the working poor under the Omnibus Budget Reconciliation Act of 1981 and the failure of state governments to adjust income eligibility standards for AFDC to keep pace with inflation" (Cunningham and Monheit, 1990, p. 82). Households with small amounts of earned income will often lose their AFDC eligibility and with it their Medicaid card. Indeed, private medical insurance is now so expensive, and employment-related insurance so rarely offered to working women, that many women find they must remain on AFDC only in order to retain the associated Medicaid benefit.

Allowing employers and employees to "buy in" to Medicaid would be one way to avoid this perverse pattern. That is, rather than sacrifice Medicaid eligibility by getting a job and going off welfare, one could be allowed to retain eligibility by having employers or workers pay a small premium (the amount of which could be indexed to earnings). An alternative would be some sort of "play or pay" scheme whereby all employers were required either to provide health insurance to all employees ("play") or to pay into a premium pool that would be used to provide insurance to those not covered through their employment ("pay"). Yet a third option, one employed with considerable success nearly everywhere else in the civilized world, is a system of national health insurance providing universal health coverage to all citizens.

NATIONAL DRUG POLICY

The scourge of drugs has descended on the inner city like a plague of locusts. It is, of course, true that drugs are a symptom more than a cause of inner city turmoil; at the same time, the spread of illicit drugs has had profoundly damaging effects on communities and neighborhoods, on the criminal justice system, and on the specific individuals involved. Thus, however epiphenomenal the drug problem may be, no master plan for the cities can afford to ignore it.

A useful beginning point for the discussion is to ask an obvious but often overlooked question, namely, why do people use drugs in the first place? Many young people *try* drugs initially as a form of experimentation, as an expression of independence, to be "cool," or to "fit in" with one's peer group. But this does not explain the habitual and continued use of illicit drugs thereafter. Nor does physical addiction provide the answer; the actual physical addictivity of the most commonly abused illicit substances—cocaine, marijuana, even crack and heroin—has been grossly exaggerated in most accounts. "Peer pressure" is (admittedly) an important factor but only serves to restate the question. (Thus, what explains the habitual and continued use of illicit substances among peers?)

People *try* drugs for a variety of reasons, but they become habitual users of drugs mainly for two reasons. First, drugs induce euphoria; they make a person feel good. And second, people use drugs habitually because they have nothing better to do with their time.

We have already explained how, in a deep sense, life in the urban underclass has become a life with no future. With no legitimate prospects for the future, life all too quickly becomes a quest for the immediate gratification of present impulses. Weighing the consequences of present behavior against their future implications thus becomes a meaningless exercise. Thus the primal attraction of drugs is that they provide *immediate* gratification. Arguments against using drugs—that one might *become* an addict or *eventually* destroy one's physical health—all require an orientation towards the future, a concern, in short, about tomorrow's consequences of today's behaviors. The correct response to the question, why do inner city youth (and adults) use drugs? is, why not?

The argument is sometimes made that legalization of drugs would take the profit out of the drug trade (and the mystique out of drug use) and would thus lower the stakes and reduce the level of drug-related crime and violence in the cities. It is no doubt true that many central city juveniles are attracted to the drug trade because of the enormous profits to be made. But the generalized absence of legitimate routes to success for inner city youth suggests that in the absence of a drug market, many or most of these juveniles would turn to some other illegitimate activity that might prove equally violent, for example, armed robbery or other predatory crimes. Even now, we hear of expensive automobiles being brazenly stolen at gunpoint while their owners sit behind the wheel at a traffic light. How much more behavior of this sort might we create if we took the profit out of the drug trade?

When all is said and done, the drug epidemic has become a convenient scapegoat for the ills of the central city, the morally reprehensible headwater from whence all other problems flow. This emphasis, however, again mistakes a symptom for a cause. A great deal of the drug problem (and the crime problem) would disappear if young people in the inner city had a future to which they could reasonably aspire. Our feeling, in short, is that the emphases we have recommended in educational and employment policy would also go a long way towards reducing the drug (and crime) problem. Idle hands, it is said, do the Devil's work. Jobless hands do drugs.

To conclude: As a first measure, we recommend a simple method to end poverty as it is presently defined, a guaranteed annual income policy that redistributes about $60 billion per year through the mechanism of a negative income taxation system and that assures all Americans a minimum standard of material well-being. The effect of the NIT scheme that we propose, coupled with an increase in the minimum wage to the NIT break-even value, is to create a system of guaranteed well-being (which is to say, a *welfare* system) in which people are always better off if they work than if they are idle. As a second measure, we recommend a system of inner city public education that is geared as a first priority towards fitting young people for useful and productive adult roles, and then a national employment policy that provides everyone access to those productive adult roles. These and the related measures we have discussed would not solve every problem that has arisen in connection with the urban underclass, but they would assuredly make a substantial dent in most of them.

What would all this cost? Unquestionably, the cost would run into many tens of billions of dollars each year, perhaps even a few hundreds of billions, at least in the beginning. But what does the alternative cost us now? As a rough guess, we have suggested a half trillion dollars a year as the approximate direct and indirect cost of poverty to the nation. If an additional hundred billion dollars a year solved a large share of the problem of poverty and all the other problems that are related to it, then the hundred billion would be a stunningly productive investment. As recent events in Los Angeles and elsewhere have dramatically indicated, the urban underclass is a time bomb ticking. It would be prudent, we think, to defuse the bomb while there is still something left to save.

NOTES

1. As a point of comparison, consider the federal response to Hurricane Andrew, a $7 billion aid package for the victims and states in question. Andrew killed fewer than 25 people, left several thousand homeless, created some (probably temporary) economic havoc for a few more tens of thousands. That degree of suffering is worth $7 billion in an instant. We price a dramatic reduction if not the end of poverty at $60 billion, or 8.6 times the $7 billion aid package. Arguably, poverty creates far more than 8.6 times the human misery that Andrew created, yet we cannot muster the necessary funds or political will to intervene effectively.

References

Abrahamse, Allan F., Peter A. Morrison, and Linda J. Waite. January 1988. *Beyond Stereotypes: Who Becomes a Single Teenage Mother?* Report R-3489-HHS/NICHD. Santa Monica, CA: The Rand Corporation.

Allen, Walter R. and Reynolds Farley. 1986. "The Shifting Social and Economic Tides of Black America, 1950–1980." *Annual Review of Sociology* 12:277–306.

Anderson, Elijah. 1978. *A Place on the Corner.* Chicago: University of Chicago Press.

———. 1989. "Sex Codes and Family Life among Poor Inner-City Youths." *Annals of the American Academy of Political and Social Science* 501 (January):59–78.

———. 1990. *Streetwise.* Chicago: University of Chicago Press.

Anderson, Martin. 1978. *Welfare.* Stanford, CA: Hoover Institution Press.

Auletta, Ken. 1983. *The Underclass.* New York: Vintage.

Bane, Mary Jo and David T. Ellwood. 1983. "Slipping into and out of Poverty: The Dynamics of Spells." National Bureau of Economic Research Working Paper #1199. Cambridge, MA.

Beeghley, Leonard. 1984. "Illusion and Reality in the Measurement of Poverty." *Social Problems* 31 (February):322–333.

Blau, Joel. 1992. *The Visible Poor: Homelessness in the United States.* New York: Oxford University Press.

Bluestone, Barry and Bennett Harrison. 1982. *The Deindustrialization of America.* New York: Basic Books.

Blumberg, Paul. 1980. *Inequality in an Age of Decline.* New York: Oxford University Press.

Brickner, Philip. W., Linda K. Scharer, Barbara Conanon, Al Elvy, and Marianne Savarese (eds.). 1985. *Health Care of Homeless People.* New York: Springer Publishing.

Burstein, Emanuel S. 1983. "Deductions, Credits, Exemptions, and Exclusions in the Federal Income Tax System: A Discussion of Public Policy Issues." *Studies in Taxation, Public Finance and Related Subjects: A Compendium* 7:68–81.

Burt, Martha. 1992. *Over the Edge: The Growth of Homelessness in the 1980s.* New York: Russell Sage.

Caplan, Nathan, Marcella H. Choy, and John K. Whitmore. 1992. "Indochinese Refugee Families and Academic Achievement." *Scientific American* 266 (February):36–42.

Caudill, Harry. 1963. *Night Comes to the Cumberlands.* Boston: Little, Brown.

Center for the Study of Social Policy. 1992. *Kids Count Data Book 1992.* Washington, DC: Center for the Study of Social Policy.

Cloward, Richard A. and Frances Fox Piven. 1974. *The Politics of Turmoil.* New York: Pantheon.

219

Cook, Thomas D. and Thomas R. Curtin. 1987. "The Mainstream and the Underclass: Why Are the Differences So Salient and the Similarities So Unobtru-
sive?" Pp. 217–264 in *Social Comparison, Social Justice, and Relative Deprivation*,
edited by John C. Masters and William P. Smith. Hillsdale, NJ: Lawrence
Erlbaum Associates.

Cunningham, Peter J. and Alan C Monheit. 1990. "Insuring the Children: A
Decade of Change." *Health Affairs* 9(4):76–90.

Currie, Elliott. 1985. *Confronting Crime: An American Challenge*. New York:
Pantheon.

Danziger, Sheldon. 1989. "Overview." *Focus* [special issue: "Defining and Measuring the Underclass"] 12(1):1–5.

Danziger, Sheldon and Peter Gottschalk. 1987. "Earnings Inequality, the Spatial
Concentration of Poverty, and the Underclass." *American Economic Review* 77
(May):211–15

Danziger, Sheldon and Daniel Weinberg (eds.) 1986. *Fighting Poverty: What Works
and What Doesn't*. Cambridge, MA.: Harvard University Press.

Devine Joel A. 1983. "Fiscal Policy and Class Income Inequality." *American Sociological Review* 48 (October): 606–622.

Devine, Joel A. and William Canak. 1986. "Redistribution in a Bifurcated Welfare
State: Quintile Shares and the U.S. Case." *Social Problems* 33 (June):391–406.

Devine, Joel A., Mark Plunkett, and James D. Wright. 1992. "The Chronicity of
Poverty: Evidence from the PSID, 1968–1987." *Social Forces* 70 (March):787
-812.

Devine, Joel A. and James D. Wright. 1990. "Minimum Wage, Maximum Hokum."
Society 27 (July/August):50–54.

Duncan, Greg J. with Richard D. Cole, Mary E. Corcoran, Martha S. Hill, Saul D.
Hoffman, and James M. Morgan. 1984. *Years of Poverty, Years of Plenty*. Ann
Arbor, MI.: Survey Research Center, Institute for Social Research.

Edelman, Murray. 1964. *The Symbolic Uses of Politics*. Champaign, IL.: University of
Illinois Press.

Ellwood, David T. 1986. "The Spatial Mismatch Hypothesis: Are There Teenage
Jobs Missing in the Ghetto?" Pp. 147–184 in *The Black Youth Employment Crisis*,
edited by R.B. Freeman and H.J. Holzer. Chicago: University of Chicago.

———. 1987. *Divide and Conquer: Responsible Security for America's Poor*. Occasional
Paper #1, Ford Foundation Project on Social Welfare and the American
Future. New York.

———. 1988. *Poor Support*. New York: Basic Books.

Ellwood, David and Mary Jo Bane. 1984. "The Impact of AFDC on Family
Structure and Living Arrangements." Working Paper prepared under grant
#92A-82, U.S. Department of Health and Human Services. Washington, DC.

Ennis, Philip H. 1967. *Criminal Victimization in the United States, Field Surveys II*.
NORC, President's Commission on Law Enforcement and Administration of
Justice (May).

Executive Office of the President, Office of Management and Budget. 1992a.
Budget of the United States Government, Fiscal Year 1993. Washington, DC: U.S.
Government Printing Office.

─────. 1992b. *Historical Tables, Budget of the United States Government, Fiscal Year 1992*. Washington, DC: U.S. Government Printing Office.

Fagan, Joel. 1990. "Social Processes of Delinquency and Drug Use Among Urban Gangs." Pp. 183–219 in *Gangs in America*, edited by C. R. Huff. Newbury Park, CA: Sage.

Farley, Reynolds and Walter R. Allen. 1987. *The Color Line and the Quality of Life in America*. New York: Russell Sage.

Freedman, Jonathan. 1978. *Happy People*. New York: Harcourt, Brace, Jovanovich.

Friedrichs, J. (ed.) 1988. *Affordable Housing and the Homeless*. Berlin: Walter de Gruyter.

Galbraith, John Kenneth. 1955. *The Affluent Society*. Boston: Houghton- Mifflin.

Gallup Organization. 1985. *The Gallup Report*, (#234: March).

Gans, Herbert. 1972. *More Equality*. New York: Pantheon.

Gilder, George. 1981. *Wealth and Poverty*. New York: Basic Books.

Glasgow, Douglas G. 1980. *The Black Underclass*. San Francisco: Jossey- Bass.

Goodwin, Leonard. 1969. *Do the Poor Want to Work?* Washington, DC: The Brookings Institution.

Griffin, Larry J., Joel A. Devine, and Michael Wallace. 1983. "On the Economic and Political Determinants of Welfare Spending in the Post- World War II Era." *Politics and Society* 12:331–372.

Gutman, Herbert G. 1976. *The Black Family in Slavery and Freedom, 1750–1925*. New York: Pantheon.

Hacker, Andrew. 1987. "American Apartheid." *New York Review of Books* 34 (December 3):26–33.

─────. 1992. *Two Nations: Black and White, Separate, Hostile, Unequal*. New York: Charles Scribner's Sons.

Hamilton, Richard F. and James D. Wright. 1986. *The State of the Masses*. New York: Aldine de Gruyter.

Harrington, Michael. 1962. *The Other America*. Baltimore: Penguin.

─────. 1984. *The New American Poverty*. New York: Holt, Rinehart and Winston.

─────. 1988. "The New American Poverty." Videotape. New York: Institute for Democratic Socialism.

Harrison, Bennett and Barry Bluestone. 1988. *The Great U-Turn*. New York: Basic Books.

Haveman, Robert (ed.). 1977. *A Decade of Federal Antipoverty Programs*. New York: Academic Press.

─────. 1988a. "The Changed Face of Poverty: A Call for New Policies." *Focus* 11 (2):10–14.

─────. 1988b. *Starting Even*. New York: Simon and Schuster.

Haynes, Cheryl (ed.). 1987. *Risking the Future: Adolescent Sexuality, Pregnancy, and Childbearing*. Washington, DC: National Academy Press.

Hopper, Kim, and Jill Hamburg. 1984. *The Making of America's Homeless: From Skid Row to New Poor, 1945–1984*. Report prepared for the Institute of Social Welfare Research. New York: Community Service Society.

House of Representatives, Subcommittee on Human Resources of the House Ways and Means Committee. 1989. Hearings on "How to Help the Working

Poor; and Problems of the Working Poor," 101st Congress, 1st Session, February 28, 1989, Serial 101–5.

Huizinga, David, Robert Loeber, and Terence P. Thornberry. Forthcoming. *Urban Delinquency and Substance Abuse: Technical Report.* Washington, DC: Office of Juvenile Justice and Delinquency Prevention.

Hunter, Robert. 1904. *Poverty.* New York. Grosset and Dunlap.

Institute of Medicine. 1988. *Homelessness, Health, and Human Needs.* Washington, DC: National Academy Press.

Jargowsky, Paul A. and Mary Jo Bane. 1990. "Ghetto Poverty: Basic Questions." Chapter 2 in *Inner-City Poverty in the United States,* edited by Lawrence E. Lynn and Michael G.H. McCleary. Washington, DC: National Academy Press.

Jencks, Christopher. 1989. "What Is the Underclass—and Is It Growing?" *Focus* 12(1):14–26.

Jencks, Christopher and Paul E. Peterson (eds.). 1991. *The Urban Underclass.* Washington, DC: The Brookings Institution.

Jones, Jacqueline. 1992. *The Dispossessed: America's Underclasses from the Civil War to the Present.* New York: Basic Books.

Kasarda, John. 1985. "Urban Change and Minority Opportunities." Pp. 33–67 in *The New Urban Reality,* edited by Paul E. Peterson. Washington, DC: The Brookings Institution.

———. 1989. "Urban Industrial Transition and the Underclass." *Annals of the American Academy of Political and Social Science* 501 (January):26–47.

Katz, Michael. 1983. *Poverty and Policy in American History.* New York: Academic Press.

———. 1986. *In the Shadow of the Poor House.* New York: Basic Books.

———. 1989. *The Undeserving Poor: From the War on Poverty to the War on Welfare.* New York: Pantheon.

Kolko, Gabriel. 1962. *Wealth and Power in America.* New York: Praeger.

Lemann, Nicholas. 1988/1989. "The Unfinished War." *Atlantic Monthly* (Part 1, December; Part 2 January):37–56, 53–68.

———. 1991. *The Promised Land.* New York: Alfred A. Knopf.

Levine, Carol and Nancy N. Dubler. 1990. "Uncertain Risks and Bitter Realities: The Reproductive Choices of HIV-Infected Women." *Milbank Quarterly* 68:3.

Levitan, Sar. 1985. *Programs in Aid of the Poor.* Baltimore: Johns Hopkins University Press.

Levy, Frank. 1988. *Dollars and Dreams.* New York: W.W. Norton.

Lewis, Oscar. 1966. *La Vida.* New York. Vintage.

———. 1968. "The Culture of Poverty." Pp. 187–200 in *On Understanding Poverty,* edited by Daniel Patrick Moynihan. New York: Basic Books.

Lieberson, Stanley. 1980. *A Piece of the Pie: Black and White Immigrants Since 1880.* Berkeley: University of California Press.

Liebow, Elliot. 1967. *Tally's Corner.* Boston: Little, Brown.

Light, Ivan H. and Edna Bonacich. 1988. *Immigrant Entrepreneurs: Koreans in Los Angeles, 1965–1982.* Berkeley: University of California Press.

Long, Jancis V. F. and George E. Vaillant. 1984. "Natural History of Male Psychological Health, XI: Escape from the Underclass." *American Journal of Psychiatry* 141 (March):341–345.

Marx, Karl. 1967 [1894]. *Capital,* vol. III. New York: International Publishers.

Massey, Douglas S., Andrew B. Cross, and Mitchell L. Eggers. 1991. "Segregation, the Concentration of Poverty, and the Life Chances of Individuals." *Social Science Research* 20 (December):397–420.

Massey, Douglas S. and Mitchell L. Eggers. 1990. "The Ecology of Inequality: Minorities and the Concentration of Poverty 1970–1980." *American Journal of Sociology* 95 (March):1153–1188.

Massing, Michael. 1992. "What Ever Happened to the War on Drugs?" *New York Review of Books* 39 (June 11):42–46.

McClanahan, Sara. 1985. "Charles Murray and the Family." Pp. 1–7 in *Losing Ground: A Critique.* Institute For Research on Poverty Special Report 38. Madison, WI: Institute For Research on Poverty.

Mishel, Lawrence and Jacqueline Simon. 1988. *The State of Working America.* Washington, DC: Economic Policy Institute.

Monkkonen, Erik H. 1984. *Walking to Work: Tramps in America, 1790–1935.* Lincoln: University of Nebraska Press.

Morgan, James M. 1974. "Family Composition." Pp. 99–121 in James M. Morgan et al., *Five Thousand American Families: Patterns of Economic Progress, vol. I.* Ann Arbor, MI.: Survey Research Center, Institute for Social Research.

Moynihan, Daniel P. 1965. *The Negro Family: The Case for National Action.* Washington, DC: U.S. Department of Labor, Office of Policy Planning and Research.

Murray, Charles. 1984. *Losing Ground.* New York: Basic.

Newsweek. 1992. "Wisconsin Is Talking . . . " *Newsweek* (January 20):6.

Noto, Nonna. 1981. "Tax Expenditures: The Link between Economic Intent and the Distribution of Benefits among High, Middle, and Low Income Groups." *Studies in Taxation, Public Finance and Related Subjects: A Compendium* 5:59–75.

O'Connell, Martin and Carolyn C. Moore. 1984. "Out of Wedlock Births, Premarital Pregnancies and Their Effect on Family Formation and Dissolution." *Family Planning Perspectives* 16:157–162.

O'Connor, James. 1973. *The Fiscal Crisis of the State.* New York: St. Martin's Press.

Orfield, Gary and Carole Ashkinaze. 1991. *The Closing Door: Conservative Policy and Black Opportunity.* Chicago: University of Chicago Press.

Orshansky, Mollie. 1969. "How Poverty is Measured." *Monthly Labor Review* 92 (January):37–41.

Panel Study of Income Dynamics, 1968–1987. ICPSR Study #7439. Ann Arbor, MI: ICPSR.

Patterson, James T. 1986. *America's Struggle Against Poverty, 1900–1985.* Cambridge, MA.: Harvard University Press.

Peterson, Paul E. (ed.). 1985. *The New Urban Reality.* Washington, DC: The Brookings Institution.

Piven, Frances Fox and Richard A. Cloward. 1971. *Regulating the Poor.* New York: Vintage.

————. 1979. *Poor People's Movements.* New York: Vintage.

Rein, Martin and Lee Rainwater. 1978. "Patterns of Welfare Use." *Social Service Review* 52:511–534.

Ricketts, Erol R. and Ronald B. Mincy. 1988. "Growth of the Underclass." Changing Domestic Priorities Discussion Paper, The Urban Institute, Washington, DC.

Ricketts, Erol R. and Isabel V. Sawhill. 1986. "Defining and Measuring the Underclass." Changing Domestic Priorities Discussion Paper, The Urban Institute, Washington, DC.

Ross, Christine, Sheldon Danziger, and Eugene Smolensky. 1987. "The Level and Trend of Poverty in the United States, 1939–1979." *Demography* 24 (November):587–600.

Rossi, Peter H. 1990. *Down and Out in America.* Chicago: University of Chicago Press.

Rossi, Peter H. and Kathryn Lyall. 1976. *Reforming Public Welfare: A Critique of the Negative Income Tax Experiment.* New York: Russell Sage.

Rossi, Peter H. and James D. Wright. 1987. "The Determinants of Homelessness," *Health Affairs* 6:1 (Spring):19–32.

Rossi, Peter H., James D. Wright, Gene Fisher, and Georgianna Willis. 1987. "The Urban Homeless: Estimating Composition and Size," *Science* 235 (March 13):1336–1341).

Rubin, Beth, James D. Wright, and Joel A. Devine. 1992. "Unhousing the Urban Poor: The Reagan Legacy." *Journal of Sociology and Social Work* 19 (March): 111–147.

Ruggles, Patricia and William P. Marton. 1986. "Measuring the Size and Characteristics of the Underclass: How Much Do We Know?" Project Report (December), The Urban Institute, Washington, DC.

Ryan, William. 1971. *Blaming the Victim.* New York: Random House.

Sawhill, Isabel V. 1987. "Poverty and the Underclass: Testimony Presented at a Hearing of the House Budget Committee's Task Force on Income Security, November 10, 1987." Urban Institute Working Paper #2002. Washington, DC.

Shapiro, Isaac and Robert Greenstein. 1988. *Holes in the Safety Nets: Poverty Programs and Policies in the States.* Washington, DC: Center on Budget and Policy Priorities.

Sheley, Joseph F., James D. Wright and M. Dwayne Smith. 1992. *Firearms, Violence and Inner-City Youth.* Draft report submitted to the National Institute of Justice and the Office of Juvenile Justice and Delinquency Prevention (March).

Shenkman, Richard. 1988. *Legends, Lies, and Cherished Myths of American History.* New York: William Morrow and Co.

Smeeding, Timothy and Lee Rainwater. 1991. *First World Poverty.* Cambridge, MA: Harvard University Joint Center for Political and Economic Studies.

Smith, M. Dwayne, Joel A. Devine and Joseph F. Sheley. 1992. "Unemployment and Crime: Age and Race Effects." *Sociological Perspectives* 35 (4):551–572.

Smith, N. 1985. "Homelessness: Not One Problem but Many." *Journal of the Institute for Socioeconomic Studies* 10 (3):53–67.

Steinberg, Stephan. 1981. *The Ethnic Myth: Race, Ethnicity, and Class in America.* New York: Atheneum.

Surrey, Stanley and Paul R. McDaniel. 1985. *Tax Expenditures.* Cambridge, MA: Harvard University Press.

Tessler, Richard and Deborah Dennis. 1989. *A Synthesis of NIMH-Funded Research Concerning Persons Who Are Homeless and Mentally Ill.* Washington, DC: National Institute of Mental Health.

Thernstrom, Stephan. 1964. *Poverty and Progress: Social Mobility in a Nineteenth Century City.* Cambridge, MA: Harvard University Press.

Thurow, Lester. 1980. *The Zero-Sum Society.* New York: Basic Books.

———. 1992. *Head to Head.* New York: William Morrow and Co.

Tilly, Chris. 1991. "Reasons for the Continuing Growth of Part-Time Employment." *Monthly Labor Review* 114 March:10–18.

U.S. Bureau of the Census. 1968. "The Extent of Poverty in the United States, 1959 to 1966." *Current Population Reports,* Series P-60, No. 54 (May). Washington, DC: U.S. Government Printing Office.

———. 1969. "Poverty in the United States, 1959 to 1968." *Current Population Reports,* Series P-60, No. 68 (December). Washington, DC: U.S. Government Printing Office.

———. 1970. "24 Million Americans: Poverty in the United States, 1969." *Current Population Reports,* Series P-60, No. 76 (March). Washington, DC: U.S. Government Printing Office.

———. 1975. *Historical Statistics of the United States: Colonial Times to 1970.* Washington, DC: U.S. Government Printing Office.

———. 1979. "Characteristics of the Population below the Poverty Level: 1977." *Current Population Reports,* Series P-60, No. 119 (March). Washington, DC: U.S. Government Printing Office.

———. 1985. *Poverty Areas in Large Cities.* Subject Reports PC80–2–8D. Washington, DC: U.S. Government Printing Office.

———. 1986. *Statistical Abstract of the United States, 1987.* Washington, DC: U.S. Government Printing Office.

———. 1988a. "Money Income of Households, Families, and Persons in the United States: 1986." *Current Population Reports,* Series P-60, No. 159 (June). Washington, DC: U.S. Government Printing Office.

———. 1988b. "Money Income and Poverty Status in the United States: 1987 (Advance Data from the March 1988 Current Population Survey)." *Current Population Reports,* Series P-60, No. 161 (August). Washington, DC: U.S. Government Printing Office.

———. 1988c. "Rural and Rural Farm Population: 1987." *Current Population Reports,* Series P-27, No. 61 (June). Washington, DC: U.S. Government Printing Office.

———. 1989a. "Poverty in the United States: 1987." *Current Population Reports,* Series P-60, No. 163 (February). Washington, DC: U.S. Government Printing Office.

———. 1989b. *Statistical Abstract of the United States, 1989.* Washington, DC: U.S. Government Printing Office.

————. 1990. *Statistical Abstract of the United States, 1990.* Washington, DC: U.S. Government Printing Office.

————. 1991a. "Poverty in the United States: 1988 and 1989." *Current Population Reports,* Series P-60, No. 171 (June). Washington, DC: U.S. Government Printing Office.

————. 1991b. "Money Income of Households, Families, and Persons in the United States: 1990." *Current Population Reports,* Series P-60, No. 174 (August). Washington, DC: U.S. Government Printing Office.

————. 1991c. "Poverty in the United States: 1990." *Current Population Reports,* Series P-60, No. 175 (August). Washington, DC: U.S. Government Printing Office.

————. 1992. "Workers with Low Earnings: 1964 to 1990." *Current Population Reports,* Series P-60, No. 178 (March). Washington, DC: U.S. Government Printing Office.

U.S. Department of Education. 1991. *Digest of Educational Statistics, 1991.* (November). Washington, DC: U.S. Government Printing Office.

U.S. Department of Health and Human Services. National Center For Health Statistics. Annual editions. *Vital Statistics of the United States.* Washington, DC: U.S. Government Printing Office.

U.S. Department of Health and Human Services. National Institute on Drug Abuse. 1990. *National Household Survey on Drug Abuse: Highlights 1988.* Department of Health and Human Services Publication No. (ADM) 90–1681.

————. 1991. *Drug Use among Youth: Findings from the 1988 National Household Survey on Drug Abuse.* Washington, DC: Department of Health and Human Services.

U.S. Department of Justice, Bureau of Justice Statistics. 1992. *Criminal Victimization in the United States, 1990.* NCJ-134126 (February). Washington, DC: U.S. Government Printing Office.

————. 1991. *Correctional Populations in the United States, 1988.* NCJ-124280 (March). Washington, DC: U.S. Government Printing Office.

U.S. Department of Justice, Federal Bureau of Investigation. Annual editions. *Uniform Crime Reports.* Washington, DC: U.S. Government Printing Office.

U.S. Department of Labor, Bureau of Labor Statistics. 1988. *Handbook of Labor Statistics.* Bulletin 2307 (August). Washington, DC: U.S. Government Printing Office.

————. 1989. *Handbook of Labor Statistics.* Bulletin 2340 (August). Washington, DC: U.S. Government Printing Office.

Waldman, Steven. 1992. "Benefits 'R' Us." *Newsweek* (August 10):56–58.

Whitaker, Catherine J.. 1990. *Bureau of Justice Statistics Special Report: Black Victims.* Bureau of Justice Statistics report NCJ-122562 (April). Washington, DC: U.S. Government Printing Office.

Wilkerson, Isabel. 1987. "New Studies Zeroing in on Poorest of the Poor." *New York Times* (December 20):26.

Williamson, Jeffrey G. and Peter H. Lindert. 1980. *American Inequality: A Macroeconomic History.* New York: Academic Press.

Wilson, James Q. and Richard J. Herrnstein. 1985. *Crime and Human Nature*. New York: Simon and Schuster.

Wilson, William J. 1978. *The Declining Significance of Race*. Chicago: University of Chicago Press.

———. 1985. "The Urban Underclass in Advanced Industrial Society." Pp. 129–160 in *The New Urban Reality*, edited by Paul E. Peterson. Washington, DC: The Brookings Institution.

———. 1987. *The Truly Disadvantaged*. Chicago: University of Chicago Press.

Wright, James D. 1988. "The Mentally Ill Homeless: What Is Myth and What is Fact?" *Social Problems* 35 (April):182–191.

———. 1989. *Address Unknown: The Homeless in America*. Hawthorne, NY: Aldine de Gruyter.

Wright, James D., Janet W. Knight, Eleanor Weber, and Julie Lam. 1987. "Ailments and Alcohol: Health Status among the Drinking Homeless." *Alcohol Health and Research World* 11:3 (Spring):22–27.

Wright, James D. and Eleanor Weber. 1987. *Homelessness and Health*. Washington, DC: McGraw Hill.

Author Index

Subject Index

232   Subject Index

Crime (*continued*)
  racial disparities and, 174–175, 178
  victimization rate and, 175, 180–181,
    182–184
Cross-sectional data, 19
Culture of poverty, 125, 127

Data on poverty, 19–20
Demography of poverty (*See also*
    Working poor)
  children and, 68–71
  contemporary information on, 71–
    75
  diversity and, 49
  elderly poor and, 39, 65–68
  rate of poverty and, 43–45
  rural poor and, 62–65
Drug abuse
  crime and, 169–173
  dealing drugs and, 167, 169
  destructiveness of, 164
  expenditures toward preventing,
    194
  guns and, 170–171, 172
  in inner city, 163–164, 168
  National Household Surveys on
    Drug Abuse and, 164, 166–167
  policy for preventing, 215–217
  reasons for, 215
  report on, 163
  trends in, 165, 169
Drug dealing, 167, 169
Drug policy, 215–217

Ecological dimension of underclass,
    86–89
Economic dimension of underclass,
    82–84
Economic Opportunity Act of 1964, 12
Economic Policy Institute report, 34
Education
  African-Americans and, 159–160
  Caucasian Americans and, 160, 161
  enrollment in school and, 158–160,
    162, 166
  illegitimacy and, 136–137
  policy, 207–212
  quality of, 162

quantity of, 162
  underclass and, 158–162
Elderly poor, 39, 65–68
Employment (*See also* Working poor)
  minimum wage and, 35–36
  opportunities of work and, 53–55
  patterns, 33–35
  policy, 203–207
  underclass and, 150–153
Enrollment in school, 158–160, 162,
    166
Episodic poverty, 83–84, 95

Family income
  crime and, 181, 182–184
  macroeconomy and, 32, 36–38
Family policy, 212–213
Farm poverty, 62–64
Feminization of poverty, 51, 53, 55
Food stamps, 16, 55
Future, lack of, 130

GAI (guaranteed annual income),
    196–197, 199–202
Gallup surveys on income, 26
Geography and poverty, 92–93
G.I. benefit bills, 9
Gini index, 32
Graduation rates, 158, 168
Great Depression, 8–9
Guaranteed annual income (GAI),
    196–197, 199–202
Guns, 170–171, 172

The Harvest of Shame (Murrow), 11
Health policy, 213–215
High School and Beyond study, 136–137
Homelessness, 49, 118–120
Homicide, 173–174, 176–177
Household income, 32
Housing vouchers, 16, 55

Illegitimacy
  African-Americans and, 139
  Aid to Families With Dependent
    Children and, 140–141, 146–147
  Caucasian Americans and, 133,
    139–140